*For the team, advisors, and members
of the Alliance of Independent Authors
from whom I've learned so much.*

CREATIVE SELF-PUBLISHING
ALLi's Guide to Independent Publishing for Authors & Poets

Copyright © Orna A Ross, ALLIANCE OF INDEPENDENT AUTHORS 2023, 3rd edition.
First edition, 2018.
Second edition, 2021.

EBOOK: 978-1-909888-16-6
PAPERBACK: 978-1-913349-74-5
LARGE PRINT: 978-1-913349-75-2
HB: 978-1-913349-76-9
AUDIO: 978-1-913349-77-6

CREATIVE SELF-PUBLISHING

ALLI'S GUIDE TO INDEPENDENT PUBLISHING
FOR AUTHORS AND POETS

PUBLISHING GUIDES FOR INDIE AUTHORS
BOOK 1

ALLIANCE OF INDEPENDENT AUTHORS

ORNA A. ROSS

CONTENTS

INTRODUCTION

Welcome to self-publishing! Or to considering that you might, some day, perhaps some day soon, publish your very own book. It's an enthralling creative adventure and I would like to guide you through all I've learned, as a novelist, poet, and founder-director of the Alliance of Independent Authors (ALLi).

I started ALLi, with my husband Philip, back in 2012 to encourage and empower authors just like you, and this book summaries everything they have taught me over the years.

In this introduction, I introduce myself and explain how to read this book (warning: it's a doing, not just a reading, experience!). I also outline the supports and resources ALLi provides to authors at all stages of publishing.

Step on in.

A PERSONAL PREFACE

This is a book about you. Your writing and publishing ambitions. Your books and your readers. Your income and influence and impact—and how you can grow each of these through self-publishing as an independent ("indie") author.

It's also a bit about me. About how self-publishing saved my writing life, not once but twice. About my mistakes and failures as an indie author, and what they've taught me. About forming the Alliance of Independent Authors (ALLi) and all that I've learned from our members, team and advisors. I share these details in the hope that you can learn from my experience.

Mostly, it's about the art and craft of publishing books when you're also the books' author. The nature of that work poses particular challenges and opportunities, for writers as creators and business owners. In this book, I aim to grapple with those challenges from a personal and creative, as well as practical and commercial, perspective.

I've learned much that has surprised me since starting to self-publish over a decade ago, from publishing my own novels and poetry books and guidebooks for authors like this one, and also from working alongside thousands of other indie authors, and the publishing services that support them, at ALLi. But three core beliefs I've held from the start have only been reinforced by those experiences.

The first is that, for authors, self-publishing is not just an alternative route to readers, it's a complete disruptor, changing everything for writers in ways that are mostly positive. The second is that *any* writer who is willing to work to acquire the necessary writing and publishing skills can now make their living from writing books. The third is that publishing (which includes book marketing, not just book production) is every bit as creative a process as writing. This book is founded on those three beliefs.

Are You Published?

At a party recently, I found myself talking to a stranger who asked me the usual just-met-you question, "What do you do?"

"I'm a writer," I said. "A novelist and poet."

"Are you published?"

"Oh yes," I said, lightly, though I knew what I meant by my answer was not what he meant by his question. I rummaged in my bag and found one of my postcards. It has pictures of my books and links to my author website on one side, and info about the Alliance of Independent Authors on the other. I carry these around and hand one over when the topic of my work comes up.

He looked down at the postcard then back up at me. "You're self-published?"

"Yes," I said, with a smile. "And with my husband I run an organization for other indie authors."

"Wouldn't you rather be published properly?" I didn't reply that I consider myself to be very properly published, thank you, having sold many more copies of my books than any of my publishers ever had. Or that my idea of a "properly published" book is one written, produced, distributed, marketed and promoted to publishing standard that generates enough income to properly pay all of those involved—*including its author*. I said: "No. I much prefer the creative freedom of self-publishing."

Nobody can argue with that and for me, freedom has been the

greatest gain. The freedom to get on with it, rather than waiting for validation. The freedom to publish when I want instead of fitting into somebody else's schedule. The freedom to choose how to present myself and my books.

I turned the conversation. "What about you?" I asked. "What do you do?" Off we went into his work as a pediatrician, social awkwardness averted.

I knew he would probably chuck the postcard I'd given him before he got home, but still I was glad to have handed it over, and to have said those words that are so important to me with pride. *Novelist. Poet. Indie author. Authors' organization.*

I'll never get over the wonder of it all. It's such a good life for an author, the life of the successful self-publisher. You set your own definition of success and choose the people you want to work with. You produce your own books your own way, and have a dizzying level of creative freedom, answerable only to your readers and your own artistic imperatives. You are as autonomous as it is possible to be in this world.

None of this is to say that self-publishing is easy. "We are all apprentices in a craft where no one ever becomes a master," Ernest Hemingway once wrote about writers. The indie author is a forever apprentice in the craft of publishing and the craft of business, as well as the craft of writing.

To be an author, to be a publisher, to run a creative business: each of these is a complex and challenging ambition. It takes time to learn to do each one of these well, and more time to integrate them all into a way that works for you.

It's done step by step, book by book, win by small win.

What is Publishing?

Publishing is not the moment when someone presses the "publish" button on a self-publishing platform, or when a third-party publisher in London or New York tells an author they think a manuscript is worth their money. It's not just printing a book or formatting a digital file, either. So what is it? The answer (as so often) lies in the root of the word: the Latin *publicare,* meaning "to make public property" (also, interestingly, "to confiscate").

Publishing takes a privately penned manuscript or typescript and transforms it into a publicly available and readable book, in one or more formats: ebook, audiobook, print book.

Commercial publishing goes a step further, aiming to sell enough of those books to turn a profit. To do that means putting the manuscript or typescript through seven distinct processes: editorial, design, production, distribution, marketing, promotion, and rights licensing.

These seven processes make up the craft of commercial publishing, for an individual author as for the world's largest publishing conglomerates. Self-publishing, taking a book from concept to completion to transaction, means mastering creative writing, creative publishing and creative business. Three challenging crafts rolled into the publishing business of one indie author.

Becoming A Writer

For me, as for most of us, my self-publishing story began with the urge to write. It's almost five decades since I first started penning stories and poems, in an Irish convent boarding school, in my woe-is-me, nobody-understands-anything teenage years.

Writing was both a survival tool and a homage to the storytellers and poets I'd met in my reading: Louisa May Alcott, Susan Coolidge, Charles Dickens, Johanna Spyri, and WB Yeats. I mention only the most influential of those earliest years. Thousands of writers have amused and consoled me across the years, distracted me from pain and delighted me with pleasure, helped me to make sense of life and shown me how it might be well lived.

When I grew up, I wanted to do for others what those writers had done for me. Could any work be more important, or more enjoyable? When I was twenty-four, on a Portuguese boat with the boyfriend who was to become my husband, I howled that I wanted to leave the steady, relatively well-paid job I didn't love and try to earn my living as a writer. He told me to go for it and I did.

I've had many writing-related jobs since then—features journalist, magazine editor, academic, writing school owner, even, for a brief time, literary agent. I became an author—in this book's definition, a writer who has published a book—at age thirty, with a non-fiction health guidebook for women, but what I really wanted was to write a novel. So in my thirties, in the background to running a freelance journalism career while caring for two young children, I began to fictionalize a true story about my father's family that had long fascinated me.

In those days, almost the only way to publish a book was to license your publishing rights to a third-party publisher, under exclusive contract. It was called "getting published" and it was every author's dream. It was my dream too, through the many years it took me to write the book, and through its rejection by fifty-four agents and publishers. Finally, on the fifty-fifth submission my publishing fairytale came true, and I landed a generous two-book contract with Penguin.

I soon learned that fairytale endings are as rare in publishing as in marriage. For me, as for many authors, my publisher Prince Charming turned out to be a bit of a frog. My title, *After the Rising*, was rejected as "too Irish", and I was advised to change my author name for the same reason and when it came to positioning the book, our creative differences were intense.

Where I (and the commissioning editor who had acquired the book), saw a page-turning, multi-generational family drama that shattered silences and explored questions of freedom and belonging, the marketing department saw what was then called "chick lit". When the book jacket arrived, the cover image was a faceless woman, in a sheer dress, wafting through sand dunes and neon-pink branding. The blurb focused wholly on the contemporary love story, making no mention of the Irish civil war that was key to the book's themes. It gave no sense that the book even *had* a historical story, though it had taken me so many years to fictionalize sensitive personal and political issues into a story that would make readers think, while it swept them away.

"It's not about how you feel, it's about drawing in readers," the publishers said, which of course is wholly right, but my objection wasn't that I didn't "like" their choices. I was thinking commercially too. How were the right readers for my kind of book—the ones we needed to capture and keep for the next book—going to find it, behind its neon-pinkiness? And wouldn't those who chose the book based on its chick-lit promise be disappointed by its sexual politics and twisty-plot intrigue?

I asked for a meeting with the marketing department but, though I had a decade of experience in media and publishing as a journalist and literary agent, they actually laughed. How naive! No, no, that *never* happened.

The strategy worked, took the book to the top of the bestseller charts. Having suffered those fifty-four rejections, I was hyper-aware of how lucky I was, but I also felt bruised and confused. Next time, on my second novel, it was even worse.

Then, while we were preparing to launch, a tornado of change hit: the collapse of the "Celtic Tiger" in Ireland coincided with breast cancer, family and friend fallouts, redundancy and more. It flung our family of four into chaos. I closed my writing school, passed the literary agency to my business partner and, aged almost 50, moved from Dublin to London, where there would be more opportunities for us all.

That's where I was when digital self-publishing burst onto the scene: recovering from cancer and its treatments, writing poetry and working on a new novel. What should I do next? Where do you go as an author when Penguin hasn't delivered? Publish yourself? *Really*?

Enter Self-Publishing

At first, I was skeptical. Despite my creative differences with Penguin, I was still grateful to them for having invested in my work. I valued what they brought to the publishing process, and doing without a publisher altogether for a novel felt unthinkable to me. I'd self-published a book for a women's group I'd worked with, but that was non-fiction and more of a personal project.

Selling fiction internationally seemed far more daunting. What about editing and cover design? What about marketing?

"We hire those services, just like the publishers do," said one of my indie author friends, recently converted and understandably starry-eyed, as self-publishing was delivering her a six-figure income and she'd just bought a new house for her parents. However, she was tech savvy and business minded, and I was neither. And while her books were great, I also saw lots of other self-publishers putting their books out before they were ready, or choosing terrible covers, or not bothering with an editor.

Everyone in the industry had an opinion. Self-publishing was only for writers who weren't good enough to find a publisher. It was a democratizing force in an elitist industry. It was a fad. It was a game-changer. "Self-publishing is devaluing books" was a common cry in those days. One much-quoted publishing executive said, "We're all going to drown in a tsunami of crap." "No, no, no. Self-publishing is the best thing to happen to readers and writers since Gutenberg," replied the increasing number of authors who were publishing ebooks through retailers like Kindle Direct Publishing, Apple and Kobo Writing Life. They were all reaching more readers, earning more money, and having the best publishing experience of their lives.

The only way I was going to know was to do it myself and see.

I started small, with a poetry chapbook in ebook format. Everyone knew poetry didn't sell, which suited me just fine, as I made my mistakes and found my technical feet, with my new-found editors, designers and other authors to help me. Pressing the "Publish" button was a heady moment and when my little poetry chapbook actually did start to sell, I was astonished.

I hadn't told any family or friends so some (dearly beloved) strangers had parted with good money for a pamphlet of my poetry. Poetry! And unexpectedly, I had completely enjoyed the publishing process. I wrote on my blog and to my (then quite small) email list to tell readers what I was doing, and made some more sales, this time using a PayPal button on my own website.

Given that 70% of each sale made through the online retailers was coming to me, and more than 90% when I sold directly through PayPal, profit was already in sight, just through the ebooks. Wow! I could also publish print books, using print-on-demand technology and, most excitingly, my readership was global in both formats. Digital publishing knew no boundaries and through the various publishing platforms all the English-speaking countries of the world—and beyond!—were now as open to me as the UK and Ireland. Wow again!

Best of all, I retained all rights. *I* was the publisher.

All the implications began to sink in. No more "Publish me, pleeeeeease". No more rejection by gatekeepers. No more "creative differences" with publishing houses. Think of all the energy *that* would save, energy I could put into writing and my own publishing. Unlike my time with Penguin when we had only a season to see how the book would do before somebody else got their marketing turn, my little book could go on selling for me for as long as I chose to market it.

I was now firmly on the side of best-thing-since-Gutenberg. I saw that self-publishing was much more than just an alternative route to market. Authors could now reach readers while retaining all rights. If we chose to claim it, we could have creative freedom *and* commercial control. This was going to change *everything*.

It was time to talk to Penguin.

Going Indie

I got my rights back in 2012, the year I started to call myself an indie author, and the year my husband Philip Lynch and I launched ALLi, the Alliance of Independent Authors, as a non-profit, global authors' organization. More than a decade later, I am still happily self-publishing and our happy organization has thousands of members all over the world.

Going indie has been the best move of my writing life. My books sell steadily on my own websites and through retailers in more than 100 countries around the world. (Thanks for the info, Kobo map!) Some have hit bestseller lists, some have won awards, and my sales long ago surpassed those made by Penguin. Those sales are now to the right readers, and my reader mailing lists and publishing business continue to build steadily month on month.

I'm telling you all this not to self-congratulate but to point up what's possible. As writers go, I'm nothing special. I've made lots of missteps and mistakes along the way, which I'll also share with you in this book. I've gone down wrong pathways, taken on too much, opened too many projects at once. I've hired poor editors and chosen the wrong covers. I once had to unpublish a whole series that I spent years working on.

Nothing special, just lucky. As are you. All authors, all creatives, are blessed to live in these digital days.

Impact of Self-Publishing

Self-published books now span multiple formats, territories, and platforms and their sales are increasing globally at what veteran publishing commentator Mike Shatzkin has described as a "staggering" rate.

Today, hundreds of thousands of book buyers spend real money to buy and read untold pages of books written and uploaded into the cultural bloodstream with no judgement, mediation, review, or pitching by the traditional keepers of the gate. [1]

By 2014, within five years of mainstream digital self-publishing taking off in the US, it was accounting for more than 30% of all recorded book sales. On Amazon.com alone, thousands of independent authors were earning more than $50,000 annually for books, audiobooks, and ebooks, with more than 1,000 authors surpassing $100,000. [2]

This doesn't count all the books sold on other platforms. Contrary to popular belief, self-publishing is much bigger than Amazon. Millions of books are sold across the world on many other platforms—Apple Books, Google Play, IngramSpark, Kobo Writing Life—and, not least, on authors' own websites.

A recent ALLi survey into indie author income[3] found that self-publishing authors earn more, like for like, than authors with an exclusive trade publisher. More than 9% of our current membership has sold more than 50,000 books in the past two years.

In a few short years, indie authors have irrevocably changed the industry: now accounting for 30-34% of all ebook sales in the largest English-language markets, depending on which source you read (and none of them tell the full story), and making real inroads into the audiobook market too, and into print, through print-on-demand.

Self-publishing sales figures are higher than anyone knows, or can know, as many self-published books sell without an ISBN, on author websites, in special consignments, at weekend markets, back-of-the-room events, and many other ways that go unrecorded. Research by Written Word Media has demonstrated that it is now possible to earn over $100,000 annually as an author without appearing on any bestseller list. In a May 2016 snapshot of 142 such "invisible" authors on Amazon.com, 105 were self-publishers.[4]

Does any of this come as a surprise to you? You won't read much that is accurate about self-publishing in mainstream media. Although hundreds of thousands of indie authors around the world are producing work of outstanding literary merit and commercial appeal, although corporate publishers, film and TV buyers, and literary agents scout bestseller lists for successful self-published authors these days, hoping to woo them with a deal, these changes have yet to be widely reflected in the mainstream literary world of newspaper and magazine reviews, bookstores, festivals, and prizes.

As director of ALLi, I see firsthand the achievements of our innovative and hardworking community, the great flowering of creative expression in the literary arts that is being unleashed, and the great variety of ways in which authors can now succeed. That's what I want to share with you in this book. If you're just starting out, or haven't yet seen the success you seek, if you're struggling to produce your book or not reaching enough readers, if you need to make more sales or don't know how to move into profit as a publisher, this book points the way.

Publisher's Block

Everybody knows all about writer's block, but block and resistance are an integral part of any creative endeavor, including publishing. For a number of years, between 2016 to 2019, I labored under my own publishing block. At ALLi I was productive, but after a strong start as a self-publisher (at one time I had three novels at the top of the literary fiction charts), I'd stopped paying enough attention to marketing my fiction and poetry.

I was always writing—I write every day—and I was still making books, but largely books like the one you're reading: how-to non-fiction. My fiction and poetry were still selling in respectable numbers, but I wasn't growing. Yes, I had a busy day job at ALLi, and I had recently hit a personal challenge, a health diagnosis within the family that was having a big impact on my life, but with hand on creative heart, I knew that wasn't the whole story. I needed to be a better publisher of fiction and poetry. But how? In what ways, precisely?

When I was a creative writing teacher, I used f-r-e-e-writing, a creative flow technique, to clear writer's block for students. (see the next chapter for more on this method). I now used the same technique to explore my publishing business block. As so often, f-r-e-e-writing delivered some surprises. What emerged as I explored my publishing business on the page was my childhood and my family.

The Ireland where we grew up was full of job insecurity and emigration. My father worked in insurance, we also owned a pub and shop, and my mother later ran a bed-and-breakfast. I had three brothers who worked in insurance, accountancy and engineering. Everyone was agreed on the need to pin down a pensionable position, but I was drawn to books and poetry and adventure.

It took me decades to reconcile my life as a woman and then mother with my life in books, but I had. Only now I wanted to self-publish, and do it well. My f-r-e-e-writing revealed how my desire to be a successful independent author was challenging the binary opposition I'd been carrying around, unconsciously, as I'd done the work first of writing novels and poems, then of becoming a novelist and poet. Living life from that perspective.

If I now wanted to also be a good publisher, if I wanted to see my novels and poetry books recognized and read, I'd have to unpack all that anti-business baggage I was carrying from being on the "other" side in my family. I saw that I wasn't paying enough attention to money, which meant I wasn't paying enough attention to everything.

One part of me wanted to sell more books but other parts of me were not adopting the necessary behaviours.

- I was **publishing across a number of genres** but I hadn't segmented my readers. Fiction, non-fiction and poetry were all mixed up.
- I had thirteen projects open at once—a severe case of **shiny object syndrome**, cutting out of projects without finishing, to start something new.
- I was **doing too much** overall, too busy with too many sub-optimal tasks.
- Most of all, beyond running a never-ending to-do list, I was **failing to plan**. As the business people liked to say, failing to plan is planning to fail.

Sustainable success for my publishing business began on that rainy night. I learned my lessons, and they are embedded in this book in the hope that you can learn from my mistakes.

I've also seen lots of other mistakes, in dealing with tens of thousands of ALLi members and hundreds of thousands of ALLi subscribers over the past decade, as well as reading all the self-publishing blogs and books, and having close relationships with owners and directors of publishing houses and self-publishing services. I bring it all together here, zooming across the globe, across time and across the seven processes of publishing, so you can see precisely where you fit in and where you are right now.

Each week on Instagram, I put out a prompt for the poetry lovers who follow my feed. The same prompt produces a unique poem from each writer, as they watermark the idea with their own imagination, artistry and individuality. It's exactly the same with creative self-publishing. No two indie authors publish in exactly the same way.

That's why we're never in competition with each other. There's always room for another writer and as authors, we turn to each other for advice. The self-publishing community is renowned for collaboration but always, as creative self-publishers, we turn first towards the quiet, creative voice within.

1. Mike Shatzkin. 2019. The Book Business: What Everyone Needs to Know
2. https://www.writtenwordmedia.com/100k-author/
3. https://www.allianceindependentauthors.org/facts/
4. https://www.writtenwordmedia.com/100k-author/

HOW TO READ THIS BOOK

This book is structured to lead you in a logical order from understanding your author identity, to creating a personal definition of success, through to the foundations you need to put in place to succeed as an author. We then cover the seven processes of publishing. They will guide you to plan a profitable publishing business that is uniquely yours and which deeply satisfies a growing band of readers.

Each step of the way, exercises offer you the opportunity to integrate the information you've learned within the context of your own creative development as a publisher.

At ALLi we recommend a "just in time" instead of a "just in case" approach to acquiring knowledge. Instead of trying to learn everything all at once, seek out the information you need, when you need it. Learn to do that one thing, in the way that's right for you, then move to the next.

So one approach to this book might be to use the contents page to start with the information you most need. If you are just starting out and in doubt as to whether self-publishing is right for you, for example, go to Chapter 6. If you want to know what the possibilities are for authors today, see Chapter 29 about business models for authors and possible income streams. Want to set up a sales-centred author website, go to Chapter 12. Constantly fighting overwhelm? Take a look at the planning method offered in Chapter 24.

If you have never self-published before, however, or if you are uncertain about your publishing choices, you might want to read the book from beginning to end, skimming parts where it gets technical. It'll give you an overview, and you can come back to these parts when you need them.

Understanding what kind of self-publisher you are, what your author identity is, and what it means to have an indie author mindset: these might seem less necessary than practical information about Amazon's algorithms or how to license your TV rights, but authors who are enjoying success have all developed such understandings.

Advice You Can Trust

Poor advice is a problem for our community. Every day, all over the internet and often at the top of the search engines, publishing services put out all sorts of questionable "advice" that trades on authors' dreams with only one aim: to get you to buy what they're selling.

Marketing and social media services are particularly adept at this. Some vanity publishers have turned misinformation into a fine art. Ditto some TV and film "producers". If we don't know enough about how publishing works, and our own publishing aims and objectives, we can be easily swayed.

Even when we are experienced publishers, clever marketing can see us purchasing tools and courses that are not quite right for us, or that we don't have time to implement.

Another problem, more unexpectedly, is helpful authors. On social media forums, authors advise each other, sometimes well but often, despite good intentions, badly. Some speak about self-publishing without ever having done it. Others generalize from their own particular circumstances, assuming that what has worked well (or poorly) for them is also a good (or bad) option for everyone else.

"An author has to be on social media"
"Social media doesn't sell books."

"Give away free stuff."
"Free books devalue writing."

"You won't get traffic if you don't blog."
"Blogging is a waste of writing time."

"You should start a podcast."
"Forget podcasting, it's so over."

"Just write more books."
"Advertise or die."

"Practice lean publishing."
"Invest for success."

"Stick with Amazon."
"Go wide for the win."

Every week on our member forum we'll get somebody asking a question like, "Are Facebook ads worth it?" Lots of authors will jump in and answer. It's striking how varied the authors' experiences have been and how there is no single right answer.

Whether Facebook ads are going to be "worth it" for you depends on so many factors—your intentions and goals, your willingness to learn, your genre and category, your time and money budget, your personal inclinations. That won't stop some well-meaning authors from issuing blanket statements about how great/useless ads are, and how you must/must never advertise. More established authors will always offer their own experience, with a proviso that "YMMV" (your mileage may vary).

Your mileage *will* vary. No two self-publishers are the same. All advice must be embedded in your personal creative intentions and capacity. That's the big difference between this book and other self-publishing guides. It invites you to put your creativity at the core of your publishing, as well as your writing.

Going Creative

One of our aims with this book is to debunk bad advice. The other is to encourage you to trust your own creative impulses and approach your publishing with a creative spirit of experimentation, exploration and learning by doing. When we work this way, we can enjoy the challenges of writing and publishing, and know that there is no such thing as failure. Each book (and each mistake) is a learning opportunity that empowers your creative growth.

It all hinges on the "creative" concept. What does it mean, at a practical level, for you as a self-publishing author?

In my thirty plus years as a writer, I've had the privilege of working with some of the world's most imaginative and innovative people: activists, actors, artists, authors, designers, filmmakers, illustrators, performers, photographers, and publishing professionals. I also spent some years in a university, teaching creative and imaginative studies from an academic perspective. Across that time, I've found that few people—even those who are highly creative themselves—can articulate what that word means.

If you ask an artist for a definition of creativity, you'll get a different answer, using different language, describing different aspects of life than if you ask an inventor, a coder, or an entrepreneur. The dictionary doesn't help: there are many definitions of creativity, some plain wrong and most incomplete.

The only all-encompassing definition is the simplest and most obvious—*creativity is self-expression.* However we each express ourselves so differently and none of us is a singular, coherent self anyway. As the American bard, Walt Whitman, famously put it in "Song of Myself": "Do I contradict myself? Very well then, I contradict myself; (I am large, I contain multitudes.)"

We completely misunderstand what it is to be creative if we think it's restricted to particular tasks—writing but not marketing, for example. Or if we see creativity as a talent or skill that some people (writers) have, but others (business people) don't. Writing can be cranked out in a rote, uncreative, commercial way while the tasks of running an author business offer countless opportunities to be innovative, imaginative and expressive. An entrepreneur can display dazzling creativity, while a writer can be a hack, routinely going through the motions.

In 2015, the Red Bull Cracking Creativity Project[1], a collaboration between the energy drinks company, a group of TED Fellows and a number of scientists at the MIT Media Lab, ran the largest review of creativity research yet done. The project examined more than 30,000 research papers and interviews with hundreds of subjects—poets, rock stars, circus performers, all kinds of people—as well as conducting their own survey to see if the question "what is creativity?" could be answered definitively.

This review arrived at an overarching conclusion confirmed by other studies before and since, and by my own experience and observation of author-publishers: creativity is not an outcome but a brain and body state. A state of being. We have little success in training people to be more creative because we treat it as if it were a *skill* producing a *product*, when really it's a *state* engaged in a *process*.

That's the understanding of creativity that underwrites this book.

There are two main occupational hazards for a self-publisher: going too fast or going too slow. Too fast means publishing too soon, putting out books that need better writing skills, more editing, improved production, a proper marketing and promotion plan. Too slow means not publishing enough, getting stuck in resistance or block, being unclear about your processes, paralyzed by choice, distracted and unable to focus, mired in your own mind. The solution to both is the same: going creative.

Going creative means connecting more deeply with your innate creative capacity. Expanding your skills with new practices and processes. Setting up processes that foster creative flow. That is what I hope this book and the creative planning program that accompanies it will provide for you—in your writing, in your publishing, in your way of doing creative business.

I don't know where you are in your writing or publishing business, whether you're just considering self-publishing for the first time, or whether you're already up and running. No doubt you are impatient to get to the practical information but as you've seen from my experience, when you don't understand your creative context, you waste a lot of time and money churning or spinning.

Yes, you need to know all about the craft of publishing but you also need to know what becoming skilled at that craft means to you—the opportunities and threats that are particular to you as a writer and publisher; the creative conditions within which you work, rest and play; your personal passion and mission; your physical and cognitive strengths and weaknesses; the particular ways in which your creative resistance presents itself.

At times, this book strays into territory that might seem strange for a practical guidebook—but that is the nature of our task. Creative writing, creative publishing, creative business are all complex processes that call for emotional as well as intellectual labor.

What's needed is a way of working that integrates them all. Such integration is not a concept, it's an *experience*. So this is not just a reading book, it's a *doing* book. For you to get the full benefit, your participation is required.

CREATIVE EXERCISES

The exercises in this book are your key to processing whatever challenges are currently presenting for you in your writing or publishing life. Creativity is a muscle. And, like any muscle, it needs exercise. When you want to build muscle, you lift weights. Want to run faster? Do sprints. Want to be more creative? Do these exercises.

The creative exercises in this book have already helped thousands of authors to dissolve resistance, banish block, and foster flow in writing, publishing and creative business.

F-r-e-e-writing

The recommended method used to complete the exercises in this book (and in the *Go Creative! In Business* planners and workbooks) is f-r-e-e-writing. Lots of writers love to journal and you're probably already familiar with the concept of free writing: you sit down for a period of time and write whatever comes to mind. The method used here—f-r-e-e-writing—is similar, but with the additional aspect of setting a time and writing as fast as you can, by hand, pen to paper, if possible.

The aim when f-r-e-e-writing is to write so fast that you get beyond the conscious mind and open a channel that receives and transmits the insights and inspirations of the subconscious mind with more ease. The acronym f-r-e-e stands for writing **fast**, **raw** and **exact-but-easy**.

Based on the research work of writing facilitators like Dorothea Brande[2], Julia Cameron[3], Peter Elbow[4], Natalie Goldberg[5], James W Pennebaker[6] and others who have researched and used various forms of expressive writing in their work, this kind of f-r-e-e-writing has been shown to have transformative effects on creative capacity and flow.

- **F = Write Fast:** Write as fast as you can, without stopping, for an allocated time or notebook space (typically 15 minutes or three A4, letter-size pages, 8.5 x 11 inches approx).
- **R = Write Raw:** Ignore punctuation, spelling, or grammar. Don't judge the writing, welcome any words that arrive. Let whatever wants to be written flow onto the page.
- **E = Write Exact:** Give sensory details of whatever you're writing about. Recall sounds, smells, tastes, thirsts, and feelings, as well as ideas and insights.
- **E = Write Easy:** Take off the reins, write in a free-flowing way. If you find yourself not knowing what to write next, just write something like "I can't think what to write, I can't think what to write," until the mind starts to move in words again.

The **TRY THIS** exercises in this book (see below) will ask you to use this core practice again and again.

You can also use a few paragraphs of f-r-e-e-writing any time to help you see and dissolve a particular writing, publishing or business block. In addition, taking a period to f-r-e-e-write—to just write whatever comes into your head, again as fast as you can—can be enormously productive and rewarding.

Find out more, and buy a f-r-e-e-writing notebook or creative business planning workbook here: SelfPublishingAdvice.org/ playbooks

Consider, Try & Do: Creative Exercises

Many of the exercises in this book ask you to f-r-e-e-write around a particular theme, but there are others that call for very different kinds of creative work, rest and play. These exercises form a scaffolding that supports you and allows you to take your creative risks from a place of safety.

1. **CONSIDER THIS: Creative Rest**—Think of this as a creative breather, a moment to stop reading, to rest and reflect, meditate and mull.
2. **TRY THIS: Creative Play**—Exercises that encourage you towards creative awareness, to do a creative experiment, or to explore a particular topic through f-r-e-e-writing.
3. **DO THIS: Creative Work**—These exercises apply a core publishing practice or creative process to your author-business.

Often, when I introduce these creative exercises to indie authors, they wail, "I don't have time for this". It's so important to understand that these exercises don't *take* time, they *make* time. Less becomes more as overwhelm, stress and resistance dissolve, and inspiration, intuition and insight emerge.

I've used every exercise in this book over the years and I've seen them make such a difference in other authors' lives that I pass them on whenever I can. But you don't need to take my word for it. As you do the exercises, you'll witness for yourself how they work for you. Don't measure the number of hours you're putting in as much the product you're putting out and your feelings as you create.

When you do this, you'll see for yourself how the exercises foster creative flow and have practical applications for you. How they keep you centered, as you speak ever more truly in your own voice, not just in your books but also on your website, in your sell sheets and author pages, when speaking to interviewers and media, and in person. How they release you from the nagging stress of too-much-to-do syndrome.

Still, no matter how well you know they work, you'll feel that inclination to resist—to skip over them, to question their value, to think you're too busy to do them. It's the same syndrome that makes one part of you procrastinate when another part wants to write. Conscious creation always comes with creative resistance in tow. Whatever way your resistance rises for you—and it will—please see it for what it is.

My promise to you in this book is that I'll distinguish between proven techniques and tools, ALLi's best practice recommendations, and my personal approach and opinion. And I'd really appreciate your promise that you'll do the exercises, so you can get the most from this book.

Workbooks, Planners and Workshops

To accompany this creative self-publishing book, I've produced a set of workbooks and planners that apply the creative process to the business of publishing.

You can purchase these **Go Creative! Business Planning Workbooks for Authors and Poets** *on ALLi's Self-Publishing Advice website at SelfPublishingAdvice.org/playbooks*

I also run a private online workshop each month based around the concepts and exercises in this book for a small group of **creative business planning patrons***. Patreon.com/OrnaRoss. These workshops are based on the business planning method outlined in this book. See SelfPublishingAdvice.org/planning/ for more details.*

1. 2015. Red Bull Cracking Creativity .
2. Dorothea Brande. 1934. Becoming A Writer.
3. Julia Cameron. 1992. The Artist's Way
4. Peter Elbow. 1989. Toward a Phenomenology of Freewriting.
5. Natalie Goldberg. 2005. Writing Down the Bones.
6. James W Pennebaker. 2014. Expressive Writing: Words That Heal

ALLI SUPPORTS AND RESOURCES

This book is first in series from the Alliance of Independent Authors (ALLi)'s **Publishing Guides for Authors** series. It is the foundational text which outlines the method and mindset that underlie all our services to our members, readers, and subscribers.

Alliance of Independent Authors

ALLi is pronounced "ally" (al-eye not al-ee), and we aim to be an ally to self-publishers everywhere. Our name is spelt with a big ALL and small i because our members are like the three musketeers in Dumas's eponymous novel: ALL working for each individual "i", and each for ALL. Our mission is ethics and excellence in self-publishing.

ALLi is headquartered in London and unites thousands of beginner, emerging and experienced indie authors from all over the world behind this mission. Most of our members are in the US and Canada, followed closely by Europe, Australia and New Zealand, and South Africa. We are a Community Interest Company (CIC) and all profits are invested back in for the benefit of our members and the wider indie author community.

Our work is fourfold:

- ALLi *advises*, providing best-practice information and education through our online Self-Publishing Advice Center, SelfPublishingAdvice.org, offering a daily blog, a weekly live video and podcast, a bookstore of self-publishing guidebooks, and a quarterly member magazine.
- ALLi *monitors* the self-publishing sector through a watchdog desk, alerting authors to bad actors and predatory players and running an approved partner program.
- ALLi *campaigns* for the advancement of indie authors in the publishing and literary sectors globally (bookstores, libraries, literary events, prizes, grants, awards, and other author organizations), encouraging the provision of publishing and business skills for authors, speaking out against iniquities and inequities, and furthering the indie author cause wherever possible.
- ALLi *empowers* independent authors through community and collaboration—author forums, contract advice, sample agreements, contacts and networking, literary agency representation, and a member care desk.

Whether you're self-publishing your first book or your fiftieth, ALLi is with you every step of the way, with a suite of member benefits that includes free guidebooks, discounts and deals, member forums, contract consultancy, advisory board, literary agent for eligible members, a community watchdog desk and more.

As well as offering access to ALLi's supportive, dynamic community and wide range of services, your membership also supports our advocacy work for indie authors globally, from Alaska to New Zealand the long way round, and everywhere in between.

When you join ALLi, you're not just joining an organization, you're becoming part of a transformative, self-organizing, global, author movement. If you haven't yet, I'd like to invite you to join us.

Find out more at: AllianceIndependentAuthors.org

AskALLi: Advice Campaign

In 2013, ALLi launched its #**AskALLi** campaign, in which we pledged to answer, with evidence-based authority, *any* self-publishing question *any* author might have. We continue this work today, through our email support desk, our member forums, and our blog posts and podcasts in the **Self-Publishing Advice Center.** Key in any search term there to get a best-practice answer to your question.

As an ALLi member, you can also jump onto our closed forum and ask other members, ALLi team, and advisors who are on hand, 24/7, for their advice.

Resource Links

Blog: SelfPublishingAdvice.org/blog: How-to blog posts, analysis and opinion on all seven processes of publishing

Podcast: SelfPublishingAdvice.org/podcast: Advice on Fridays and Inspirations on Sundays

Conference: SelfPublishingAdviceConference.com: The largest annual online gathering of independent authors, each October

Planning: Small group creative planning programs run by Orna Ross: Patreon.com/OrnaRoss

---

PART I

THE INDEPENDENT AUTHOR

In Part I we look at the different kinds of self-publishing writers and the success measures for independent authors who want to make a living from writing and publishing books. As an indie author, you may begin as a writer, but you must also become a publisher. We outline some self-publishing success stories and begin the process of establishing your definition of success as both writer and publisher.

1

WHAT KIND OF SELF-PUBLISHER ARE YOU?

T he first thing you need to know about the self-publishing sector is that it is diverse. It embraces artistic authors who produce experimental books no third-party publisher will touch, and entrepreneurial authors who want to make a killing on Kindle. There are those who are publishing one book for family and friends, and those who want to make writing and publishing their life's work. There are authors who want to pay a service to do as much as possible for them, and those who are fiercely DIY. Artisans who produce premium books of exceptional design, and minimalists who've nailed a super-simple process to facilitate rapid release. Somewhere, in the middle of it all, there's you.

The only assumption this book makes about you is that you want to be a good publisher as well as a good writer. Depending on where you are in your development as an indie author, you may not think about it in that way. It's commonplace in our sector to hear people talk about "author careers", for example, but publishing your own books and selling them to readers is not a career; it's a business.

An independent author is a business owner, and the business is book publishing and book selling—a confusing sector. Publishers come in many structures and sizes: corporate, medium, and indie; trade, academic and children's; hybrid, assisted and vanity; and now author-publishers too.

At ALLi, we have identified three kinds of self-publishing authors. Which kind are you?

THREE KINDS OF SELF-PUBLISHERS

1. The One-Book Self-Publisher

This kind of writer is not interested in writing for a living or in publishing lots of books. They want to make a particular book out of their own need, or the needs of a group of people—their grandchildren, their activist group, their local historians, their client base. Whether they are publishing for family or friends, for posterity or self-development, to boost their business or fulfil a long-held dream, the term *self*-publishing is most appropriate for this group.

For the family, friends, and community writers, it's about personal storytelling, as an act of *self*-expression. For the non-fiction author making a book to boost their brand, or business, or expertise, it's about *self*-promotion. Generally for one-book publishers, the focus behind the writing and publishing is as much about the author as the reader, and more production than sales driven.

2. The Independent "Indie" Author

Indie authors self-publish commercially. As well as the intrinsic creative rewards of publishing, they also want the extrinsic rewards of income and influence. This is not "vanity publishing," paying an inflated sum to a service that flatters and deceives the author while posing as a publisher. Neither is it skipping the work of honing writing and publishing craft. This is taking charge of your own team and becoming the creative director of your own writing and publishing business.

In some ways, *self*-publishing and *indie* authorship are misnomers for this group of writers. A good book is always a collaborative process and indie authors must put their books through the same processes as any other publisher. They must have production and profit plans, they must work with editors, designers, marketers, aggregators, agents, assistants, sales platforms and more to see their books produced and published to standard.

Independence is a heady word, conjuring up values like freedom, rebellion, and self-reliance. Compared to authors who sign exclusive deals with a single trade publisher or a single self-publishing service, indie authors are relatively independent, yes, but only when they embrace that empowerment.

At ALLi, we define an indie (independent) author as follows:

- You have self-published at least one book.
- You see yourself as the creative director of your books and your own publishing business.
- You are proud of your indie status and carry that self-respect into all your ventures, negotiations, and collaborations, for the sake of other authors, as well as yourself.
- You expect your status as rights holder and creative director to be acknowledged in payment, terms and conditions.
- You see your connection to your readers as your primary publishing relationship.

Until recently, received wisdom assumed that writers "just want to write," but the self-publishing revolution has revealed this sizeable band of authors who very much want to publish their own books, their own way.

3. The Authorpreneur

Authorpreneurs are indie authors who have mastered the three sets of skills needed to make a good income from publishing. They understand and practice good writing craft, good publishing craft, good business craft. They produce great books and sell plenty of them, not as a one-off sales spike, but again and again. They may also produce premium books and other products. They have built a tribe of readers who value their work and look forward to hearing from them.

In many cases, they are licensing rights to publishers and other rights buyers. In some cases, they are publishing other authors too.

In 2019, ALLi changed the name of its top author membership tier from Professional Member to Authorpreneur Member. One member felt so strongly about the move that she left the organization, saying, "I really dislike that made-up word and I really dislike 'entrepreneur' being linked to 'author' in any way, shape, or form." We went ahead nonetheless, not just because so many other members felt positive or neutral but because no other term seemed as accurate. It perfectly describes the new breed of author who blends books and business, authorship and entrepreneurship. A new word for new publishing.

When you publish your own books, you become part of a contemporary disruption to the world of work that is much wider than our own sector of writing and publishing. Over the past decade, an abundance of new innovations—social, personal, sexual, spiritual—have arrived into the marketplace, transforming how we work and live together.

A rural farmer in Africa today has more computing power in her pocket than the entire NASA facility had when it launched Apollo 11 in 1969. People now connect through social media groups and digital dating, electronic assistants and voice technology, text messages and memes. Many have job titles that didn't even exist ten years ago: data scientist, app developer, green-building consultant, internet coach and yes, authorpreneur. It was important for our organization to name the entrepreneurial attitude that distinguishes these authors.

At time of writing, authorpreneur members make up almost 9% of ALLi's membership. These authors have sold 50,000 books or equivalent in the two years prior to joining. We look forward to seeing that percentage grow as more authors acquire the creative publishing and creative business skills that bring success. But, of course, not all self-publishers want to be indie authors and not all indie authors want to be authorpreneurs.

CONSIDER THIS: What Kind of Self-Publisher are You?

A one-book self-publisher? An indie author, aiming to earn a living from your writing? A fully fledged authorpreneur, creating a high-earning publishing business, perhaps publishing other authors too?

Or perhaps you haven't even decided whether you will self-publish at all?

While this book, and the Alliance of Independent Authors, provide everything a one-book author needs to publish well, our focus here is mainly on the indie author and authorpreneur. Those who want to make a living from writing and publishing books, or are succeeding in doing so, while creating a body of work, earning a good income, exerting an influence that enriches the world, and leaving a legacy when they're gone.

If that's what you want, you can have it. There's no barrier to entry, beyond your personal abilities and disabilities. There are no gatekeepers, no rejection letters, no pile of manuscripts in the corner labelled "slush". You don't have to go to the right parties or know the right people. You don't have to have an Oxbridge or Ivy league degree, you don't have to have any degree at all. It sounds hyperbolic, but it's true: you can just do it.

Of course, there are things that you *do* have to do, and nobody else is going to do them for you. Write words that resonate with readers. Produce books that are properly designed and edited. Set up effective supply chains. Establish a brand that explains your work to the world. Create marketing and promotion processes that get your books into the right reader's hands. And do all this at a profit.

Does it sound daunting? Don't worry, at ALLi we are surrounded by authors who can point the way. Let's look at a few examples to see the many ways it can be done.

2

SOME SELF-PUBLISHING SUCCESS STORIES

The publishing industry has long labelled any kind of author-funded publishing as "vanity," but self-publishing is something that sincere, talented and skilled writers have always done, even when it was far more challenging than it is today.

The list of venerable self-publishers from the past is long, and includes such luminaries as Margaret Atwood, Jane Austen, E. E. Cummings, Beatrix Potter, Alfred Lord Tennyson, Henry David Thoreau, Leo Tolstoy, Mark Twain, Walt Whitman, WB Yeats and countless others.

"We're thinking of starting a printing press, for all our friends' stories," wrote Virginia Woolf to a friend in 1916, about the decision she and her husband Leonard had made to purchase a hand-press. "Don't you think it's a good idea?" A year later, when the press was up and running, she confessed to another friend that she was loving self-publishing. It was "the greatest mercy to be able to do what one likes—no editors, or publishers, and only people to read who more or less like that sort of thing."[1]

In addition to these individual authors, educators have always published books for their students, libraries, galleries, and museums. Other institutions have always published books for their visitors, and companies have always published books for their clients. All of this falls into the realm of "self"-publishing.

And now that we no longer need printing presses, the roster of distinguished self-published authors is growing at a rapid pace. As you read through the following author's stories, notice the breadth of their choices and pathways and consider which of their pathways most appeal to you.

INDIE AUTHOR EXAMPLES

1. The Record Breaker: LJ Ross

Ex-lawyer, LJ Ross, tells everyone that deciding to self-publish a novel was the best decision she ever made. Her first novel, *Holy Island*, was an instant success on Amazon's Kindle Direct Publishing platform (KDP) and at time of writing—just a short five years later—Ross has published nineteen more books, sold around 4.5 million copies, and topped Amazon's Kindle ebooks bestseller list seven times in 2019, a record for the platform.

Ross also has her own print imprint that supplies paperbacks to UK bookshops. Her books straddle two genres, romantic suspense, and crime fiction and though "everybody" advised her against mixing it up, she went ahead. "The benefit of remaining independent is that you can take your own creative and business decisions," she says.

Despite approaches from traditional publishers, Ross has yet to be tempted. With the exception of audiobooks and some foreign rights (rights to publish in other countries outside the UK), which she says she publishes along more traditional lines, she wants to remain within the self-publishing sphere.

"In my case, it's been a very sustainable means of income and has allowed me to work as a full-time author from the beginning," she explained. "I know that there are thousands [of other authors] out there who have been able to... work part-time as an author, alongside all of the other full-time indie authors who have been able to give up the day job. Self-publishing has been a liberating, life-changing experience for many writers."

2. The Fiction-Activist: Lisa Genova

The neuroscientist and novelist, Lisa Genova, writes stories that are equally inspired by brain science and the human spirit. Her breakthrough book was *Still Alice*, a moving story about Alzheimer's Disease and how it affects relationships based on Genova's experience of watching as the disease "systematically disassembled the woman I knew as my grandmother".

It was self-published in 2007, having spent a year on the pitch-and-rejection cycle. The last agent who looked at the manuscript warned Genova not to self-publish, telling her that it would kill her career forever. The author went ahead, publishing the book and "selling it out of the trunk of my car... trying to create a buzz on Myspace, Goodreads and Shelfari and local book signings." She invested in a PR agent and *Still Alice* subsequently sold well and went on to net lucrative publishing rights deals, including a movie starring Julianne Moore.[2]

At time of writing, Genova has published four other novels, signed trade deals with a number of publishers, and received many awards, including the Pell Center Prize for "distinguished storytelling that has enriched the public dialog," the Sargent and Eunice Shriver Profiles in Dignity Award, the Global Genes RARE Champions of Hope Award, and the American College of Neuropsychopharmacology Media Award. Just as well she didn't listen to that agent.

3. The Movie Blockbuster: Andy Weir

Andy Weir is a computer programmer and self-described "space nerd" who, having been repeatedly turned down by literary agents, initially published his science fiction book, about a NASA astronaut stranded on Mars, in serial form on his blog. Requests from his readers led him to make the book available in its entirety and it quickly became an Amazon bestseller within the science fiction genre, selling in excess of 35,000 copies in less than a month, thanks to the author platform Weir had built on his blog.

He licensed the audiobook rights and it became a bestseller too. A subsequent hardback edition hit the Top 20 in the New York Times bestseller list and the film rights were sold to Twentieth Century Fox. The book was adapted to a major Hollywood movie starring Matt Damon,[3] and Weir received the John W. Campbell Award for Best New Writer in 2016.

4. The Booker Prize Lister: Jill Paton Walsh

Jill Paton Walsh was a self-publishing pioneer in the 1990s, another story born out of rejection by the trade. "My third adult novel was rejected by the publisher of the first two and I could not understand the criticism offered… the book in question, *Knowledge of Angels*, felt to me the one I was born to write." Paton Walsh's agent did succeed in licensing it to Houghton Mifflin in the US but, try as they might, they couldn't find a UK publisher. Before publication day, her US editor phoned: did she want a few extra copies so her British friends could read it? "The nineteenth London rejection was on my desk," says Paton Walsh. "My husband said: 'Fuck them all–we'll do it ourselves.' We rang back and said: 'Can you make that 1,000?' In a burst of furious activity, we got an ISBN, mocked up a British title page and swift-aired the books across the Atlantic." With the help of indie publisher friends, they organized a sales rep, an invoicing programme, a warehouse, and a publicist.

The book was distributed and began to sell in significant numbers for a literary philosophical novel. It went into reprint, foreign rights began to sell, and Transworld bought the paperback rights. And then it made the longlist for the 1994 Booker Prize. And then the shortlist.

"I didn't win the Booker, but by then I really didn't need to; our action in self-publishing the book in Britain was vindicated."[4]

5. The Trade-Publishing Escapee: Adam Nevill

Adam Nevill has nineteen trade-published books, all of which sell respectably and some of which have won awards and been made into movies. He switched to self-publishing because he was frustrated by dwindling earnings for his books in trade publishing and also by the industry's view of the horror genre. In a nutshell: "outside comfort zones".

His first self-published novel, *The Reddening*, was released in October 2019 and it's already out-sold a number of his trade-published books, for which he credits ACCESS marketing campaigns you'll read about in Chapter 21.

In 2016, Adam's first year as a self-publisher, he wrote an excellent post on his blog. "The best strategy I tried initially seemed both counter-intuitive and counter-productive and that involved producing free books and linking them to my website and author newsletter. I feared devaluing my own writing, but in all of the courses I studied from professional and successful indie authors, they recommended this marketing strategy.

"I then watched my mailing list surge and even saw one of the free ebooks downloaded 30K times in a couple of months. These were mostly new readers too, who'd never read or even heard of me. I'd never, so quickly, reached so many new readers of horror.

"The learning curve was steep, and the process of acquiring new skill-sets, setting up the company, and publishing three books... consumed my mental capacity and nearly all of my time [for] eight months. What I ended up with at year's end was an automated author platform... It pretty much runs itself now."

Adam continues to thrive as an indie author today, with an ever-growing list of fans and a semi-automated marketing system.

6. The Millionaire Poet: Rupi Kaur

In 2016, a young Sikh-Canadian poet outsold Homer with her first collection, *milk & honey*, which famously stole the position of best-selling poetry book from *The Odyssey*.

The poet, Rupi Kaur, takes her punctuation style from her Punjabi heritage's *gurmukhi* script in which there are no uppercase letters.

"I asked a creative writing professor once how to get published but i was told it was too difficult. poetry basically never got published. when i asked about the self-publishing route i was told no: to surpass the gatekeeper would be looked down upon by my literary peers."

But in November 2014, Kaur self-published a print book through Amazon. "it didn't occur to me to even reach out to publishers to submit unsolicited manuscripts because of years of being told 'there was no market for my poetry' [and] creative control was most important. i wanted to design the cover. i wanted to lay the book out. it was my heart on paper. i wanted to pick the size. font. and colors. years of study in visual rhetoric and design led me to fall in love with print and graphic art." (Kaur does not use capital letters, or any punctuation marks other than a period.)

Critics have publicly dismissed her work as "not poetry" but that is to misunderstand her mission and her *modus operandi*. "all the dozens of poems together were themselves one poem. all the parts/poems came together to make one body. to pick off pieces isn't right." She also illustrates her poems herself on Instagram and has a carefully honed aesthetic that matches her mission and the kind of meaning her fans are seeking from her work.

Her fans get it. She has a following of millions, many of whom are poets themselves, now also enjoying writing workshops and shared writing time with her.

From that first poetry pamphlet, Kaur has gone on to make the Forbes "thirty under thirty" list, and licensed publishing rights to third-party publishers all over the world. Today, her book tours sell out world stadiums more commonly associated with rock stars.

7. The Business Owner: Daniel Priestley

Business mentor, Daniel Priestley, is founder of Dent, an accelerator program for small enterprises that works with 500+ entrepreneurs each year to develop their businesses. An entrepreneur at twenty-one, he had built a multi-million dollar marketing and management business before the age of twenty-five. Now he raises up to $100,000 for charity each year. He is also a prolific self-publisher. His first two books were trade-published but then he turned to working with ALLi Partner Member, Rethink Books, to help him plan, write and publish his books himself.

Like most business book self-publishers, for Daniel, his books are his calling cards. "The reason I write books is to get a message out there to connect with a lot of people. For me, it's more important that the book is out there doing its job, as opposed to just simply trying to sell the book. The books fit within a broader context of a bigger business."[5]

8. The Children's Book Bestseller: Karen Inglis

UK and USA bestseller, Karen Inglis, first started writing for children when her sons were toddlers. The three books she wrote then sat in a box for over ten years while she went back to her day job, but in 2010 she decided to rewrite and edit them and prepared them for self-publishing.

Since then, Karen has seen hundreds of thousands of sales across her titles, mostly in print, alongside several foreign rights deals, with more in progress. At time of writing, her bestselling book, *The Secret Lake,* has had over 400,000 print sales and more than 10,000 star reviews, an astonishing achievement for any children's book publisher.

9. The Gamer Turned Author: Paul J Bennett

Paul's interest in writing started in his teen years when he discovered the roleplaying game, Dungeons & Dragons (D&D) and began to create realms, worlds and adventures that pulled other gamers into his stories. In his thirties, Paul started designing his own roleplaying system, and his first book originated from a fantasy game that he ran like a TV show, with seasons of twelve episodes, and an overarching plot.

When the campaign ended, he knew all the characters, what they had to accomplish, what needed to happen to move the plot along, and was inspired to write his first novel. Like many indie authors, Paul is self-taught, and has spent many hours researching how to write and self-publish. He is now working on his fourth successful series based on his fantasy world. An ALLi authorpreneur member, he makes an excellent living from self-publishing.

10. The Self-Publishing Adventurer: Anna McNuff

A self-described adventurer and mischief maker, Anna McNuff is best known for her attempt to run 100 marathons through Great Britain, in her bare feet. Her books chronicle her adventures, from exploring the wilds of New Zealand on foot, to cycling through every state in the US.

Her fourth book, *Llama Drama*, in which she and her friend Faye travel the Andes, "with a limited grasp of Spanish, and the hope of meeting as many llamas as possible", won the Kindle Storyteller award in 2020.

She's been named by Condé Nast Traveler as one of the fifty most influential travellers of our time, and is the UK Ambassador for Girl Guiding, and co-founder of Adventure Queens, a women's adventure community.

"Some of the best things in my life have come from spontaneous moments and that's how I started self-publishing," McNuff says. "It's brought me to this place in time. I can't wait to go on my next adventure."

These are just ten stories plucked from hundreds of thousands of possible success stories, here at the start of this book to inspire you—to show you what's possible and also to show that success for indie authors takes many forms. Different authors and different books require different pathways and plans.

Scan ALLi authors to see the great range of possibilities. We have thousands of author members who have published one or more books, and hundreds of authorpreneur members who are earning an excellent living from writing and publishing books and associated products.

Go to: AllianceIndependentAuthors.org/author-search/ and click "ALLi Authors" to survey author members.

Search "Authorpreneurs" to bring up our authorpreneur members only. These authors have all sold at least 50,000 books, or page-read/business equivalent, in the past two years and are making a good living from their self-publishing.

Your Publishing Challenges

You too can have the success you seek. No matter where you are now, whether you're writing your first book or your fifteenth or your fiftieth, you can deepen and develop your writing and publishing skills.

Every indie author who is succeeding today began in the same place—with an impassioned idea, a sense of purpose, and a desire to shape words into a book. They found time, between day jobs and personal commitments at a kitchen or café table, in a garage or study to put in the hours. They wrestled, as you must, with an invisible underbelly of doubt, fear and resistance, but they had enough creative confidence to get started and keep going, without waiting for validation or permission, without knowing how things were going to turn out.

An overnight success is never what it seems. The creative action all happens inside, down deep, across months and years. What you see when an author emerges into public consciousness is a result of a thousand tiny moments, day after day of applying creative principles, practices, and processes.

Let's begin by asking you those publishing questions I put to myself in my study, on that rainy night, to get a clearer picture of what's going on for you, as a publisher, right now.

TRY THIS: Your Definition of Self-Publishing Success

Are you running a successful publishing business right now?

Are you happy with your book making? (Writing and writing habits, editorial, design, production)

Are you happy with your book positioning? (Distribution, marketing)

Are you happy with your book sales (promotion, rights licensing)

Do you earn enough from your publishing business at the moment? (Yes / No) How does that make you feel? Choose a precise single adjective, like elated, content, downcast, frustrated. On a scale of one to ten, rate the intensity of that emotion for you, right now.

Write a paragraph about when you started to feel this way and why.

What would it take for you to become a good publisher?
What's the most important thing for you to do next?

1. JH Willis, Jr. Leonard and Virginia Woolf as Publishers. The Hogarth Press 1917-41
2. "Still Alice (novel) – Wikipedia." https://en.wikipedia.org/wiki/Still_Alice_(novel). Accessed 30 Jun. 2017.
3. "The Martian (Weir novel) – Wikipedia." https://en.wikipedia.org/wiki/The_Martian_(Weir_novel)
4. https://www.theguardian.com/lifeandstyle/2010/oct/24/jill-paton-walsh-a-life
5. https://extraordinarybusinessbooks.com/episode-72-book-as-business-development-with-daniel-priestly/#:~:text=I%27ve%20al-ways%20thought%20of,trying%20to%20sell%20the%20book.

3

YOUR DEFINITION OF SUCCESS

To create a book or a publishing business, you need to get clear about the specifics. What does success look like for you?

Poet Maya Angelou said, "Success is liking yourself, liking what you do, and liking how you do it." Novelist Paulo Coelho said success "is being able to go to bed each night with your soul at peace." The great non-fiction writer Samuel Johnson said, "No man but a blockhead ever wrote, except for money."

When I started out in my twenties, like many aspiring writers with an overactive imagination, my definition of success was fame and fortune—I would become a bestselling and prizewinning author. I smile now at the mental conversations I used to have with imaginary chat-show hosts who were fascinated by my (not yet written) first book.

Eventually I got real, wrote the book, edited it a hundred times, found a publisher, got some actual media placements, and saw behind the smoke and mirrors of publicity and publication.

Fame and fortune, when they finally came, were not at all how I'd envisaged them and now that I've gone past bestsellerdom and prizes,

I have three definitions of success that are quite different to the early, ego-fuelled dreams of my naive young self.

- To earn my living from writing and publishing fiction and poetry. For me, that's success.
- To help other authors and creatives succeed. For me, that's success.
- To play my part in the evolution of humanity to a more expanded and progressive consciousness. For me, that's success.

TRY THIS: Your Definition of Success.

1) What is your definition of success? Is it lots of money? Extrinsic rewards like big cars, upscale houses and jewelry? Or intrinsic: independence, autonomy, personal growth? Is it the freedom, time and money to live where you like, doing what you most love? Is it inspiring or empowering or educating others? Or something else?

2) Where do you think this definition comes from? Why do these things spell success to you?

The compulsion to compare your accomplishments to others is an occupational hazard for indie authors, known in creative circles as "comparison-itis". Whether it's a negative or positive comparison is irrelevant. As an indie author, you are surrounded by authors who are doing better than you and also those doing worse than you. You see some doing extraordinary things: turning over exceptional amounts of money or inordinately impacting their niche, and others who seem determined to self-sabotage at the first sound of opportunity's knock.

When comparison-itis threatens to take over, it is your personal definition of success that will sustain you. Another author's way is not your way, and the more you are following your own true path, the less the doings of others will distract you—and the more your readers will love it.

Partly, this is about knowing your genre(s). Books fall into one of three broad mega-genres: fiction, non-fiction and poetry. I write across all three. Writers who stick to one genre, one category, one niche or, even better, one teeny-tiny micro-niche have an easier time. Their readers know what they do and what to expect. One glance at their website and a new reader can tell whether their books are for them, or not. That's what you want.

Alas, those of us who write all over the shop can't help but indulge our multi-passionate natures. It makes us happy, deeply satisfies our creative impulses, and keeps us in flow. So that's how we must go. With self-publishing, there's room for us too, once we understand the extra work involved in marketing and promotion, and staying in touch with our own success measures.

Success Measures

In addition to your personal definition of success—which we'll explore in more detail in Part VI: "Creative Business Planning"—there are universal measures for all self-publishing authors. The four key indicators of a healthy author publishing business are productivity, platform, profits, and pleasure.

Productivity: Your output, expressed as:
- writing productivity: words drafted or self-edited
- publishing productivity: books published.

Platform: Your readership, influence and impact, expressed as:
- reach, the number of readers, patrons and subscribers
- engagement, the number of comments, messages, shares

Profits: Your financial rewards, expressed as:
- business profits
- personal income

Pleasure: Your personal satisfaction, expressed as:

- a reading from one to ten based on internal self-observation, one being misery and ten creative bliss, what I call your *creative happiness quotient (CHQ)*.

In his book, *On Writing*, Stephen King says:

Writing [is] about enriching the lives of those who will read your work, and enriching your own life, as well. It's about getting up, getting well, and getting over. Getting happy, okay? Getting happy.[1]

— STEPHEN KING

"Getting up, getting well, and getting over." King was referring to overcoming the alcohol and drug addiction he still regrets, decades on from going sober.

This is the difference between creative business and business as usual, which often sacrifices people for profits. Creatives value process as much as the end product. It's not just what we do, but also how we do it. Measuring our personal happiness, is how we stay connected to the how as well as the what, our process as well as our products.

The truth is that you are likely to have more than one definition of success. We contain multitudes. In one mode, our mind fancies money or fame, in another it wants to show sniffy establishment types or the folks back home what's what, in another it wants to deeply affect a reader's heart or mind.

All of these are the surface expressions of the deeper desire to connect—to connect with our readers, but also to connect with our own creative desires. Your publishing success is embedded in your writing motives—sometimes so deeply embedded, so natural and obvious to you, that you might not be consciously aware of it. As you connect the line of success from your writing to your publishing, and back again, you are forced into awareness.

Writer You thinks you're writing for everybody, but Publisher You must choose a genre and a category for your book. Writer You needs to go into the creative cave to focus, but Publisher You is curious about other authors in your genre. Writer You might not like marketing, but Publisher You knows it's a non-negotiable. Writer You is a perfectionist. Publisher You knows the work doesn't need to be perfect —just good enough. Good enough at writing to please your readers. Good enough at publishing to persuade enough of them to buy. Good enough at business to give yourself, and your writing and publishing team, fair return. Writer You would be content to throw the work out into the marketplace and see what sticks, but Publisher You knows just how valuable reader attention is and wants to make the connection.

Success for an indie author is integrating the writer and the publisher in ways that feed and nourish them both. When it works, everything you learn as a publisher about *who* you're doing this for feeds back into your writing which further improves your publishing. Once in this benign loop, you grow clearer all the time about *what* you do and *how* you do it.

And making you happier all the time too.

Publishing, like every creative field, is full of dreamers and posers, wannabes and pretenders, not to mention scammers and con artists, all of whom want the rewards without doing the work. They are all massively missing the point—and have the misery to prove it. Creative happiness is generated by meeting the challenges we've set for ourselves.

As we transform our experiences, sufferings and joys into words, then into books, then into reader communities; as we build our own self-penned and self-published body of work; as we increase our income and influence and impact, we generate many kinds of happiness, from humming contentment, to dopamine hits, to raptures of bliss. The more creative we are in how we write, publish, and do business, the more variety and intensity of happiness we'll experience. There is no limit to how good this can get.

You may feel you are a long way off at this point, but it begins with caring less about the outside world, what others think and do, and more about your inner world, particularly the ideas and impulses you hold most dear. That's how we achieve independence.

---

1. Stephen King, 2021. *On Writing: A Memoir of the Craft*

PART II

GOING INDIE

In this section we do a quick look back at the history of books to see where today's indie author fits in. We present the various pathways to publication now open to authors and explore your author identity, and how creative independence is an outlook and your most important asset as a self-publishing author. We also consider the question of whether self-publishing is second-best, and ask what it means to be properly published and properly independent.

4

A QUICK HISTORY OF BOOKS AND AUTHORS

W hen we set out to write and publish our books, we are stepping into a long and venerable tradition. The history of writing and publishing books is at least 7000 years old and has engaged the finest human minds, hearts and souls that have walked this world. Understanding that tradition shows us where we fit in and where we'd like to break away.

Human beings have lived through many evolutions and revolutions in authorship. For countless centuries, storytelling and verse-making were not written but oral—a tradition that lives on today in stand-up, performance poetry, and storytelling gigs. Elite families hired bards, troubadours, and balladeers to elevate their ancestors and themselves, put a spin on their invasions and battles, and entertain their troops. Druids and monks and sages and witches passed on the wisdom traditions of their tribes. Alongside the oral stories, older civilizations also recorded their lives in cave drawings or stone carvings.

Then came writing. Ancient African writing is the largest and oldest collection of script, dating to around 5,000 BCE, with Ancient Egypt developing three significant writing systems using symbols and images: hieroglyphics, hieratic and demotic. The first alphabet was developed by a Semitic people living in or near Egypt and quickly adopted by neighbors to the east and north, the Canaanites, the Hebrews, and the Phoenicians.

The ancient Egyptians were also the first to use "pages", by weaving together stems of a papyrus plant, pounding them flat, and pasting them together into a scroll. The Greeks and Romans soon adopted this technique which was used for hundreds of years until the 8th century CE when writers began to use parchment made from calf or deer skin treated in alkaline.

Chinese books began as thin slips of bamboo or wood connected by thongs and used like paged books or scrolls for official documents and literary texts. Bamboo or wood documents were sometimes considered drafts, with final editions written on silk. In China, woodblock printing began to replace hand copying around 700 CE, growing out of religious demand for copies of Buddhist and Daoist scriptures and secular demand for the reproduction of classical texts used in civil service exams.

The first book we know about is a series of Sumerian poems *The Epic of Gilgamesh,* a mythic retelling of the life of an ancient ruler, builder and warrior, "knower of all things on land and sea". The oldest version dating to 2100 BCE, written on tablets.

The first book to be penned on paper was in China, where mulberries, hemp, bark and even fish were used for pulp that was pressed and dried in sheets and later printed on with ink, using wooden printing blocks. *The Diamond Sutra,* a Buddhist book made using this method in Dunhuang, China around 868 AD has survived.

For centuries, a religious, monastic culture supported scribes in the making of long books, decorated with colorful, hand-drawn illustrations. These "illuminated manuscripts" were mostly devotional religious works, and stories about sages and saints that put a religious spin on older folk tales. Scribes also penned texts about astronomy, medicine, and natural history.

Medieval times saw manuscript culture transition to the marketplace, with the growth of cities and the rise of universities. Movable metal type surfaces first in the 14th century, with the *Jikji,* a collection of Buddhist Zen teachings printed in Korea.

In 1439, inventor and printer Johannes Gutenberg became the first European to use movable type and he created a mechanical device he called "a printing press" that used a casting system and metal alloys to press inked letters against paper or cloth. The printed book, as we know it today, was born.

AUTHOR HISTORIES: ARTISAN AND ARTISTS

Throughout all these changing forms for transmitting words across time and space, the author's status in society and ability to make a living from writing adapted to changing circumstances.

While those who write books have never been a homogenous group, looking back we can see how, since Gutenberg, Anglo-American and European cultures have experienced four revolutions in how authors work and earn, train and trade.

Society generally saw the working author as an *artisan* up to the 17th century, as an *artist* with the launch of the Romantic movement in the 18th and 19th centuries, and as a *career professional* in the 20th century. The revolution now underway is that most authors are becoming *publishers*, also known as the *indie authors* or *authorpreneurs*.

The Artisan Author

The invention of the printing press was the most significant cultural event in the second millennium and it invested those who owned the presses with great power. Books could only be made using one of these large, heavy presses housed in a printing factory, all of which required considerable upfront investment.

Occasionally, enterprising authors invested in printing presses and sold their own work, but mostly the machines were owned by commercial publishing houses. Publishers paid author advances for sure winners, but mostly books were commissioned by wealthy patrons to whom the work was dedicated.

They protected their investment by curating books that pleased the paying public (trade publishing), by gathering sufficient subscribers in advance to fund the print run (subscription publishing), or by charging authors for the cost upfront (vanity publishing).

Within this system, authors were artisans. Today, we call Shakespeare a literary genius but in his time the artisan-author was not weighted with concepts of high art and there was no great distinction between work of the hand and head. All that came later. Then, wheelwrights made wheels, shipwrights made ships, and playwrights made plays. Gifted and prolific writers were respected but not revered or seen as a separate class.

In the social hierarchy, writers were somewhere in the middle to lower middle class, above yeomanry and laborers but below monarch, nobility, gentry and merchants. They served apprenticeships, like other craftsmen, learning from "journeymen" and "master" writers, but they didn't sell the products of their craft. At this time, copyright was a publisher's right and copyright law (instigated in 1710 in England and 1790 in the US and a century later across Europe) institutionalized publisher power.

The Artist Author

The author-as-artisan lasted from the establishment of the medieval guilds until the end of the 18th century. Then came the Romantic movement and its belief in the superiority of the imagination and insistence on isolation and melancholy. As science demolished the beliefs of conventional religions and the church's claim on truth was discredited, high art was where many people now turned for connection to life's higher truths.

Alongside a lucrative commercial appetite for serialized fiction producing great wealth for publishers and authors, ran the concept of the writer as literary high-priest, solitary and unworldly, touched by vision, inspiration and mysterious gifts from beyond. The man of genius (yes, always a man) was believed to possess almost superhuman creative powers arising from a life devoted to Art and the shunning of money.

Artist authors needed great courage and made great sacrifices, living a hand-to-mouth existence that put them in danger of illness, even death from starvation. And the image of the solitary, starving artist toiling on a masterpiece in a garret in Paris or New York, seeking to express pure truth and beauty, still exerts a powerful hold on the collective imagination today.

AUTHOR HISTORIES: CAREERS VERSUS BUSINESS

The Career Author

In the 20th century and particularly after the Second World War, with the spread of mass literacy and education, the new copyright laws granting copyright to the creators, and the introduction of English literature studies into schools and universities, authorship became a career. Aspiring writers no longer served apprenticeships or locked themselves away to starve in a garret. Instead, the most typical trajectory was reading English Lit. at university, then finding a day job while submitting manuscripts to agents and publishers.

Some got a permanent, pensionable job in education or some funded institution that allowed them to write their books alongside. Some supplemented book income with freelance writing—pitching newspapers and magazines for paid articles, essays, stories, poems and reviews.

Like any employee or contractor, writers traded their time, labor and expertise. Progress depended on pleasing existing members of the literary establishment—a boss, an institution, a publisher, a prize-giver —who would open the gate and usher them through.

This era is now passing, as professional income and opportunities dwindle but many of us writing today have grown up in it and it is still how we think about how authors work. This is why we talk of indie authors having writing careers instead of publishing businesses.

The Entrepreneurial Author

Today we are in the era of the author as a publisher. Advances in digital tools and technology, machine learning, and most recently, artificial and augmented intelligence allow authors to reach potential readers at a speed and scale that was unthinkable in the artisan, artist, or career eras. Today in countries like the US and UK where self-publishing is most advanced, more than a third of novels, non-fiction and poetry books are profitably published by their own authors.

Indie authors are the creative directors of their books and their businesses, integrating all their efforts—from their media appearance to their social media posts—into a creative business enterprise.

Working this way calls for a significant mental and emotional change in authors who still think of themselves as artisans, artists, or career professionals. We all carry aspects of the history of publishing in how we approach our writing, as artisans, artists, career professionals and entrepreneurs.

- The **artisan author** sees success as making great books.
- The **artist author** sees success as achieving a perfection of truth and beauty.
- The **career author** sees success as being recognized by literary gatekeepers and influencers, pleasing other companies, organizations and institutions.
- The **entrepreneurial author** sees success as a thriving publishing business.

All of these ways of being an author are available to us today. How we approach our work will vary hugely, depending on which conception of "author" we're working from.

Many authors and poets are unconsciously carrying inherited, conditioned beliefs that influence how they meet their work each day and week, living in the age of entrepreneurial author while thinking of themselves as artisans, artists, or professionals.

That's not a problem if it's a conscious choice and we've figured out a way to make our preference work for us. There is no "correct" way to be an author, there never was and there never will be. Artisan authors are still found at craft fairs around the world, selling their books and other products, alongside other creativepreneurs. Professional author careers are still to be had, for a few. Artist authors still take themselves off to Paris to drink cheap wine and work on their masterpiece—if only for a gap year. It *is* a problem, though, if we're locking ourselves out of today's opportunities by working from, perhaps even clinging to, the ideas and ideals of the past.

If you're finding it difficult to finish a book, or to sell books that you've already published, it might be due to your concept of authorship.

TRY THIS: F-r-e-e-write Your Author Identity. *What beliefs do you hold about what being a writer is, or should be? Do your actions betray other contrary, perhaps unconscious, beliefs? How are your beliefs serving you?*

DO THIS: Allocate a Percentage. *What percentage of you is artisan, artist, career professional, and authorpreneur?*

5

PATHWAYS TO PUBLICATION

A ll publishers, from the largest corporation like Penguin Random House to the micro self-publisher, have to bring a manuscript through the seven processes of publishing: editorial, design, production, distribution, marketing, promotion and rights licensing.

We'll go into these processes more in detail in Part V of this book "The Craft of Publishing". In this chapter, we consider the various pathways to publication that a book can take.

THIRD-PARTY PUBLISHING

As a sector, third-party publishers are often referred to as "traditional publishing" or sometimes as "trade publishing", though different kinds of companies and houses fall into this category.

1. **Corporate publishers**, the so-called Big Five (formerly the Big Six): Penguin Random House, HarperCollins, Hachette, Macmillan, and Simon and Schuster (currently looking for a buyer). Each of these large conglomerates has dozens of

imprints. These publishers bear most of the financial risk associated with publishing, aside from the writing. Authors signing a third-party publishing deal don't have to pay any editorial, design or marketing expenses. Instead, they license their publishing rights to the publishing house and receive a small percentage payment—somewhere between 5% of net receipts to 15% of recommended retail price—as a royalty payment. They may also receive a non-refundable advance payment on their royalties, based on the number of books the publisher expects to sell. Most books don't earn more than the advance, but when they do "earn out", authors receive further royalties on each sale, usually payable once or twice a year. Corporate publishers have a pre-existing relationship with the physical books trade—wholesalers, distributors and bookstores, as well as publicity and review outlets in mainstream media.

2. **Indie publishers**. Smaller, independent presses vary in size, from mid-sized, long-established boutique presses to digital start-ups with little publishing experience. Authors may not receive advances but may get larger shares of the profits. It is harder for smaller presses to get books into bookstores and to get mainstream reviews and publicity but, like indie authors, they are more nimble, and have increasing options open to them. Many are highly creative and specialized and have a unique relationship with their fans.

Like the self-publishing sector, third-party publishing has been revolutionized over the past ten years, embracing new technologies, tools and techniques. The "traditional" term implies it belongs in the past, but we will always have third-party publishers who want to invest in author talent. And we'll always have authors who want to work with those they believe can help them reach more readers.

Third-party publishing can be a harsh system for most authors. Many authors and their agents struggle to change even grossly unfair contractual terms and conditions[1].

The longer I am out of this publishing system, the more clearly I see how it exploits the majority of authors. The editors and marketers and sellers who work in publishing and bookselling are, in the main, a delightful group of people—thoughtful and dedicated, highly qualified and intelligent, they could all be earning more money in another sector but are in publishing because they love books. That love extends to "their" authors, whom they admire and respect, sometimes even revere.

Those are the individuals in the system. The system itself, though, is indifferent and harsh, a business model built on author failure as collateral damage. Does that sound like an exaggeration? Alas, it is not. Every stage in third-party publishing is built on author failure.

- **Rejection**: Most submissions go unaccepted and most authors won't ever be offered a publishing contract.
- **Signing**: Most publishing contracts take as many of the publishing rights as possible, for as long as possible, across as wide a territory as possible, without ever exploiting most of the rights.
- **Orders:** Most of the books signed by a publisher won't be ordered in by bookstores.
- **Marketing**: Most of those books that are ordered won't be selected for significant, front-of-shop promotion.
- **Rejection Reprise:** When the books don't sell, most authors are dropped
- **Remuneration:** Most of those who are kept on struggle to earn a pittance from their books.

That's the grim truth. Of course, there are also the stars, the writers we read about in the newspapers who've sold millions, or at least enough to keep going. But for every winner it creates, third-party publishing shrugs off vast swathes of losers.

And it's getting worse. Veteran publishing consultant and commentator, Mike Shatzkin, has written that the "troubling truth about today's book business" is how the biggest publishers today are delivering bigger profits from a flat or declining sales base.

The core asset base of a book publisher is "performing titles": the books that are delivering measurable revenues. The more of them there are, the healthier the business is. Thirty years ago, big publishers were adding to that core title base and, in fact, it was the effort and investment required to deliver new titles into the marketplace that made short-term profits harder to earn. Today's reality is that new titles are much harder to introduce successfully, and publishers have responded to that by flattening and even reducing new title production.[2]

— MIKE SHATZKIN

Shatzkin writes about US publishing but it's the same all over the world. Technology has masked this trend, as for the past decade publishers haven't had to invest in new titles. Their ability to digitize their back list, creating ebooks and audiobooks where they previously only had print, is what is keeping them in profit, and seeing the select band of winning authors taking even more of the publishing pot.

From the publisher's perspective, all of this is completely understandable, a matter of business. The effect on the author community, though, has been devastating.

All of this is not to say that indie authors don't cut publishing deals. The more successful you are as a self-publisher, the more likely you are to be approached by publishers, at home and from overseas. At ALLi, we encourage our members to opt for print deals, translations and other offers *if they add value*. We work with partner members and a dedicated literary agent to facilitate selective rights deals for our qualifying members—but there's a key difference in approach. Indie authors do *non-exclusive* deals and *selectively* license rights. They don't give all rights to one exclusive publisher.

The indie way for an author to approach a publishing deal is to see a third-party publisher offering a contract as a potential business partner. One publisher doing a deal with another, not an author being rescued from oblivion by a savior or validator.

Once you've experienced self-publishing for yourself, and had some success, your attitude changes from, "Publish me, please," to "What are you, the publishing service, bringing to the table for this particular book? What do I give up? What do I gain?"

This position can only be taken by an independent author, with some publishing experience, not by the tyro author with an unproven, first-time manuscript.

ASSISTED PUBLISHING

Assisted self-publishing—hiring a company that offers publishing packages as well as individual services, for a fee—is known by many names: *subsidy publishing, hybrid publishing, cooperative publishing,* and more. Vanity publishers also use these terms sometimes.

The defining difference between assisted self-publishing and independent self-publishing is that assisted publishing services package the elements and processes of publishing, while the independent author separates them out, using their own competencies, and a mix of different services and assistance, to produce and promote their books.

It is impossible to generalize about assisted publishing companies. Some are ethical and excellent providers, others are incompetent, still others are racketeers, trading on authors' dreams and charging dearly for it. These are called *vanity publishers,* as they often pose as publishers, flattering the author about the quality of their book, fooling them into thinking that their book is going to be "published", then presenting an exorbitant invoice.

Until the advent of digital publishing, most self-published books were published through such services, Let's deal with them first, because the advice there is clear. Just say no.

Vanity Publishing

A vanity publisher is a publishing service that uses bait and switch tactics to take advantage of new authors' lack of knowledge about publishing and self-publishing to offer overpriced services that under-deliver, at best. Vanity presses charge unfairly, aggressively up-sell, and often use unethical tactics, purely with the intent of extracting maximum money from authors for minimal service.

Why is vanity publishing still thriving today, even though there are so many better self-publishing options for authors? The sector is expert at marketing, particularly digital advertising, where their deep pockets allow them to prominently advertise under the keywords that new authors are likely to search, outbidding valid self-publishing services and information. Publishers don't advertise, but inexperienced authors don't know that.

If you key in the term "self-publishing" to Google or other search engines, you'll be presented with a list of ads from these vanity operators. The worst of the vanity presses take a disproportionate share of profits, grab rights, charge inordinate fees, and make it hard for an author to get out of the contract.

ALLi warns authors, and monitors the self-publishing services sector in a variety of ways:

- a Watchdog desk: Allianceindependentauthors.org/watchdog where authors can alert us to poor services and get help if they've signed up for a bad deal.
- a rating of the best and worst self-publishing services SelfPublishingAdvice.org/ratings.
- a partner membership for approved and vetted services. Selfpublishingadvice.org/directory ALLi Author members also have access to these partners through a searchable service database. (Members log in and navigate to "Find a Service.")
- a contract advisory service for members. (Members log in and navigate to "Contracts.")
- A variety of sample agreements to compare to the ones you've received or to use yourself

Unlike vanity operators, good assisted publishing services charge a clear fee for a quality service, with all costs upfront and transparent, from the start. The author who is bankrolling the book retains all rights and income, and has control over titles, editing and cover design.

As the quality of services and the terms of contracts vary so widely, authors considering any kind of assisted publishing arrangement first need to ask themselves *why*. Why the particular service they are attracted to, but also, why assisted publishing at all?

Does what the service is offering represent value? What is that value proposition? Could you receive those services in a more cost-effective way, if you did some more research?

You also need to fully understand the contract terms, including the rights management, what services will be included, and at what cost, and to which party. While many indie authors are attracted to hybrid arrangements, the author generally bears the cost if a book doesn't sell, just as they would in self-publishing—but they've given up much control and sacrificed revenue that may not flow back to them.

Don't assume a known brand-name means you're in safe publishing hands. Penguin had an association with Author Solutions, the most notorious of the vanity presses, for years. Simon & Schuster's assisted publishing wing, Archway, charges exorbitant fees and holds out a meeting with top S&S executives as one of the benefits of their overpriced packages. Vanity, vanity, vanity.

The Financial Flow

James D Macdonald, an indie author well known for his advice about literary scams, coined what he called "Yogi's Law," which states, "Money should flow toward the author". We use this guiding principle at ALLi too.

This doesn't mean authors shouldn't ever pay for services or shouldn't ever hire an assisted publishing service. Every business requires investment, and different authors require different levels of support. It means, whichever form of assistance you choose, do your sums. Verify that money flowing away from you is likely to return, multiplied. If not, you need to be happy to lose the money or else find another way to get at your end goal.

Too many indie authors, and those embedded in traditional

publishing, see all assisted services as problematic. If I invest money, will I make more money? With vanity services, the answer is no. With good assisted services, the answer is maybe. It's your responsibility to see whether that service is likely to deliver a return on investment for you, or not. The principle of *money flowing to the author* is a more nuanced guide to contemporary publishing.

For some self-publishing authors, time is more precious than money and they are very happy to pay more for an all-in solution. The born indie is empowered and exhilarated by having control over all the publishing tasks but for those who are slowly coming around to self-publishing, or those who have it thrust upon them, it can be overwhelming and paralyzing at first. Authors who quail at the thought of all the tasks can value the help of an assisted service, especially for their first book.

If that's you, better to pay over the odds on your first book than to be derailed forever by the challenge of doing all there is to do. Longstanding ALLi member, Kathryn Guare, explains her transition from assisted to indie publishing.

For my first effort in self-publishing, like many first-timers I was vulnerable to the exploitative assisted publishing companies that have been superbly documented by the ALLi Watchdog group.

Many of the most disreputable have an approach that is essentially a cheap imitation of the "traditional" publishing structure. In my opinion (not scientific) the people most vulnerable to them are those who still have that traditional model firmly in mind and want something that mimics it, so they end up paying for the privilege of getting bamboozled into bad contracts and useless services that take advantage of their naiveté.

I think those less vulnerable are the ones who have a more business-like approach ("I'm creating a product here") and are simply looking for the services to get it done. Again, I fell into the latter category.

Looking back on my experience, I don't think I got scammed,

but I paid an exorbitant amount of money for services I could have done myself—and for my subsequent books, I did do them myself. I paid too much, but I also know that given my level of intimidation, if I'd tried the pure DIY approach I wouldn't have made it. I'd have given up.

Right now, instead of working on the final cover design for my next book, I would have one manuscript in a drawer, gathering dust.[3]

— KATHRYN GUARE

In her blog post for ALLi, Kathryn advises those who opt for an assisted publishing package to catalogue everything learned along the way, so that you'll be more informed and confident, next time out.

Finally, be aware that it's harder to evaluate costs when services are packaged. All-in-one publishing packages can be padded with what ALLi watchdog, John Doppler, calls "high-cost, low-value fluff" that can complicate the task of evaluating whether the package is value for money.

Hybrid-publishing arrangements, where payment to the publisher is by way of a percentage, in addition to or instead of fee, need particular attention. Do the services on offer warrant the percentage of revenue you'll give up? Are you actually left with all the most challenging bits (writing, marketing) with the publishing service providing what you could quite easily, and far more cheaply, arrange for yourself—editorial, design and distribution.

INDEPENDENT AUTHOR PUBLISHING

This is the choice for most self-publishers who want to make a living from their writing. The independent author is a creative and commercial director, overseeing the writing and publishing process from concept to completion—writing and self-editing the book, then hiring freelancers such as cover designers, editors, ad managers, content marketing strategists, and rights managers, to create and sell books in three formats: ebooks, print books and audiobooks. Over time they build a team that helps them to produce and promote their books in ways that turn a significant profit.

Indie authors tend to focus on digital publishing: ebooks and audiobooks delivered by digital download, and print-on-demand books. Digital publishing hugely expands an author's readership. Digital also favors publishing for a targeted readership, so even if your topic or way of writing is very niche, you can make income from it, if you write and publish well enough, because you now have a global readership who buys online, not a national readership confined to nearby bookstores.

At ALLi, we have many members who are completely unknown outside their niche, who do not appear on any bestseller lists, including Amazon's, but are making a living (or in some cases, a killing!) from publishing their own work.

Digital also means there is no such thing as "out of print" and authors can continue to promote backlist titles, long after launch date.

In short, for the independent author, profit lies in digital downloads, which maximize income, impact, and influence—while minimizing risk. This is far less complex than producing consignment print runs for physical distribution in bookstores, a demanding business model which is under increasing pressure, even for major corporations.

We do have some members who handle consignment print books through bookstores with aplomb, and we know that many author-publishers want to have their books in bookstores and work hard to make that happen.

If that's you, see our guidebook by Debbie Young, *Your Book in Bookstores: ALLi's Guide to Print Book Distribution for Authors,* available for purchase in all formats at: SelfPublishingAdvice.org/bookstores. Members enjoy free access to the ebook.

Finally, it's worth noting that the book buying landscape is shifting in the direction of the author. It's part of the growth in what's being called the creator economy, direct sales from creator to consumer.

Today's self-publishing author is ideally placed to take advantage of this trend.

Indeed, when it comes to publishing, indie authors today have much more in common with other creatives running passion-powered businesses than with authors who choose to exclusively license all their rights to one of the three publishers.

CONSIDER THIS: independent or assisted? *Given your current competencies and creative conditions, which pathway to publication will you take with your next self-published book: independent or assisted?*

Perhaps you are still unsure whether any form of self-publishing is the right pathway for you? If you haven't yet published and you still feel that self-publishing is second-best, if you're troubled by the poor quality of the majority of self-published books, if you long for the sense of validation that can only be won by somebody else investing in your book, if you see yourself as more artist or professional than business person, the next chapter is for you.

Authors who are already publishing, already operating from an indie author mindset, and already clear about their definition of success might want to skip ahead (over the next two chapters "Is Self-Publishing Second Best?" and "Independent Author, Independent Mindset", plus Part III: "Creative Expectations", which explores publishing passion, mission and values), to move directly to Part IV "Publishing Foundations".

For more on publishing services, and to assemble the perfect team for your book publishing, see the second book in ALLi's Publishing Guides for Indie Authors Series: Choosing the Best Self-Publishing Services by the head of the ALLi Watchdog desk, John Doppler.

---

1. Are Contracts Enough? Research by Professor Rebecca Giblin, Director, Intellectual Property Research Institute of Australia (IPRIA)
2. Mike Shatzkin. 2019. The Book Business.
3. https://selfpublishingadvice.org/assisted-services/

6

IS SELF-PUBLISHING SECOND BEST?

Recently, I found myself chatting to Brian, an academic and literary novelist who's unhappy with where he finds himself. Brian is a recognized expert in his field of trauma psychology, who has worked with respected academic publishers across three titles for his non-fiction, and another imprint of the same publishing house for his two novels. He works long hard hours but earns less than his wife, an accounts executive. They cannot cover the bills on their London home and Brian is thinking of giving up writing and teaching altogether and starting over again in a "more sensible career."

I told him (as I tell anyone who will listen) about the digital opportunities now available. He could get his rights back from the various publishers who were underselling his books and publish them himself. And he could turn his university course into an online asset that would bring him a global audience and earn him more money with more ease than his untenured university work.

"You're not listening," I said, as his eyes glazed over.

"I can't do those things," he said.

"Why not?"

"I just can't." He shrugged.

Oh, that shrug. I've seen it so often. It says: self-publishing is too much work / too low status / doesn't give me the validation of a publisher and the university / would interfere with my art / insert favorite assumption here. I wanted to shout at him, "Brian! You could find far more readers and earn far more money! You could free yourself from work politics! You could support your family doing what you love! Instead, you're talking about having to give up your life's ambitions. And all you can do is *shrug!*"

Not minding my own creative business is one of my failings. It's landed me in trouble many times, so I said no more to Brian.

Don't get me wrong, I'm not one of those indie activists that think third-party publishing is doomed—there will always be a role for third parties to assist authors with publishing—and I do understand that there are many reasons why authors might not want to self-publish.

You might think it's not the best way to get your books into bookstores or win a certain literary prize that you want. You might feel it associates you with the second-rate work that will always be part of an uncurated literary marketplace. You might hate the idea of being in business, considering it to be the very opposite of what attracted you to writing in the first place.

All valid things to think about. What bothers me is not when writers ask these questions. It's when they *don't*. When they reject self-publishing out of snobbery or a need for validation. When they cut themselves off from opportunities because they unthinkingly think that self-publishing is second best.

Self-Publishing Myths

Many moons ago, as authors began moving into self-publishing in huge numbers, all the arguments against it were given an airing in *The Guardian* newspaper. Mystery writer, Sue Grafton, kicked it off when she described self-publishers as "too lazy to do the hard work" of going through the submission and rejection process she saw as a necessary part of an author's apprenticeship. Comparing self-publishing "to a student managing to conquer 'Five Easy Pieces' on the piano and then wondering if s/he's ready to be booked into Carnegie

Hall", Grafton said, "I don't believe in short cuts when it comes to the arts."

The indie author community erupted.

In a follow-up article, ALLi advisor Adam Croft responded that this was "outrageous... [when] the complete opposite is true." Independent authors had to be hardworking and dedicated to succeed. "I don't even have the slightest desire to enter the negotiation stage with any publisher as there's no way any of them could offer me what I'm able to do for myself."

Another ALLi member, Society of Literature Fellow and award-winner, Catherine Czerkawska, said Grafton's comments displayed an "unacceptable ignorance of [recent] changes to the industry."

The debate became raucous with publishers also weighing in. Founder of Profile Books, Andrew Franklin, declared self-publishing was always a bad idea because the "overwhelming majority" of self-published books were "terrible–unutterable rubbish."[1]

To her credit, Sue Grafton took the critiques on board and a few days later issued an apology.

It's clear to me now that indie writers have taken more than their fair share of hard knocks and... are actually changing the face of publishing. Who knew?!... I can see that a hole has been blasted in the wall, allowing writers to be heard in a new way and on a number of new fronts. I will take responsibility for my gaffe.[2]

— SUE GRAFTON

Not every trade-published author was as reasonable. Jonathan Franzen (in an article later removed by the paper) said the self-publishing model favored "yakkers and tweeters and braggers". Richard Russo spoke about how Amazon KDP puts "great" young writers in peril. The thought of self-publishing, he said, "literally chills my blood"[3]. Jodi Picoult advised authors: "DO NOT SELF PUBLISH", large caps here[4].

Years on, *The Guardian* was still giving the corner-for-the-prosecution full-feature treatment, with literary novelist, Ros Barber, writing:

For me, traditional publishing means poverty. But self-publish? No way! ... Self-publishing is a terrible idea for serious novelists.[5]

— ROS BARBER

According to Barber, self-published authors spend 10% of their time writing and 90% of their time marketing; the "vast majority" of indie authors have tweet-streams that are 90% adverts; a self-publisher can't receive the critical acclaim and literary prizes that are the only way to build reputation and following. All of this is ignorance and prejudice posing as fact. No aspect of literary success is closed to the self-publishing author—including award-winning acclaim or validation from a respected peer or institution—once a book attains the necessary quality of writing and publishing. Once the author becomes a good publisher as well as a good writer.

Grafton was closer to the mark. Learning how to write long-form work takes many years of dedicated toil. The higher and more complex the writers' ambitions, the longer it takes. Few first-time authors spring into publishing brandishing a prize-winning, peer-approvable book. Most must go through the creative process of exploring and experimenting, learning and improving. The difference is that the self-publishing author learns through feedback from readers. Indie authors make their mistakes in public, sometimes with first books they later unpublish. They find their way through publishing, rather than through private pitching of publishers and agents.

Publishing Smoke and Mirrors

One reason why authors think self-publishing is second-best is that they don't know enough about how third-party publishing operates.

Few authors speak openly about what happens after signing a traditional publishing contract, or after they've been moved to the backlist. They don't want to be disloyal, and they may fear repercussions.

So the prevailing narrative that most unpublished authors hear is a fairytale in which a publisher Prince Charming comes sweeping in, waving a magic contract that will allow the writer to just write happily-ever-after, while somebody else takes care of the marketing and promotion that will make them rich and famous. I understand the power of this narrative. I was invested in that fairytale for years, partly because, back then, it was the only choice, but also because I wanted the validation of some independent arbitrator saying my writing was "good enough."

I was a journalist with a wide network of media and publishing contacts I could have used to get a publishing contract without the 54 rejections. Instead, I anonymously sent my manuscript off to one publisher and agent after another. It was a point of honor to me, that my book should succeed on its merits.

My series of rejections worked for me in exactly the way Sue Grafton suggests, as a writing apprenticeship. Each time my manuscript came back, I worked on it some more before sending it out again. I no longer believe that's the best way to serve a writing apprenticeship, and I'm overjoyed that we now have more options.

When I finally got my "Yes" call from Penguin, I was as overcome as any Cinderella. I didn't know then what I'd actually won was a ticket in a literary lottery. Others may think a publishing contract is a sign that our writing is good enough, but the approval of one person is too subjective to be meaningful. Just ask the editors who turned down Harry Potter. Rejection or acceptance of a manuscript is much more about the publisher's commercial needs than the writer's creative skills.

Third-party publishing is a star system where a few authors do well and most fail. As we saw in Chapter 5, this is no accident. The sector runs on deeply ingrained practices built around author celebrity and author failure that it rarely questions. We've all heard about the countless authors who, like me, suffer serial rejections. We hear far less about the equally countless authors who *were* signed, but then find themselves demoted, or dropped, or destitute. Through loyalty to their publishers and agents, they don't speak out, which perpetuates the illusion of the publishing deal happy-ever-after.

How many writers have fallen away over the decades, creatively dispirited and defeated by this in-or-out system?

Closed Literary Establishment

Another reason an author may be hesitant about self-publishing is the kind of prejudice within the literary establishment that still sees the most prestigious literary prizes, most respected lists, and most illustrious events, rejecting independently published work.

Once a book is properly published, unless you dig deep into the metadata and do some research, it's difficult to tell whether it has been put out by its author, or by a third party. Yet too many literary events, festivals, prizes, reviewers, booksellers, government bodies, and other interested parties still take the lazy option of a blanket ban on self-published work.

It's 100% reasonable for a book to be rejected because it's not to standard, with a shoddy cover or content, but to be rejected because it lacks a publishing imprint's name on its spine, even though it's a match for a third-party published book in every other respect, is snobbery or prejudice—especially when it's a blanket ban.

Literary and publishing organizations that renege on the challenge of opening up to indie authors are failing the reading and writing community they exist to serve. They are cutting away the work of the most vibrant, hard-working, forward-thinking, and entrepreneurial authors in the writing community, and denying them the support, acknowledgement, and access they deserve.

ALLi runs an ongoing campaign, Open Up to Indie Authors (AllianceIndependentAuthors.org/openup), to encourage and aid any individual or organization in the literary or publishing sector who wants to include self-publishing authors in their programs, events, listings and reviews. There are four components to this campaign:

1. **Our campaign guidebook:** Open Up To Indie Authors offers best practices and urges prizes, festivals, events, bookstores, libraries and others to include self-publishing authors in their programs. (This book is available for purchase in multiple formats in our bookstore: SelfPublishingAdvice.org/openingdoors. Members enjoy free access to the ebook.)

2. **Email campaign:** We run an email campaign where we encourage inclusion of indie authors by sharing best practice with organizations and programs.

3. **Information gathering:** Please contact us to commend those who are opening up to indie authors and let us know about those who could do better. We work with ambassadors and author organizations around the globe. Write to us at: campaigns@allianceindependentauthors.org

4. **Sharing opportunities:** We share success stories where organizations have opened up to indie authors and we encourage indies to make the most of those opportunities, so that they can enjoy greater success and visibility throughout the publishing industry.

The good news is that publishing *is* opening up, albeit slowly in some quarters. For example, on the prizes front, the Arnold Bennett Prize; the Arthur C Clarke Award; the Bord Gáis Energy Irish Book Awards; the British Book Awards; the Commonwealth Book Prize; the Rathbones Folio Prize; the Jhalak Prize; the Kitschies; the Lambda Literary Award; the Lindisfarne Prize for Crime Fiction; the Peters Fraser + Dunlop Young Writer of the Year; the Pulitzer; the Nebula Award; and the Romantic Novelists' Association Awards (the RoNAs) are all open, now, to self-published authors.

Self-Publishing Stigma

Another reason an author might be reluctant to self-publish is because they don't want to be associated with the many sub-standard self-published works on the market.

Some authors, especially beginners, push the "publish" button long before their book is ready, releasing books riddled with typos, questionable content, and poor cover designs that shriek home-made. Some authors refuse to submit their golden words to proofreaders or even grammar checkers. Some have no idea how far short of readability standards their book falls. Most of the books published this week, this month, this year, will be ignored by readers, and deservedly so, if the writing or the publishing is not up to standard.

None of this matters to, or has anything to do with, those who write and publish well. It has no effect whatsoever on good books reaching the right readers. The odds are very much against the average self-published book, but the odds are very much *for* a book published by a savvy and skilled author-publisher.

To appreciate why, we need to understand how self-publishing has disrupted the books marketplace. Traditionally, when books were primarily sold in print format in physical bookshops, publishing worked from a scarcity model grounded in commercial principles. It selected a few books to be published and protected their value with copyright. Today, the digital revolution means we work within an abundance model, grounded in creative principles.

Succeeding in publishing now requires a change of mindset from scarcity thinking to abundance thinking, from commercial imperatives to creative. Creativity is never orderly and neat; it's colorful and chaotic and kaleidoscopic. In an abundant, creative model, excess and redundancy are not causes for concern. This is, after all, how nature, the fundamental model for all creativity, works. An oak tree throws a lot of acorns to get one baby oak.

Yes, self-publishing enables more poor-quality books to be published than ever before, but, in an abundance model, what's important is not how many bad books are enabled. They quickly fall into invisibility as nobody reads them. What matters is how many good books are enabled.

The unprecedented wave of literary expression that self-publishing is facilitating is actually a beautiful thing when viewed through a creative lens rather than a critical or commercial one. Throughout cultural history, in renaissance Italy, in Elizabethan England, in transcendentalist America, in literary revival Ireland, whenever new creative forms and formats flourish, an opening-up occurs. The means of expression become available to more people. And while this facilitates more tyro and aspirant work—our exec's "tsunami of crap" —it also results in more accomplished and virtuoso work. More masterpieces emerge.

CONSIDER THIS: Are You Ready to Self-Publish? *If you are resisting the challenge of running your own self-publishing business, why? In what ways? What do you think you can get from trade-publishing that you cannot have as an indie author? If validation is highly important to you, why? Where does that come from? Is there a person in your past who has made you seek approval or feel like you've something to prove? Is your mindset around this question serving you well?*

---

1. https://www.theguardian.com/books/2013/jun/11/self-published-ebooks-20-per-cent-genre
2. https://www.theguardian.com/books/2012/aug/29/self-published-laziness-charge-sue-grafton
3. https://www.theguardian.com/books/2012/aug/29/self-published-laziness-charge-sue-grafton
4. https://www.thedailybeast.com/jodi-picoult-on-writing-publishing-and-what-shes-reading
5. https://www.theguardian.com/books/booksblog/2016/mar/21/for-me-traditional-publishing-means-poverty-but-self-publish-no-way

7

INDEPENDENT AUTHOR, INDEPENDENT MINDSET

A t ALLi, we spot when authors adopt an attitude of creative independence. We call it "going indie". They begin to explore where their books fit in the marketplace and the value they're bringing to readers. They begin to set creative intentions for their marketing, to assemble a team of publishing professionals, to adopt new techniques and tools, to claim autonomy and responsibility, to accept that they are the captain of their own commercial and creative fate. And to understand that the primary relationship, between them and their readers, is the most important one to nurture. This leads them to new technologies, tools and techniques, and to finding a personal creative routine that can fulfil their ambitions.

They move beyond thinking like a writer and start thinking like a publisher too. Soon they are up and running, on the creative ride of their life: making mistakes and enjoying successes, reaching more readers, selling more books, moving into profit.

An independent mindset develops in different ways for different authors. To distort Shakespeare's fine line in *Twelfth Night*, some authors are born independent, some choose independence, and some have independence thrust upon them.

The born indies come straight into writing and self-publishing, together. For them, it's the obvious and only choice. Most of these are younger writers who have grown up sharing their writing on Wattpad, social media, or blogs. Publishing a book is just their logical next step. Their followers are keen for them to produce a book, follow their journey through writing and production, and buy the book as soon as it's released. It soars to success and though it all seems to happen organically, from a publishing perspective what's happened is that the marketing work has been done upfront.

Then there are those who consciously choose self-publishing for its creative and commercial rewards: the speed, the control, the freedom, the direct relationship with readers. With time and dedication, they also do well.

It's those who come to self-publishing reluctantly, because they've repeatedly tried and failed to get a publisher, who have the hardest time. Most indie authors need support when starting out, as there's a lot to learn, change and implement, but an author who is dreaming of a publishing contract from a third party is rarely in the right mind mode to do the work of becoming a good publisher themselves.

They are the ones most likely to fall away, defeated not so much by the job of self-publishing as the mindset they've brought to it.

INDIE AUTHOR MINDSET

The rock on which you build your publishing business as an indie author is your intellectual property (IP), as protected by copyright, and your appreciation of your copyright's value.

The laws in most Western countries gives you automatic, exclusive, legally-secured rights to reproduce and distribute your own work. To publish, perform, or record them. To profit from them and to authorize others to also. Authors have this power, but every day disempower themselves by naively signing away their rights, by choosing poor self-publishing services, or by working from assumptions about publishing that are outdated, or just plain wrong.

Here are some authors I've personally spoken to in recent months.

- Bob writes philosophical non-fiction. After trying and failing to find a trade publisher, he turned to self-publishing in frustration. He'd never bought an ebook or digital audiobook himself and didn't even consider publishing in those formats. Instead, he paid a publishing service thousands of dollars for a consignment of print books. He contacted ALLi because having paid his bill, he found the books were poorly edited and designed, and the company had no distribution or marketing structure to get them to readers.

- Danny puts all his young adult (YA) fiction and business books in Amazon's exclusive ebook program, KDP Select, seeing Amazon as the "800-pound gorilla" in the self-publishing sector. He spends a four-figure sum on advertising on the platform, but his book-sales have recently plummeted, and his income has crashed. Fearing to pause his Amazon ads and unable to get the answers he needs from Amazon, he is steadily amassing debt.

- Barbara built a successful self-publishing business in the romantic suspense genre but has just signed a 13-book, all-rights, life of copyright deal with a third-party publisher. She could have tried a single book or series with them to see how it would go. Instead she signed their contract without hiring an agent or sending the contract to ALLi for review. At the time, she was so delighted to get the offer she barely read the terms, but now is (rightly) concerned about some of the clauses.

- Tess has been self-publishing historical fiction for two years and is at work on her third book. Her reviews are good, she has spent a lot of time and money on design and editing, has a website, and distributes her books widely, through online retailers and aggregators. She says she "loves writing but hates marketing" and "just wants to write" but she also wants to make an income from writing. She has no marketing plan and, unsurprisingly, her books are not selling.

Bob and Barbara are upset with their publishing services, Danny is upset with Amazon, and Tess is upset about "the lot of authors today" compared to a past golden era she has constructed in her mind, when publishers did all the marketing.

For all of these authors, and for countless more who contact ALLi each month, untried ideas and unconscious assumptions about self-publishing are holding them back. As long as these mindsets remain fixed, their commercial and creative progress is stalled. Bestselling UK novelist Adam Croft, who runs a Facebook Page called the Indie Author Mindset, has written about how his outstanding success only became possible once he'd adopted this approach.

I'd always been fine with writing stories, and I'd run businesses in the past but bringing those together and getting that commercial side of the brain to work alongside the creative side of the brain was the challenge. Once those two were brought together, everything started to work.[1]

— ADAM CROFT

So what is this "indie author mindset" that you need to have or develop in order to succeed in self-publishing? What are its features and qualities?

INDIE AUTHOR CHARACTERISTICS

Indie authors are independent, entrepreneurial, collaborative, resilient, lifelong-learning creatives.

Independence

Indie authors choose ourselves. We don't need somebody else to tell us that our work is good enough. We trust in our own skills and our ability to improve them. We invest our time, money and energy in our own books, producing regularly, learning by doing, and improving our processes as we go. We take responsibility for the risks, as well as the rewards, of publishing ourselves.

CONSIDER THIS: *Can you ignore mob mentality and put yourself out there, without anyone else to blame if things go wrong? Step out of your comfort zone and challenge yourself? Embrace the abundance and opportunity that self-publishing affords?*

Entrepreneurship

Successful self-publishers don't tend to be the kind of writers who say, "I don't care about money" and rely on a benefactor, day job or supportive spouse to survive. We measure income alongside impact and influence and have an entrepreneurial outlook, open to new ways to reach readers, new communities who might be interested in our books, new opportunities to get our message out. Just as entrepreneurs must create a product or service, test it, raise funding, recruit a team, and find interested buyers, so must the indie author.

CONSIDER THIS: *Can you be proactive and plan for the outcomes you want, investing in your author business and yourself, taking mindful risks where necessary in order to achieve your intentions? Can you follow your passion and mission all the way into successful selling? Can you process problems and overcome challenges, let go of a method, a mindset or a person that does not serve you well? Can you inspire, mobilize, and direct a team of creatives?*

Collaboration

The camaraderie, collaboration and co-operation within the indie author community is outstanding. Maybe we need each other more than other authors, but successful indies tend to operate out of *ubuntu*, the African philosophy of interconnectedness that says, "I am because you are". Even if they are not that esoteric about it, indies are likely to work from the co-opetition model, where competitors co-operate for mutual benefit—sharing techniques and tools, news and views, telling each other about good services, warning each other away from vanity outfits and shoddy services.

In fact, indie authors are sometimes criticized for being *too* supportive of each other, encouraging the production of sub-standard books. It's not that we don't see flaws, mistakes or infelicities (our own and others'), it's that we're creatives, not critics. We see failures as creative teachers, that facilitate learning and growth, if taken with the right attitude. We know a critical hammering can derail a sensitive author, who might well have done better next time. We know how important it is to keep ourselves creatively motivated, positive and focused. We support each other in that.

We are all trying, failing, and, as Beckett said, trying again and next time "failing better". Sometimes, a bad book is a step towards a brilliant book.

Again and again, ALLi members attest to the benefits of sharing and learning from each other in this way, as they work together for each other.

Beyond this emotional support and information sharing, many indie authors work profitably together on products and projects.

CONSIDER THIS: *Can you be a giving participant in literary and publishing culture? Treat other authors and influencers with respect and help others to grow? Spend time and energy investing in your networks, giving more than you take, acting without expectation of reciprocation? Can you work with other authors to write more books and reach more readers?*

Resilience

It takes courage to create, and risk is a daily activity for an indie author. We risk time on ideas, or promotions, or concepts that may come to naught. We risk money to pay for editorial and design upfront. We risk confidence and reputation every time we strike out. But that's the job. Indie authors are open to failure and willing to learn from mistakes and excited by the prospect of new projects and creative collaborations.

As ALLi's Creative Advisor, Mark McGuinness says in his book *Resilience: Facing Down Rejection and Criticism on the Road to Success,* "Anyone who says 'don't take it so personally' doesn't understand what it's like when you are hit by a major rejection or biting criticism. Successful indies have found ways to acknowledge the pain—and bounce back from the impact."

CONSIDER THIS: *Can you break out of the pessimism that's endemic in publishing and the wider world and believe in your own creative potential? Get over the inevitable moments of self-doubt and creative discomfort and do the next necessary task? Can you be flexible, bounce back from disappointments, turn things around when they go wrong, see the opportunities in failure? Take care of yourself physically and mentally, take time out for renewal and recharge? Build more resilience every day so that you become unassailable over time?*

Curiousity

"Being a writer is like having homework every night for the rest of your life," the Oscar winning screenwriter Lawrence Kasdan once quipped. Being a publisher and creative business owner doubles up the homework. We indie authors love our jobs but we all have a constant stream of tasks awaiting attention, and there's always the next book to be written.

Indie authors nonetheless invest time, energy and commitment in educating ourselves about writing craft, publishing craft and creative business craft.

We work smart, keep up with the latest trends, recognize opportunities, and figure out how to make the most of them, all without derailing our writing.

CONSIDER THIS: *Can you show up to your book and your author business, day after day, when it seems like nobody cares, you've got a bad review or been trolled? Can you see beyond any laurels you've earned to learn how to do things even better?*

Courage

As we employ our imaginations in our books and our book marketing, we reveal our attitudes, beliefs, desires, fears, ideas and values. This requires us to be vulnerable, to take emotional and cognitive risks that push us out of our comfort zones. We may also need to employ courage in defying familial and social norms and expectations.

CONSIDER THIS: *Roland May wrote in* The Courage to Create: *"If you don't express your own original ideas, if you don't listen to your own being, you will have betrayed yourself. Also, you will have betrayed our community in failing to make your contribution to the whole." Do you agree? How does that make you feel?*

Creativity

Indie authors apply their creativity widely, not just in the words they write but in the covers they put on their books, the marketing they use to position their books and develop their author platform, the promotional projects they undertake to reach the right readers for their books. They allow their creative impulses to lead them.

CONSIDER THIS: *Where does your creativity show up in your publishing?*

GOING INDIE

Having done this kind of thinking about his personal success measures, Bob is now reworking his book with his own chosen editor and intends to republish under his own steam, in three formats, as soon he judges it ready. He is setting up his own transactional website and a book marketing and promotion plan on Google, Apple, Kobo and others, as well as Amazon.

Danny still has all his books in KDP Select but now understands the choice, and the risks involved, and intends to go wide with his next title. Tess is learning to love marketing and has a marketing plan that integrates a growing email list, Facebook, and Twitter presence, with her wider goals. Barbara is now under contract and waits to see whether her publisher will deliver for her. She has promised to let us know.

All are now happily writing their next books, alongside their publishing tasks. All know how to measure whether things are going in the right direction. And all have embraced an indie author mindset, in which they appreciate that they are the publisher.

They appreciate they earn the moniker "indie" in their approach to publishing, and in their willingness to take risks and take responsibility. And they earn the moniker "creative" when they learn from each new change and decision that they implement.

Is Self-Publishing for You?

Self-publishing allows you to define your own goals, costs and timeline, to earn a higher percentage per book sale, and to market your work how you prefer. All very exciting but, yes, all these responsibilities can easily become draining and overwhelming too.

Truth is, failure dogs the self-publishing sector too. The majority of authors who set out to self-publish will also fail. It's just the nature of the obstacle that's different. In trade-publishing it's somebody else who causes the failure. In self-publishing, it's ourselves.

Most authors fall away because they don't see publishing through a creative lens, as a craft which they must learn and grow into, just like writing. Just as it takes more than one draft to make a winning manuscript, you may need a few iterations to get the publishing process, and the business process, to come out right.

As writers, we know that if we set good creative intentions for our writing and learn what we need to know about the craft, if we keep on keeping on with the intention of improving and learning from our missteps, if we add enough time and energy and practice, we *will* write something worthwhile. We know that success is inevitable. That's how the creative process works if we show up and play our part, if we don't get defeated by doubt or resistance.

It's just the same with publishing and with creative business. If we set good creative intentions for making the book, positioning the book, selling and licensing the book, if we learn what we need to know about publishing craft and business craft, if we keep on keeping on with the intention of improving and learning, if we add enough time and energy and practice, we will establish a creative business that meets our mission while turning a profit.

Yes, it's inevitable. If we show up and play our part, if we don't get defeated by doubt or resistance.

When we stop feeling that business is beneath us (while simultaneously feeling inadequate about marketing or tech or finance), we are liberated. Once we see publishing and business as an intrinsic part of what we do as writers, we can tap into our own creative capacity, harness our own creative flow, and start working from our own sense of what works for us.

I often say that indie authors are like Bob Dylan, on a never-ending tour. Not just because, unlike a trade-published author who must fit into their publisher's schedule, we can put marketing muscle behind any of our books, any time. But also because as self-publishers, we must find a process that allows us to continuously and sustainably do what we do: writing, making and marketing our books.

For those of you too young to know, in 1988 Bob Dylan, one of the foremost songwriters and performers in the world, found himself burnt out, artistically. He found himself with "no connection to any kind of inspiration" and a future as "an old actor fumbling in garbage cans outside the theater of past triumphs."[2] To save himself, creatively, he took to the road.

For thirty years—until stopped by the COVID-19 pandemic—Dylan did more than 100 concerts a year. It became known as the Never Ending Tour and it gave him back his artistic mojo. Traveling by bus, staying in less-than-deluxe hotels, taking his dogs along, he carved out a life for himself where he could just get on with his work.

That's what self-publishing has done for me. Allowed me to keep rock-and-rolling on, faithful to the magic of the written and published word. I don't know where I'd be today if digital self-publishing hadn't emerged as an option. It's not just that publishing my own books myself got them back out there and brought me more of the right readers than ever before. It's how it returned to me two values that are very precious to me, which were so devastated when corporate publishing was my only choice: creative freedom and creative confidence.

Will it be like that for you? I can't say for sure but what I do know is that if you don't try it, you'll never know. That's why I believe every author should self-publish, at least once. There are so many myths and misconceptions swirling around, and so many people speaking emphatically from a place of ignorance, while in the burgeoning creator economy, each self-publishing experience is unique.

The only way to know how it will shape up for you is to do it and see.

You have little to lose and much to gain. You'll learn more about your readers' preferences, what resonates with them, and how to build and nurture a loyal reader base. You'll have a better understanding of where you fit in the marketplace, In short, at worst you'll have lost some time and money but everything you learn about publishing from putting a book out will feed back into your writing.

And who knows, you may even find, as I did, that self-publishing is the best move of your writing life.

---

1. Orna Ross personal interview with Adam Croft
2. Bob Dylan. 2004. Chronicles Volume 1

PART III

CREATIVE EXPECTATIONS

In this section we explore how publishing, just as much as writing, is powered by personal creativity. You are offered exercises that explore and define your creative mission, passion, and purpose and shown how you derive many practical benefits from establishing your creative motives as a writer and a publisher. You will also discover your core publishing value and the framework that best supports it.

8

CREATIVE PASSION, CREATIVE PROCESS

C reative self-publishing is a two-way motion. First, we focus inwards, connecting creatively with ourselves; then we focus outwards to connect in a similar fashion with others. The heart of this pulsing dynamic is our creative passions.

A creative passion is not a fleeting emotion or momentary inspiration, but a drive that motivates us to push beyond our apparent ability and capacity. If you teach young people, as I once did, you'll know there are always a few in each classroom who don't like the subject you're teaching. An inexperienced teacher might make an assumption about a student's intelligence or capability based on their performance in class, but you'll soon find that the same youth who has no memory skills for, say, historical dates can recite hundreds of football league scores. He has passion for football and none for history.

If we stay on the surface, playing safe, distraction and dilettantism lie in wait. When we give ourselves over to what we most love, when we allow it to express itself through us in a unique and personal way, our books become a reflection of who we are and what we believe. Others who share similar passions and interests are drawn to this work. It touches their own thoughts, feelings, and ideas.

The deeper we dive into our creative passion, the more sustaining it becomes, ensuring that we never grow stale.

Our passion can be rooted in something small and very personal: an unusual interest or unusual combination of interests, a little inner voice whispering an intuition, a huge ambition. Sometimes it's so much part of us that we don't even recognize it. Once we do, we can consciously bring our passion into our publishing as well as our writing.

You may already know where your reading and writing passions lie. If you don't, this simple exercise will give you your starting point.

CONSIDER THIS: What Do You Love? *Reflect on what most excites you about your own writing and the books you most love to read? What do they have in common? If you're like most people, you have a number of passions reflected in your reading and writing.*

TRY THIS: Identifying Creative Passions. *Answer the following question under the four headings of theme, character type, setting, and style. What do I most enjoy reading and writing about?*

These exercises may give you instant answers or you might need to take time to do more exploration. It's worth investing time in this now as it can save you months or years of frustration later.

This approach is the opposite approach to writing to market which many still insist is necessary for publishing success. Writing to market is creating content specifically tailored to what's currently popular, or in demand. The idea is to maximize the chances of commercial success by writing what readers are actively seeking. You research popular genres, tropes, and themes and follow current trends e.g. writing a post-apocalyptic sci-fi novel because that genre is currently trending.

While writing to market may make it easier to garner sales and reader interest, it can also constrain your creativity and interfere with developing confidence, uniqueness and authenticity. At one time, it may have been the only way, but in this era of global audiences and the internet, even niche subjects can find significant readership, especially when you consider the 'long tail' effect of digital markets. While mainstream bestsellers might get the majority of attention, a vast array of niche interests have emerged over the past decades, each with their own significant global market.

Connecting with your passion means you're more likely to create engaging, high-quality work that resonates with readers. In these days of AI bots, readers are drawn to authors with a human touch, writing with authenticity and passion. Even if the subject matter or approach isn't mainstream, it can find sufficient readers to make a living.

Of course, passion alone is not enough. Success also depends on your level of writing skill and publishing skills, and sometimes just on chance, but there's never been a better time to succeed by writing about what you truly love. So why wouldn't you?

Accessing the power of your passions doesn't just ensure that you enjoy your work and increase your creative energy and capacity. It has practical application in your writing, book production and marketing, clarifying your options and honing your focus.

When you've identified your creative passion, you can more easily track down and connect with those readers who are most interested in what you're interested in. These are the *right readers* for your work. They have already self-identified, and organized themselves in groups that you can access, through trade magazines, online message boards, social media accounts, hobby groups, and other ways. This is how your writing passion fuels your publishing, as well as your writing.

GENRE AND NICHE

As you share your passion with your readers, you'll find it has delivered you all the way into your genre, niche and micro-niche. This is where you set up camp.

By understanding your creative passions and using that knowledge to identify your book's genre, niche, and micro-niche, you can better target your marketing efforts and improve your chances of connecting with readers who will truly appreciate your work.

Once you have a clear understanding of your passion, research existing genres and niches that align with your interests. Look for books, authors, and trends that share similarities with your work and help you determine where your book fits within the larger market.

As you explore the market, think about how you can further refine your book's positioning. This might involve identifying a specific sub-genre or a unique combination of elements that distinguishes your work from others. By way of example, I write across all three macro-genres: novels, non-fiction and poetry.

FICTION
Genre: Historical fiction
Niche: Historical mystery
Micro-niche: Historical family murder mysteries

NON-FICTION
Genre: How To
Niche: Self-publishing
Micro-niche: Profitable publishing for dedicated indie authors

POETRY
Genre: Inspirational poetry
Niche: Feminist inspirational poetry
Micro-niche: Spiritual inspirational poetry for male and female feminists

With your niche or micro-niche in mind, you are then in a position to select categories and keywords that accurately represent your book.

DO THIS: Brainstorm categories and keywords. *Using tools like Google's Keyword Planner or Amazon's search bar suggestions, research keywords and popular search terms related to your passion, niche, or micro-niche. These should be terms that readers might use when searching for books like yours.*

Your niche and micro-niche might broadly align with the categories you put your book into when uploading to distributors, but they are not your categories. They are for you, as writer and publisher. They should be broad enough to allow room for creative expansion and evolution while being focussed enough to answer questions around design and aesthetics, book descriptions and marketing campaigns.

Taking the time to do this work on your creative passions will help you when it comes to your books, improving your chances of connecting with readers who will truly appreciate your work.

Creative Process

Process is what turns passion into projects and products.

Most people who start to write a book never get to type "The End". Most published writers fail to reach a readership. Most indie publishers and bookstores go under. There are lots of specific reasons for these failures, but there is also a single, universal reason. Somewhere along the line, the creative process broke down.

Whenever we want to consciously create something, we are entering a process that begins with intention (a goal) and ends in completion (attaining the goal). Whatever we're aiming to make, this creative process always goes through the same seven stages. A paragraph of fine writing, an ebook or audiobook, a thriving business —all begin with an intention, a sense of the outcome we want, and then proceed through seven stages to deliver that outcome.

Or not.

When we're making something that comes easy to us—a short story, breakfast, $5 profit—we don't notice the stages. We go from intention to completion without even thinking about it, especially if it's something we've made often before. When something's new to us and when it's a stretch—a long novel, a 50-seater banquet, a successful publishing business—it helps to be more aware of the process.

The creative process is both universal and unique. Give the same prompt to a hundred writers and you'll get a hundred completely different stories or poems. Give a hundred indie authors a blank business plan and you'll get a hundred completely different publishing businesses.

The seven stages of the creative process are **intention, incubation, investigation, formation, elaboration, clarification** and **completion**. I've written them out in a row below to better understand them—but the creative process is not linear. Each stage melds into and interweaves around the other, in an interactive waltz.

The creative process is always unfolding, whether we are conscious of it or not. Awareness just ensures that we follow the right steps at the right time—and that we enjoy the dance.

The seven stages of the creative process can be organized under three phases: **vision, making, and revision,** as follows:

THE CREATIVE PROCESS: 7 STAGES

The Vision Phase

1. Intention —> Survey, choose, commit
2. Incubation —> Meditate, f-r-e-e-write, cogitate
3. Investigation —> Research, explore, experiment

The Making Phase

4. Formation —> Plan, draft, design
5. Elaboration —> Deepen, develop, expand

The Revision Phase

6. **Clarification** —> Refine, correct, contract
7. **Completion** —> Finalize, finish, release

Each stage of the process calls for different skills and approaches. Without awareness of what phase and stage we are at in our projects, we can easily derail ourselves by bringing in thoughts and behaviors that belong to another stage. A common example in writing is to start self-editing (stage 6) before early ideas and insights have been given time to develop (stage 2) or solidify (stage 4).

A common example in publishing is pressing the production button (stage 4) on a manuscript that needs more developmental edits (stage 3). Or rushing to market (stage 7) a book without sufficient preparation (stages 2, 3) and positioning (stages 4, 5).

All of these issues are fixable later. One of the great things about self-publishing, about any creative project, is the ability to go back and do better. But we have an easier and far more enjoyable time when we recognize that the creative process is infallible and takes as long as it takes. Paradoxically—and to go creative is to take up residence in the land of paradox—it all happens faster when we stop pushing.

When we allow the process to lead, when we trust it and follow its natural flow, it finds its own way. The creative qualities of insight and inspiration, perception and enlightenment, emerge. We stop seeing blocks and obstacles as insurmountable. We imagine more expansive possibilities, while surrendering to the process. We integrate different aspects of ourselves. We align with flow.

Applying the Creative Process to Writing

The Vision Phase

1. Intention —> Decide on your idea
2. Incubation —> Invite in insights and intuitions. Brainstorm your idea, meditate and f-r-e-e-write to deepen your thoughts.
3. Investigation —> Gain a deeper understanding of the subject e.g. online research, books and journals, interviewing experts or individuals, visiting museums and libraries, observing and experiencing events or situations.

The Making Phase

4. Formation —> Write the first Draft

5. Elaboration —> Deepen and develop the draft. Add details or expand information. Refine language, develop characters or setting, add sub-plots, paragraphs, even chapters as necessary to fill all gaps and make sure the reader understands what you need them to understand.

The Revision Phase

6. **Clarification** —> The self-editing phase. Everything up to now has been expansion. Now it's time to refine, correct, contract, delete, and eliminate.
7. **Completion** —> Finish the manuscript and prepare to release it to beta readers or editors.

As creatives, we can use our knowledge of the process to accurately pinpoint where we are meeting creative resistance and block. This applies to our publishing as much as our writing.

Applying the Creative Process to Publishing

The Vision Phase

1. Intention —> To become a good publisher of the kinds of books you will release.
2. Incubation —> Do some deep thinking and f-r-e-e-writing about the kind of publisher you want to be and how you can reach more readers and sell more books (which is what all good publishers do)
3. Investigation —> Research how other similar publishers do what you want to do and sourcing the tools and team you'll need.

The Making Phase

4. Formation —> Deciding on a framework and setting up your publishing and business structure. Drawing up your publishing schedule and putting out your first books.

5. Elaboration —> Developing and expanding your business, based on the learnings. Trying new things.

The Revision Phase

6. **Clarification** —> Understanding what books and publishing approaches do best for you and letting the others go. Consolidating systems to support regular production. Refining your team and tools.
7. **Completion** —> Establishment of a mature publishing business that generates a profit and supports your writing without consuming too much time, attention or resources.

We can clearly see how the process is ignited and sustained through the seven stages of the process by directed passion.

For most indie authors, the biggest challenge is to keep moving forwards while still enjoying the ride. Too often, life, work and responsibility weigh them down, and they lose track of what they need to do. It all feels too much, and they become vulnerable to the hucksters and hype-sters. When that doesn't work, they come back to their project, a little more jaded each time.

Creative passion directed through the creative process opens the way for the author-publisher to experience deep and sustaining satisfaction.

CONSIDER THIS: Writing Process. Think about the book you're currently writing. What stage of the creative process are you in?

CONSIDER THIS: Publishing Process. Think about your publishing business. What stage of the creative process are you in?

9

CREATIVE MISSION AND VALUES

I f you write or read fiction, or watch movies or TV, you know how your characters' life choices are shaped by a matrix of personal values. We all know that a person's values tell us a lot about them and shapes how they live life. This is knowledge we can take into all aspects of our creative work.

Values aren't just conceptually held—they guide and drive our actions. We decide what is good or bad, justified or illegitimate, worth doing or avoiding, based on possible consequences for our most cherished values. And so do our readers.

Whether they realize it or not, values underpin our readers' emotional responses to our books. The particular words and images we choose convey the book's values and affect our readers' decision-making and buying choices.

Knowing our values can aid us in a variety of ways as authors and publishers—easing decision-making, increasing our confidence, focusing our actions, and guiding us through when things get confusing or difficult.

In this commencement address at Jackson State University in 2016, Michelle Obama made a clear statement of the values that sustained her and her husband, Barack, as First Lady and President of the US. These values also lie at the heart of her memoir, *Becoming*.

When they go low, we go high. We choose faith. Faith in ourselves and the power of hard work. Faith in our God...

We choose love. Our love for our children. Our commitment to leaving them a better world. Our love for our country which has given us so many blessings and advantages. Our love for our fellow citizens: parents working hard to support their kids, men and women in uniform who risk everything to keep us safe, young people from the toughest background who never stop believing in their dreams...

And we choose excellence... No cutting corners, no taking shortcuts, no whining. We give 120% every single time, because excellence—excellence is the most powerful answer you can give to the doubters and the haters.[1]

— MICHELLE OBAMA

Many book marketing experts suggest that publishers should create customer avatars for their ideal readers, establishing demographic and other socio-economic information about them—age, sex, income grouping and so on. On social media advertising platforms like Facebook and Instagram too, people are organized into male or female, where they are from and what age they are. Such factors are relevant but what's more important is the emotional resonance generated by shared values.

Why should a reader buy your books, share your social media posts, follow you from your books to your website or vice versa? Why should they care? The answers lie in understanding why you care. Your values.

Once we understand which of our personal values we're projecting in our books, and which values guide our readers' decisions, we can draw these together more deliberately in our book production and marketing. Our covers, our book descriptions, our sell-sheets, our promotions can all reflect these shared values. This helps us to focus our efforts, drive better engagement, and turn casual browsers into true fans.

Connection around personal values is at the heart of every warm human relationship and the writer-reader relationship is no exception. Values, and the value you offer your readers, must be placed at the heart of your author business.

DO THIS: Note Your Values. *Go to SelfpublishingAdvice.org/ValuesWorkbook and see the list of values there. With a pen and notebook in hand, read through them and write down any that feel important to you. Aim to note at least 50 out of the 150, the more the better. Add any unlisted values that are important to you or f-r-e-e-write any thoughts about values prompted by the list.*

DO THIS: Select Your Values. *List the seven values that are most important to you. Look again. Make any changes you want and settle on a final seven.*

DO THIS: Order Your Values. *Now list these in order of priority, with #1 being that which is most important to you, #2 the second most important and so on.*

TRY THIS: My Values, My Story. *F-r-e-e-write some parts of your life story, from a values perspective. How did those values come to be important to you? Mention other people, stand-out situations, and breakthrough moments.*

CONSIDER THIS: My Values, My Books. *Think about how these values are already reflected in your writing. Are there things there, in your writing, that you weren't conscious of as you wrote? Then turn to your future writing. How might what you now know about your values shape your books to come?*

We will come back to these personal and ethical values many times in this book. You also have values as an author and as a publisher and these vary and interconnect in unique ways. Each of these value-sets shapes your work as a writer and publisher, influencing your relationship with your readers, and your approach to every aspect of your publishing and marketing.

In Book 3 in this series, *Reach More Readers, Sell More Books: ALLi's Guide to Book Marketing for Authors and Poets*, we go into this topic of personal, author and publisher values in more depth.

CREATIVE MISSION

The written word is the most powerful tool for anyone who wants to consciously make a difference in life. Most writers do—and I assume you do, too. "Making a difference" is a cliché, of course, and a fuzzy one at that. Everybody who has ever lived has made a difference. The question for writers, and especially authors who self-publish, is: what kind of difference do we want to make?

What do we want to be *known* for? The answer to this question is our creative mission.

If you don't know what your mission is, if you feel disconnected from any particular sense of purpose, you are not alone.

One way to find your creative mission is to tap into your angers and connect them to your writing and publishing. Destructive when mindlessly unleashed, anger mindfully observed and harnessed is a powerful creative fuel—and key to connecting with your mission.

CONSIDER THIS: Exploring Angers. *What would you like to change in the world, if you had the power? What would this mean for your books, for your publishing business?*

You can use f-r-e-e-writing to uncover your mission and produce a mission statement, a written declaration of what your writing and publishing business seeks to become.

CONSIDER THIS: Sales or Acclaim? *Are you motivated more by the idea of selling books to lots of appreciative readers, or of receiving acclaim from your peers (other writers you respect) and from respected others (rights buyers, critics, prize givers)? These are not mutually exclusive, but it's good for you to know which your primary motivation is.*

TRY THIS: Creative Past *1. Look back at your own school days. How were your creative impulses stifled? What would you like to have questioned? Make a list. 2. What's the most important thing on your list? F-r-e-e-write for 20 minutes, going deeply into why.*

TRY THIS: What "Givens" Would You Like To Question? *Make a list.*

CREATE A MISSION STATEMENT

Companies and organizations often create mission statements to inform their teams and customers about their aims and values. We can create similar statements to help remind ourselves, our assistants, our readers why we write and publish.

A mission statement can help us stay clear, focused, and motivated when it comes to preparing book descriptions, author bios, and other marketing materials. It can guide what we write and the order of publication.

As independent authors, we need mission statements for ourselves both as writers and as publishers.

Mission Statement 1. Writing Identity

What kind of a writer are you? We explored this in Chapter 4 from the perspective of the author's status in society and ability to make a living from writing, but before any of that happens, you have a writing identity, a way of meeting the world and the words you use to describe it.

Your unique perspective, voice, style, and worldview fall into a category of writing. For example:

Reporter authors write books that aim for objectivity and detachment and assemble old facts in new ways.

Explorer authors write books that go beyond the facts to uncover how something happened.

Prophet authors write books that do the same but go deeper, seeking to explain the unknown and kindle the spirit.

Activist authors write books that persuade and bring about social change.

Performers write books that need to be read aloud, brought to stage or screen.

When you understand your writing identity, you can deliberately tap into your own personal experiences, emotions, and perspectives to deepen and develop it. Dolly Parton put it like this: "Find out who you are and do it on purpose."

Authentic, genuine writing builds trust with readers, as they sense that you are true to yourself, and not afraid to own your individuality. This is particularly important in the age of artificial and augmented intelligence (AI), which is now producing excellent elementary text far more quickly and easily than you and I ever can.

Owning your writing identity also helps you to set realistic goals for your writing business, and make informed decisions about the types of projects you want to undertake.

CONSIDER THIS: Writing Identity: *Are you a reporter, explorer, prophet, activist, performer? A mix of more than one? Something else?*

TRY THIS: Writing A Mission Statement. *F-r-e-e-write a statement of your writing identity in the following format: "I am a _____ author who wants to make a difference by _____."*

If you write across different genres or niches, you'll need to create separate writer mission statements for each niche.

Mission Statement 2. Readers

With the work you've done around your values, motivating passions and author identity, explore your book reviews, reader emails, and any other feedback you've ever had from readers, if you have any. This, together with what you want your readers to experience in reading your work, should form the basis of your reader statement.

DO THIS: Reader Statement. *F-r-e-e-write a reader statement in the following format: "My reader connects with my _____ (mission), particularly my top three values: _____, _____, and _____. I want them to experience _____ when they read my books."*

If you write across different genres or niches, you'll need to create separate reader statements for each niche.

Mission Statement 3. Originality

Thinking about the change or influence you want to bring about through your writing can help you to understand what makes you stand out from other writers. Again surveying your values, passions and writing identity, celebrate what makes you *you*.

It could be your unique perspective, experiences, writing style, or the specific subjects you tackle. A special interest or skill? A life experience? A unique upbringing? A nonconformist outlook? A weird sense of humor?

Whatever aspect you highlight should connect to your passion, personal values, and definition of success.

DO THIS: *Write an originality statement in the following format: "Others might not love it, but I like that I _____ and am _____".*

Mission Statement 4. Purpose

Our sense of purpose is highly individual and each of us has to determine it for ourselves. As you've done this work (you *are* doing the exercises, aren't you?) you'll have come to see how your values, mission, and passion have a point of connection—your creative purpose.

Once you know your purpose as an indie author, what you're all about as a writer *and* as a publisher, you'll enjoy a burst of creative energy. You'll feel ready to face fears and take risks. You'll be able to work with intent focus without feeling drained.

Everything has been leading to here, you'll realize. Now you know exactly where you want to go.

TRY THIS: F-r-e-e-writing Creative Purpose. *F-r-e-e-write about the links between your mission (what makes you angry) and your passion (what you most love), first as a writer, then as a publisher. How are they the same? How do they connect? Where do they differ?*

When I first did this work, like most people, a few surprises jumped at me. I found that what I most valued in life was the quiet power of the non-worldly world, what I've come to call "the feminal" —the invisible, the peaceful, the womanly, the creative. I came to see that all my work was part of a long social movement towards personal empowerment, gender liberation, and creative expression.

I felt nurtured by all the writers and publishers, past and present, and all the social and political activists who've worked peacefully for the same aims. I came to see how writing, publishing, and digital creative business all feed these values of creative empowerment and self-actualization that I prize so highly. And that creating community and content, blogs and podcasts, was part of my body of work, every bit as much as my books.

My three-part mission statement about me, my reader, and my personal purpose, has helped me to define my poetry, fiction, and marketing material. And I return often to these exercises, to reconnect with or refine my mission and passion statements. They are a source of tremendous creative energy for me, a reserve that I draw on again and again when I'm feeling tired, when I get trolled or get a lousy review, when I hit a setback or make a mistake.

In these digital days, your challenge as an author is not scarcity of information or lack of opportunity, the challenges I grew up with. The big challenge is managing abundance and overwhelm. Passion, mission, and purpose are filters. They focus us, enabling us to avoid detours and distractions, doubts and dithering. They keep our creative energies flowing in the right direction.

Staying on purpose keeps you authentic, ensures that what you offer is original, uniquely you. You don't waste creative energy trying to project an image. You find your place among other people who think the way you do, care about what you care about, consume what you want to create. That's where you find your readers and customers, fans and followers, your team and tools, and your genre, niche, and micro-niche.

Find what you're good at, what you're probably already thinking about, what you're possibly already doing, what you know that you love. Channel that uniquely-you aspect that's already in your writing into your marketing and bookselling and everything you do.

Finding your purpose aligns your books and your marketing and optimizes your business for both creative pleasure and commercial profit. You come to understand that creative success isn't somewhere out there, but embedded in your mix of passion and mission, expressed not just in your writing craft but in all aspects of your publishing craft too.

All of this feeds into the creation of a publishing business that is integrated and harmonious.

---

1. https://obamawhitehouse.archives.gov/the-press-office/2016/04/23/remarks-first-lady-jackson-state-university-commencement

PART IV

PUBLISHING FOUNDATIONS

In this section, we look at how to set up your publishing business on firm foundations that minimize risk and maximize creative and commercial benefits, over the long term. These include basics like copyright, metadata and employing wide distribution for your book across as many formats, outlets, and territories as possible, including your own transactional website. The importance of understanding the reader journey and how readers become fans and superfans are also covered as foundational self-publishing skills, together with the need to pay yourself first.

10

PUBLISHING VALUES AND PUBLISHING MODELS

Your publishing model is closely linked to your values. As we explored in the last chapter, our values are what give us our publishing passion and mission, principles and priorities. They are the foundations of our success. We have values as an author and we also have values as a publisher. In fact, as a publisher you have one guiding value and once you know what it is, everything becomes easier.

There are **three guiding publishing values: productivity, connection, and originality.** It benefits every indie author to decide which of these three they most value.

Of course, all three of these values are important to all authors. We all want to produce and sell more books, enjoy a closer connection to our readers, and improve our craft. But which is your number one? Connection, productivity, or originality?

Knowing your top publishing value does nothing less than give you the framework for your book business. Those who value productivity and output most highly should employ a **volume publishing** model. For those who most value connection and reader feedback, an **engagement publishing** framework is optimal. Authors who most value originality do best when they work a **craft publishing model**.

- For **volume publishers** the number one value is *productivity* and the number one publishing priority is *rapid release*.
- For **engagement publishers** the number one value is *connection* and the number one publishing priority is *reader relations*
- For **craft publishers** the number one value is *originality* and the number one publishing priority is *artistry*

If you find you're running around, (*doing. all. the. things*, as the latest creative community catchline puts it) it may be because you don't know your core publishing value. Or you're trying to operate a publishing model that's anathema to you.

Let's look a little closer at each of the three guiding publishing values and the publishing models associated with them.

Volume Publishing: Productivity

As a volume publisher, you write fast and sell as many books as possible to price-sensitive readers. Your publishing priority is rapid release and your framework delivers best in the genres that attract whale readers. You publish early and often, perhaps hiring other writers as ghostwriters or collaborators.

Volume publishers analyze data and push their advertising towards online retailers, especially Amazon, taking actions that influence algorithms. They may limit themselves to Amazon Kindle's KDP Select program. An example is Deborah Bladon, a New York Times, USA Today and Wall Street Journal bestselling indie author who, at time of writing, has sold over 3.5 million books through KDP only. On her website she apologises to readers who can't find her books on other platforms. "This was a tough decision... Ultimately, the stories come first and the most seamless way to guide readers through this network of characters is with the Kindle Unlimited Program."

- **Books:** Commercial fiction, non-fiction and poetry
- **Social Media:** Volume Publishers may not use social media at all and if they do, they employ a "broadcasting" model, automating updates on as many platforms as possible, and engaging only when it suits, if at all.
- **Sales and Marketing:** The focus is on digital algorithm marketing, using pay-per-click advertising, discounts, and value pricing to win advantages over other publishers in bestseller lists.
- **Team:** Volume publishers build a streamlined, online team that keeps your costs as low as possible through savvy automation.

Engagement Publishing: Connection

As an engagement publisher, you have a highly honed understanding of your readers' needs and wants. You trade in special editions, customized services, and tailored products. Your publishing priority is reader relations. You set up a structure that allows you to communicate effectively with your readers.

- **Books:** Signed, customized, reader driven
- **Social Media:** High engagement, giveaways, contests, quizzes, providing answers to readers' problems
- **Sales and Marketing:** Social media marketing and sales, online and physical events, hand selling
- **Team:** Actively engaged, receptive to readers' needs, reactive and nimble in your responses.

Brandon Sanderson's $41 million crowdfunder is an example of the power of engagement publishing. Sanderson's famous and record-busting Kickstarter was built on decades of carefully managed reader engagement.

He not only dutifully answered all his fan mail since he started writing, he has publicly posted his reader mail responses on his website for years—including listing the books and websites of his students and followers who have themselves published. He runs regular workshops and courses for writers, all posted on YouTube, and constantly updates the Brandon Sanderson "knowledge base" on his website. Sanderson invites fan fiction within carefully delineated limits, and has an active Twitter account with almost 400k followers. He also does regular giveaways and contests. And he loves to get out and about to meet his readers.

Sanderson's message on his newsletter signup demonstrates his commitment to engagement. He invites subscribers to list the metro areas (or reasonably small states or countries) where they live. "General and unambiguous is better than specific, he says. "And avoid smaller cities with the same name as larger ones," helpfully giving examples: "Utah Valley, Orange County, Bay Area, Washington DC. If you're in southern British Columbia, put Vancouver or Victoria. If you're in Vancouver WA, put Portland. For Portland ME just put Maine. For London Ontario put Toronto. In the UK, put the nearest large metro area: London, Manchester, Birmingham, Leeds, Glasgow, Liverpool, Southampton, etc."

Yes, Brandon Sanderson has published a lot of books over many decades. Yes, he now has an operation that keep the titles coming, fast and often, but the foundation of his success is how he has prioritized reader engagement and special editions, all carefully focused to meet his different reader groups' particular needs, including adults, YA and children.

This engagement publisher has devised brilliant strategies that involve his readers in his world in ways that do not derail his writing and publishing process. It has all culminated in the most successful publishing crowdfunder of all time.

Craft Publishing: Originality

As a craft publisher, you trade in unique books or a unique approach. You offer high-end literary or design values, and highly treasured products or services. Your publishing priority is creativity.

Not many authors tell readers not to buy their book, but in the first book of his Brother Hermitage series, Howard Matthews, known to his readers as Howard of Warwick, says: "If you are a lover of the historical detective genre, if you have a deep respect for the worlds created, don't read this book. It'll only upset you."

It's all part of Matthews's comic take on 11th century crime fiction. Publishers and literary agents told Matthews it would never fly, as they rejected his crime-solving medieval monk for a lack of commercial appeal. They were wrong. Brother Hermitage is now a 20+ book series with hundreds of thousands of happy readers.

Every aspect of Matthews's books, from the cover and blurb to the digital ads, feeds his original and unusual premise.

Books: high production values, premium editions.

Social Media Focus: Book trailers and author explainers that show your work and your value proposition, compelling crowdfunders.

Sales and Marketing: Special promotions, premium offers, creative campaigns.

Team: You build a culture of creativity and quality, and ensure your publishing team and assistants appreciate your mission to offer unique, highly prized products and experiences

---

Core to any creative project is *selection*. Most authors, like most creative people, find they can do lots of things rather well and tend to be attracted to new things. That's all fine and completely lovely if you're creating for yourself, but if you want to sell your books to readers, you have to focus.

Your reader needs to be crystal clear about the kind of book(s) you're offering and what they can expect if they read them. Otherwise they will pass over your book on the shelf and move on to titles and authors that don't leave them scratching their heads.

You need to be able to balance your writing and your publishing tasks if you're to reach enough readers to run a profitable publishing business. Without knowing your core publishing value, this is all but impossible. You don't know your priorities. You don't know which advice to follow, and which is only meaningful for others. You don't know how to best set up your marketing and promotion.

When you prioritize your kind of publishing, and lean into that, everything gets easier—especially marketing and promotion.

Choosing A Model

These publishing models apply for third-party publishers too. Large corporate publishing houses are generally volume publishers. They use economies of scale to survive the cut-throat margins of bookselling. While they have craft imprints, which release the books that get submitted for prizes, generally the more lucrative volume business funds their literary offerings.

What big publishers cannot do as well as indie authors is engagement publishing. For readers, the writer, not the publisher, is the brand. The indie author is both and has a great head-start as an engagement publisher.

In the self-publishing sector, we often meet an assumption that the best way, even the only way, to self-publish profitably is to write fast and publish often. Yes, that is one way to succeed, but no, it's not the only way and it's a model that's most effective with certain genres and in certain book categories.

Self-publishing has liberated into visibility those writers who sell the most books and earn the most money, who have traditionally kept the book industry (and most "literary" authors) afloat. Little wonder that they are now highly vocal about how they do things. Problems may arise, however, for authors who are trying to fit into that model when it doesn't suit them or their books.

Many writers won't complete a book a year, never mind a book a month (yes, that's happening!). If they try, they'll quickly run themselves to the ground and may feel like they've failed (failed to be productive enough, failed to fix their mindset, failed to follow advice…). If there was a failure, it was a failure to understand that they are an engagement or craft publisher and shouldn't be organizing themselves as volume publishers.

The sooner you understand and begin to work from your model, the better. Deciding on your publishing model is ideally one of the first tasks you undertake as a publisher but many of us stumble upon our model eventually, through trial and error.

And things can change over time. Some craft publishers turn to a volume model when they work out how they do what they do. Some volume publishers switch to a long-held passion project that uses a craft publishing model. Multi-passionate authors may run different models for different pen-names.

It's all good.

DO THIS: Write down the pros and cons of the publishing model you currently use. *How different would your business or day look like if you switched to another model?*

TRY THIS: Which Model is Right for You? *F-r-e-e-write your answer to this question. Have a think about how you work as an author. What feels most comfortable yet challenging enough to be fun?*

11

PUBLISHING WIDE

To "go wide" is self-publishing jargon for distributing a book via multiple platforms, such as Apple Books, Google Play, or Kobo Writing Life, in addition to Amazon and your author website. Indie authors who publish wide adhere to the principle of non-exclusivity (see Chapter 20).

Discoverability—having your books available for readers to find—is key to building a long-term, sustainable business as an indie author. ALLi advices authors to be where your readers are and provide books in the format they like. Making your books available where more readers might find them gives the strongest foundation for consistent, long-term income. For that reason, and while recognizing that there are always particular circumstances for an individual author, ALLi encourages its members to publish wide, time and other factors allowing. More on this below.

The intention in publishing wide is to reach as many readers as possible by being available through as many distributors as possible, in as many formats as possible, and across the world in as many territories as possible. As colorfully described by Kevin Tumlinson, Director of Marketing at aggregator service Draft2Digital, you "create a nicely packed powder keg that, ultimately, will explode in a mushroom cloud of sales that covers the widest possible area. If your goal is to be known for your work... in all the corners of the world, then the only path to that success is wide distribution."

These global territories which respect copyright are where self-publishing is growing exponentially today.

The opposite approach to publishing wide is to distribute exclusively through one outlet, and in the self-publishing sector, that usually means Amazon-only.

Exclusivity in publishing means limiting your publishing to a single outlet. In third-party publishing, exclusivity is the default option. Though a publisher might put a book out in multiple formats or territories, from a contractual perspective, the agreement is exclusive. The author cannot publish anywhere else, including their own website. A third-party publisher investing in a book needs to know that a competing book by another publisher, is not going to pop up and cannibalize sales. Most of all, a competing book by the author.

Exclusivity in third-party publishing may also refer to distribution of print books i.e. distributing exclusively in the United States, or United Kingdom and the Commonwealth, for example. Such contracts are how third-party publishers traditionally protected their investment in manuscripts, as the "gentleman's profession" in London and Manhattan divided the English-speaking world between them, agreeing not to publish in each other's territories.

This was never a closed system. In Europe and other parts of the world, tussles between the American and British editions of books are common and in much of the world, copyright is not respected at all. There, pirated print copies circulate freely. But the system worked well enough throughout the 20th century for everyone in the publishing and bookselling business to make a living—except, as we've seen, the authors.

The dawn of digital publishing burst through these boundaries. The world can't be compartmentalized like this anymore, and third-party publishers now increasingly seek world rights for print, as well as ebooks (though without paying more for the privilege, a trend that authors and agents are pushing back against, with varying degrees of success).

By contrast, self-publishing agreements with online retailers like Amazon KDP, Apple Books, Google Play, IngramSpark and aggregators like Draft2Digital, PublishDrive and StreetLib, are non-exclusive by default. The rights-owning author's business partners distribute and, in some cases, retail the book, taking a commission from each sale as payment for the use of their platform. It's a completely different model to rights licensing, and royalty is the wrong word for these commissions.

Uniquely, Amazon offers an exclusivity program through its Kindle Direct Publishing (KDP) Select for ebooks, and ACX exclusivity option for audiobooks. These programs offer benefits like higher royalty rates, inclusion in subscription programs, and other marketing tools in exchange for exclusivity. In addition, on their platform, Amazon downgrades print-on-demand books that have not been published through their own service, KDP Print, e.g. books from IngramSpark, making them seem unavailable or less attractive to consumers. They may appear with an "out of stock" label, for example, or "available in 8 to 10 days".

These tactics—combined with clever positioning, some arguably unfair behaviors and some excellent tools—have given Amazon market dominance in the territories they're in. This market dominance is constantly being challenged in the US courts where their head office is based.

If you publish exclusively to Amazon, you're closing yourself off from many sales channels and avenues for discoverability. And just as some readers prefer audio or print to ebooks, some are loyal to their Nook (Barnes & Noble), Kobo e-reader, or Apple device and the ease of their associated apps.

PUBLISHING WIDE: ADVANTAGES & DISADVANTAGES

Wide publishing is definitely more complex, with multiple retailers and aggregators to think about, unless you work with just one aggregator like Draft2Digital, PublishDrive or StreetLib, for all platforms. And the industry has not yet given us great tools for tracking sales across all outlets.

The main disadvantage to publishing wide is that marketing can be slower to build. Building a readership takes time, work and probably money on all platforms, but Amazon's page reads, perks and on-site promotions can shortcut the process for some. When you are dealing with multiple outlets, each one needs attention.

Your foundations are firmer, more sustainable and scalable, but it can take longer to become profitable. Kevin Tumlinson again: "Authors can become frustrated with the process just before they see solid results—the proverbial 'fifteen feet from gold.' Keep going, wide authors. Give it time."

AMAZON EXCLUSIVITY

Amazon's self-publishing services KDP and ACX run the most widely used exclusivity programs in the self-publishing sector. Amazon does not demand exclusivity but opting into their KDP Select (for ebooks) or ACX exclusivity program (for audiobooks) allows you to experience the full benefits of their reader algorithms.

KDP

If you choose to publish your ebooks through KDP Select, you cannot publish them elsewhere for ninety days, though you can then decide whether to renew or cancel the arrangement. In return for exclusivity, your books will be available in the Kindle Unlimited (KU) program. This subscription service for readers offers a monthly subscription to read an unlimited number of books, often likened to "Netflix for authors".

As a KU author you are paid by borrows and pages read, through Kindle Edition Normalized Page Counts (KENPC), rather than books purchased in the traditional way. Your payment is a percentage of a fund allocated by Amazon each month.

Once a book has been enrolled in KDP, it cannot be unlisted for 90 days. You have to unsubscribe before the expiry date, or your books will automatically enroll for another 90-day period.

ACX

Amazon ACX provides an exclusivity program for audiobook self-publishers. At time of writing, opting into exclusivity at ACX means your audiobook can only be made available on three channels: Amazon, Apple Books and Audible. You are not permitted to distribute or sell your audiobook in any other format on any other store, including your own website.

In return you earn a higher commission on each book you sell through the platform (though not as high as it seems, see below), and can come to a royalty-share agreement with a narrator sourced through the platform.

In ALLi's opinion, these benefits do not justify exclusivity with ACX, a company that has been a poor publishing partner to authors, so much so that an ongoing author campaign, Audiblegate, has been protesting terms, conditions, and a lack of transparency and fair dealing since 2020.

Exclusive Promotional Tools

Amazon exclusive authors have access to other promotional tools. You can offer your ebooks free to readers for up to five days for the length of their enrolment in KDP Select and you receive higher commissions in certain countries (e.g. India and Brazil).

You get other promotional tools like a Kindle Countdown Deal, currently available only on the Amazon.com and UK stores. There are also payment incentives for top performing authors each month on KDP (All-Star bonuses).

Publishing exclusive can also make your books more discoverable by readers on the Amazon store, especially if you are chosen for Prime Reading, which is only open to you if you go exclusive. If selected, your book is offered as a free download to Amazon's millions of Prime members which is a significant visibility and revenue boost.

The great advantage of the single outlet, exclusive model is the simplicity. You only have to upload and manage your titles once, cutting down on admin time. Exclusivity can sometimes encourage a self-publishing service to promote a book—though not always directly, or on demand.

If a book is available exclusively through a specific vendor, and it shows signs of doing well (lots of readers picking it up, reviewing it, etc.), authors may get a friendly and helpful boost from that vendor. They may find their book listed in a promotional email or placed in a prominent position on a results page. These sorts of perks may happen anyway, if the book is doing really well, but are more likely in an exclusive environment.

Amazon Exclusivity: Advantages & Disadvantages

Certain genres and books thrive more in the exclusive environment than others. At ALLi, we see every week how exclusivity to Amazon is a boon to many authors, but it can also hurt others. We've seen authors' income plummet, or even dry up, without apparent cause. We've seen accounts closed, without explanation.

We've also, since the arrival of Amazon advertising, seen authors spend increasing amounts of money on advertising to maintain their page reads in KU, while relying on bonuses from Amazon to make it worthwhile. This is a very dependent business model. Stories of sales crashes among Amazon-exclusive authors are frequent and highlight the risks to other authors, but many are unaware.

Placing all books in one basket leaves authors vulnerable to volatile market changes. Every time KDP or ACX changes its rules, or algorithms, or releases a new service, a number of Amazon-exclusive authors find their livelihoods devastated.

In 2014, ACX slashed its commission rates to writers and narrators, from 50-90 percent of net income on an exclusive title, and 25-70 percent on a non-exclusive title to just 40 percent on exclusive and only 25 percent on non-exclusive. Even these significantly lowered numbers overstate the actual percentage that authors receive from most of their books (see Chapter 20 on book distribution for more). Amazon KDP (ebooks) and KDPP (print) could do the same any time.

Indie authors are grateful to Amazon for their excellent publishing platforms and tools. They were a true publishing innovator, the first to truly allow authors to make a living selling books online, but ALLi and other author advocacy groups advise against exclusivity for very sound business reasons.

There are also questions about data use and monopoly abuse by Amazon and other Big Tech companies. At the time of writing, governments are bringing pressure to break up what amounts to a monopoly or price-fixing by Amazon, where authors and publishers are unable to set the price of a book they've invested thousands to produce. Authors who are Amazon exclusive are likely to be affected.

The savvy author holds to the principle of non-exclusivity, with Amazon, as with any other partner.

WIDE PUBLISHING AROUND THE WORLD

Until recently, indie authors have been understandably focused on the world's biggest and second-biggest ebook sales territories: the US and the UK. Although these markets are huge, they're still a small slice of the overall global pie.

Those two countries combined currently have a total of 390,000,000 citizens. That's only a third of either China or India. More to the point, the US and UK markets are mature, those in other parts of the world are just beginning to adopt digital reading of ebooks and listening to audiobooks. These nascent digital markets are now growing far faster than the more mature UK and US markets.

US and UK authors also over-estimate Amazon's global power because it is such a powerhouse in those two territories but 95% of the world, and some important publishing territories, don't have Amazon's dominance.

An author who is Amazon exclusive reduces their visibility and discoverability around the world—and in countries where it is far easier to find a foothold today.

It is not a foregone conclusion that Amazon will win the online marketplace war in every market. At the time of writing, Amazon is rolling out KDP and KU in the biggest book markets globally, so the number of readers is increasing but is, as yet, only active in thirteen countries in the world and only ten of those are eligible for Amazon

Prime, the popular subscription service for Amazon shoppers. By comparison, Apple is in 52 countries, Kobo in 70+ and Google Play in 110.

In Germany, which many agree is the next big market for ebooks, Amazon currently has 40% of the market. Apple Books and Tolino (an ebook reader and associated stores run by a group of German publishers) sell the majority of ebooks in Germany. In April 2019, Amazon pulled out of China, closing its marketplace due to unbeatable competition from Alibaba. Most ALLi members sell most of their ebooks in Canada through Kobo.

While the US is still (just about) the world's biggest ebook market in dollars, it's not the biggest by volume. That honor goes to China, a country with 854 million internet users, compared to 312 million people online in the US. And whereas the US has nowhere to grow, China is only at 59% internet penetration and will easily top one billion internet users later this decade.

China is not an easy market to access, but there are ways and means. It is also an exciting market for print and for audiobooks. In fact, its audiobook market is huge, with 560 million listeners and a valuation on par with the US audiobook market.

India is next in the Internet stakes, with 560 million people online, and India is only at 40% internet penetration. The USA has 240 million Facebook users, for example. India has 251 million with huge potential for growth from there.

While Kindle India is still accessible through KDP, there are challenges. Readers in India are used to very low prices for print books, and indie print-on-demand editions might be too expensive. On the other hand, India's ebook market is growing fast and well worth exploring.

Unlike in our western bookish world, most readers in India buy at book fairs. The same is true of the Middle East and Africa. The biggest book fair in the world takes place in Cairo, Egypt. In 2019, it saw over four million visitors pass through its doors (160 times more than the London Book Fair and 13 times more than the Frankfurt Book Fair).

COVID-19 forced a change in the world's book fair calendars, with readers, writers and publishers all driven online.

Going Global

Global markets won't come to you. You need to go to them, but it's not hard to build a following in another country, if you give it time and attention.

So how do you connect with readers in these countries? Just as you do more spontaneously in your home market, engage with them where they are.

By default, our Facebook, Twitter and other social media accounts, and our search engines, give priority to notifications from our own country, but social media platforms allow us to target other areas. As an example, here's how to make a start on Facebook in India:

- Begin on your own website. Make it clear that you are a global author interested in India (or whatever territory you are targeting).
- Use the Facebook search bar at top left of the page and explore keywords like "India writers", "Indian authors", and "thriller authors in India" etc. to make a list of comparable authors in that territory.
- Follow author pages and join groups that are relevant to your genre and niche, just as you would at home. Join in the conversations.
- Target Indian markets with ads.
- Use an alerts system like Talkwalker or Brandwatch (much better than Google Alerts) to get emails about Indian writers and readers' groups, blogs etc.
- Measure your progress and adapt, depending on what works best.

If you spend just one quarter of a year on a territory, you can establish a presence there and then move on to another, while maintaining the first.

Step outside your home box, truly engage with other territories, and the opportunities quickly open up.

For more on going global, see ALLi's occasional International Insights column in our Self-Publishing Advice Center, at: Selfpublishingadvice. org/global.

As well as our member forum, ALLi recommends two other Facebook groups, if you're looking for tactics to help you sell more ebooks more widely Wide for the Win, and Marketing Audiobooks Wide for audiobooks.

12

SALES CENTERED WEBSITE

As a creative business, you need your own transactional, product promoting website. Most authors have a brochure-type site that shows off their books and points to a retail link elsewhere, usually Amazon. That's fine for authors who are traditionally published and only receiving a single-figure percentage of each sale. Indie authors reverse the financial take from each book or another product sold when they sell direct, earning 90% or more of each sale (minus expenses).

In addition to the many benefits of selling direct (see below), there are many other reasons to have a product promoting and transactional website. Yet I constantly meet authors, even those who have published a few books, who are not convinced. Some even question the value of having a website at all.

ALLi member Keith put the objections succinctly in a recent question to ALLi's monthly Member Q&A.

I'm set to publish my first novel. Should an author website really be part of my marketing plan? I mean, who actually sells any significant quantity of books via their website, or who tallies up a sizeable email list with it? And not all writers find value in blogging for the sake of it. I get that we don't want Amazon to rule the indie publishing world, but while lousy boring websites are cheap, keeping a good up-to-date, commerce-capable site is a significant investment in time and money. Why not just rely on Amazon and Goodreads, and page reads, and BookBub and all those sorts of things? I just don't understand why I need a website.

The answer is that characteristics we established as the core characteristic for an indie author: independence.

Owning your own website instead of relying on social media pages is like owning your house rather than couch-surfing with acquaintances. As cozy mystery authorpreneur, Morgana Best, said in her interview on ALLi's Inspirational Indie Author podcast, "Why build your empire on rented land? Own and develop your own real estate. Send readers to your own website or your own app—to anything you own."

This is excellent advice, and ALLi is seeing more of our most successful members selling their books from their own websites. This isn't about ignoring the other retailers and services mentioned in Chapter 11 "Publishing Wide". They are all great services and ALLi Partner Members. It's about realising just how important your own website is to your publishing business.

If a reader looks you up, do you really want them to find your Amazon or social media page, with all the shiny distractions around, all leading to what Amazon or the social site wants them to do? When you have a website, Google and other search engines make it the first thing readers find when they search for your author name. While those readers visit, they are immersed in what you are all about, without any distractions from other authors or books. Your words. The look, feel and content you want to emphasize.

On your own website, you control what they see, and how they navigate your information. You offer a magnet to encourage them to sign up for your mailing list, as well as the opportunity to buy your books and other products or experiences. For as long as you can keep them on your site, they are paying over an invaluable currency: reader attention. And then, hopefully, financial currency too.

You can sell your books and other products directly to them there, in your own words, in your own way.

These direct sales not only bring higher revenue, they allow you to learn more about your reader, get their all-important email address, and create a direct relationship with them.

Other Retailers as Marketing Platforms

This is *not* a recommendation to take books off other retailers. It is a recommendation to use other platforms strategically.

Customers buying books from online bookstores generally fall into two categories. The first are *browsers*, searching for a certain kind of book without a specific title in mind. The second are *seekers*, searching for the book by title or author name, because they read a review, or heard a podcast, or saw the author's book launch online, or followed an ad, or somehow discovered the book outside of that retailer's platform.

In the first case, you want to be discoverable on all platforms, so the browsers find you on their favorite store. In this case, the retailer can introduce those readers to your book and make a sale for you that you otherwise wouldn't have had.

In the second, it's your marketing—your ideas and creativity and hard work—that got the book noticed by the reader seeking a title like yours. Doesn't it make a lot more sense to guide them directly to your website for that sale, instead of over to another service?

I see so many authors spending a fortune on Facebook ads every week to send their readers over to Amazon. Yes, that can be a valid strategy, if you are using Amazon's algorithm to drive your book up their sales charts, to win more visibility. In that case, you are using the service to find new readers for you. If you have more than one book, it can make sense to put your energies behind one title in this way, to win more readers that you otherwise wouldn't find. Similarly, Amazon exclusivity for one title might make good sense. What's being questioned here is unthinkingly making Amazon or any other third party your main outlet.

It works for some, but too many authors are just doing it without thinking, and leaving it that way, even when it clearly is not working for them.

Retailers can be used to aid discovery of your website, or they can be used as your primary sales vehicle. Deciding which method you use is foundational work. Most authors do best over the long term by making their own website the hub.

Online retailers like Amazon, Apple, Kobo and others make amazing things happen for authors every day. It's not either/or, it's both. What you need to watch for is the direction of traffic. It should be towards your hub, not away, as it is on so many author websites that offer only an Amazon button. You should set up your Amazon pages, your social media pages, your Apple, Google, IngramSpark, Kobo and aggregator pages, to bring the reader over to your website.

To sell books and other products directly to readers in this way, your website must be transactional. You offer your own store as a main option, but you can also point to other sales outlets, for those readers who won't be weaned off their favorite e-reader or retailer. On my website I offer a "Buy from Orna" or "Buy from Others" option that includes Amazon, Apple, Barnes & Noble, Google Play, and Kobo.

Today's tech makes it easy to streamline sales across multiple channels, creating one point of purchase that shows readers all their buying options. I use Wordpress and WooCommerce for this, and lots of authors use the Universal Book Link provided by Books2Read.

Your website can also host your blog, vlog or podcast, display social media accounts, generate coupons and other incentives for targeted book promotions, host crowdfunding projects, invite patronage and showcase special projects. It can gather traffic that makes you attractive to others as an influencer.

When deciding what to put on your website, think about your own favorite authors, and what you would love them to do for you.

SETTING UP YOUR WEBSITE

When developed with a sales and marketing perspective, your website becomes a powerful tool for building your author brand, engaging with your audience, and selling your books. Let's break down the essential steps and components to setting up an author website that works to sell your books, 24/7.

Domain Name and Hosting

Start with selecting a domain name—the web address where visitors find your site. Ideally, this should be your author name or pen name. Having your own domain (www.yourname.com) looks professional and aids in improving your visibility and searchability online.

Next, you'll need a website host, which is where your website's files are stored. Several companies offer this service, often with additional features such as email accounts and WordPress installation.

Content Management System (CMS)

A CMS is a software application that allows you to build and manage your website. WordPress is a popular option due to its versatility and user-friendly interface. Other platforms like Squarespace and Wix are also solid choices, offering intuitive drag-and-drop website builders.

Design and Layout

Your website should reflect your publishing values and author style. Consistent use of colors, fonts, and imagery that align with your genre and approach go a long way in establishing your author brand. Simplicity is key—avoid cluttered layouts that can confuse or distract visitors. Make sure your website is mobile-friendly, as a significant portion of web traffic comes from mobile devices. You can find much more about branding and website design in Book 3 in this series, *Reach More Readers, Sell More Books: ALLi's Guide to Book Marketing for Authors and Poets.* This guide is free to ALLi members and available for purchase at Selfpublishingadvice.org/ReachMoreReaders.

Essential Pages

Here are the key pages every author website should have:

- **Home Page**: This should give a snapshot of who you are and what you do. Feature your latest book, include a short bio, and guide visitors to the most important parts of your site.
- **About Page**: Share your story—how you started writing, what inspires you, and personal anecdotes. Show your personality and let readers connect with you on a personal level.
- **Books Page**: Showcase all your books. Include covers, brief descriptions, and links to buy them. Make sure it's easy for visitors to become customers!
- **Blog/News Page**: Regularly updated content helps with SEO and gives visitors a reason to return. Share writing updates, behind-the-scenes insights, or blog posts on topics related to your books.
- **Contact Page**: Provide a way for visitors to reach you—be it an email address, contact form, or links to your social media.
- **Newsletter Signup**: An email list is a direct line to your most dedicated fans. Offer an incentive—a free chapter, a short story, or a behind-the-scenes look—to encourage signups. The newsletter sign-up is an incredibly important tool for authors allowing you to communicate directly with your readers without the interference of algorithms on social media platforms or reliance on third-party retailers. You control the frequency, content, and tone of the message, ensuring it reaches your readers just as you intended. More about this in the Chapter 21 about marketing.

Keep your website content fresh and up-to-date. Regular updates not only give visitors a reason to return but also signal to search engines that your site is active, which can boost your ranking.

Calls-to-Action

Guide your visitors towards actions that further your marketing goals with calls to action. See this post on the ALLi blog for more on this: Selfpublishingadvice.org/calls-to-action/

DIRECT SALES: ADVANTAGES

There are immediate advantages to selling books directly on your author website.

Better income

Instead of moving through a chain of distribution and retail intermediaries, all of whom take a cut from the profit on the sale, you can net the full profit on the book, minus a small fee for the transaction.

For example, if you use a basic PayPal gateway, that fee is currently 2.9% of the payment plus thirty cents per transaction. WooCommerce (an open-source payment solution developed for WordPress) uses PayPal powered by Braintree on a WordPress website. The first $50,000 in transactions is free, and after that the fee is the same as PayPal per successful credit card or digital wallet transaction. It also allows payments using Stripe: again, credit card payments cost 2.9% plus thirty cents per successful credit card transaction, as long as the total yearly charges is below $1 million.

Even premium solutions like Payhip charge only 5% per transaction. All these charges are a lot lower than the minimum 30% deducted by retailers like Amazon, Kobo and others.

Paid immediately

Owning a transactional site allows you to cut out payment lag, as well as the intermediary fees. When we publish through a rights buyer like a traditional publisher, royalties can take many months, even years, to arrive. Publishing through online platforms like Amazon, Kobo, Apple, Google and others, means we get paid sooner, usually thirty to ninety days after the sale. Sell directly to readers on our own website, and we receive the money immediately.

Reader connection

If you publish through a traditional publisher, you don't get any information about your readers. The same goes for the self-publishing platforms. Readers' details and data are assets that belong to those companies, and none of them share reader email addresses or other information with authors.

When a reader makes a purchase on our website, we receive their email address and thus a direct line to them. That open line of communication is invaluable.

Commercial control

As we've seen in earlier discussions, authors' fortunes can fluctuate. At ALLi, we have seen authors with healthy sales (some in six figures) on Amazon or another outlet suddenly finding their sales plummet. They don't know why. They *cannot* know why, as the services have set it up that way. The authors have no control, no data, and no way to leverage years of work and investment.

The only way to avoid this fate is for authors to build their own publishing real estate. That way, you don't get the boost to revenue that retailer algorithms can deliver, but if things go wrong, you can examine why. You can take steps to rectify it.

Similarly, if you are experiencing success, it won't be a mystery. You'll know what you did that made it happen. You'll be able to assess your return on investment (ROI)—and do more of that.

Creative Freedom

Direct selling delivers the highest possible level of independence and flexibility. How authors publish, promote and sell books is limited only by our own creativity, the quality of our offerings, and our ability to attract readers. We are free to experiment and explore, communicate directly with readers, ask for feedback, and realize all the creative advantages of being truly indie.

DIRECT SALES: CHALLENGES

There are some disadvantages to selling directly from your author website and some key challenges to overcome.

- **Loss of sales ranking:** sales do not count toward any kind of ranking (whether on Amazon or a media bestseller list). A lot of authors use their success on online retailers to increase their discoverability, as the retailers' own algorithms promote strong-selling titles to other readers. Books sold directly on your author website don't contribute to the tallies for bestseller charts.
- **No Exclusivity:** if a title is being sold on an author's own website, it isn't eligible for exclusivity programs such as KU. (But complete exclusivity is not recommended by ALLi or other author advocacy groups).
- **Tax:** in the EU there are tax issues as VAT is due in the country where the purchaser is located, rather than the seller. Some digital sales services deal with taxation issues, but not all do so adequately. Authors should therefore check their tax reporting responsibilities if they sell books direct, and the terms and conditions of any service they use.
- **Time:** the initial setup and strategy for direct selling can take a good deal of time and thought.

Right now, direct sales are only a small proportion of most authors' income, and few are making it a central plank of their author business but ALLi's indie author income survey showed how many of the highest earners are selling directly and doing crowdfunders. We predict this is a trend that will only increasing among independent authors.

Many use self-publishing retailers like Amazon to deliver some sales, and to direct readers to their own websites at the back of the books, while simultaneously recognizing that they are in competition with those retailers for those sales. They point their social media and advertising links to their own website for digital file downloads. They take time to persuade their readers to buy directly.

Authors who are set up for direct sales are also well prepared for an incoming technology that many feel has the potential to further decentralize publishing and revolutionize the way creators get paid: the blockchains. See ALLi's guide to *Authors and the Blockchain* for more on this.

Getting Readers Involved

Whether using blockchains or through our own author websites or apps, we need to persuade readers to buy directly from us. Few readers understand traditional publishing, and most are shocked to discover that when they spend $10 in a bookstore the author receives less than $1. They mostly have no idea about:

- How many hours authors have to spend on websites, blogs, and other marketing activities.
- How they can support authors in their endeavors and why they might want to do that.
- What a difference it makes to authors when they buy directly, instead of from another online store.
- How much a donation or other form of patronage means to authors' ability to keep going.

We need to tell them.

Authors often underestimate the influence they have with readers.

Most readers value words, and once they love an author, a series or a book, they are more than willing to help them. Authors can help readers to understand the changes that are happening in publishing, why these are positive for both authors and for them, and how they can become part of the publishing adventure. When readers understand what a difference it makes to authors if they are a patron, what a difference it makes if they buy direct rather than from somebody else, they want to help with that.

Certain readers love to buy directly from an author. They'll buy your books, they'll buy other products, they'll buy your presence— have you turn up to their book club, for example, to chat about your book.

The economic tide is turning in favor of the smaller, more personal outlet. The rise in the maker movement, in personal branding, in mindful consumption, in mobile phone sales are all favorable consumer trends for authors and SelfPub3.

Today's indie authors are taking their most loyal readers into their publishing adventures, through patronage, crowdfunding, and premium products. Some creators are building a dependable income from supporters by providing newsletters, livestreams or audio chats.

Sam Yam, the co-founder of Patreon, predicts a future with fewer social-media giants and creator-economy brands like his own, and more individual creators, each with their own custom-built platform.

When you look at self-publishing from a creative business perspective, it's clear that the best insurance an author can have against any seismic change in our industry is a large and growing group of engaged readers—true fans—connected to them on an owned, and self-controlled outlet.

---

*As part of our SelfPub3 campaign we provide **Buy Direct** badges that say: "Support indie authors, buy direct, browse my bookstore." One is designed for your own website, to encourage readers to support you and buy your books directly from you. Another is a badge for readers, booksellers and anyone who would like to demonstrate their support for author empowerment.*

Scroll through the SelfPub3 campaign page at AllianceIndependent-Authors.org/selfpub3 to download your badge.

13

READERS, FANS, AND SUPERFANS

Becoming a good publisher starts with understanding your readers. Knowing your genre and micro-niche and what your readers expect of you is key to your ability to make and market books. For an indie author, the right reader is king, queen, prince, and princess. Our writing serves our readers, as does our publishing. Our reader is what it's all about.

Our job as a publisher (and as author-publishers we have a clear advantage here) is to lead the reader along the pathway we want them to go—from never having heard of you or your book to becoming a raging superfan.

You sell books and create fans by attracting your readers through a funnel. At the widest end of the funnel are those who haven't heard about you and your book, but might like the sound of it. At the narrowest end are your superfans who buy every book you write directly from you, review your books when they come out, tell their friends to buy too, and are also open to buying premium products from you.

Your aim is to pull as many readers as you can through your funnel, and take them as far in as possible, deepening your connection to them in ever more rewarding ways as they go.

Don't skip this work. It is core foundational work for your author business. It begins by understanding the reader journey.

THE READER JOURNEY

Conventional business has long mapped customer journeys as a way to understand the steps a customer takes, from not knowing a brand at all, to buying and recommending its products. The customer journey concept is important in book marketing and sales too. In publishing, it's known as *the reader journey*.

The reader journey varies slightly, depending on whether the reader is buying print books or other physical products in a physical environment, or discovering and buying books online. Its progression is, nonetheless, remarkably consistent across formats, genres and purchasing practices.

It starts with *discovery*, the reader becoming aware of you or your book. Before this, you're a nobody to them and they've never heard of your books. Now, somehow, something's caught their attention. Maybe they read a review, had your book turn up in their "also-boughts" on Amazon (the books that Amazon highlights as "people who bought this book also bought these"), noticed your cover while scrolling on social media, found you on a shelf beside their favorite author while browsing in a bookstore, or had you turn up on a search in Google. There are many ways that a reader can discover your work and the more ways you can get yourself in front of them, the better.

That's not an invitation to do everything you think of, willy-nilly. You can't do everything, but start thinking about how you can increase the touchpoints with the right readers for your books. How do you make your book more discoverable?

After discovery comes *deliberation*. Will they buy this book, or won't they? They may be pulled across the line on first sighting. More commonly, they may go away and come back again. Marketing wisdom suggests it can take up to eight encounters before a potential customer feels they know, like and trust you enough to buy from you. You can increase the likelihood of a purchase or a sign up by the quality of your copywriting in book descriptions and marketing material and images, audio or video that helps the book to come alive for them.

This is the heart of the reader journey, the first investment, the *deal* —usually the first book sale, or a free book download in exchange for an email address.

After that comes *reading*. Yes, that's a separate stop-off in the reader journey. Lots of people buy books without reading them. Estimates indicate that one in two purchased books goes unread. (I know, I *know*.) More happily, and the high-point of the reader journey from the author's perspective, is *endorsement*—the reader sharing their love of your books and your author brand with other readers.

The intention is to turn browsers into readers, and reader into true fans, or maybe even superfans.

True Fans

In 2008, Kevin Kelly, technologist, author, founder of *Wired* magazine, and astute commentator on the digital age, wrote an influential article about the value of a creator having 1,000 true fans.[1] Kelly posed an alternative to the star system for authors and other creators. Instead of trying to blast your books out to as many readers as possible, you aimed to please just 1,000 true fans.

He defined a "true fan" as a fan who "will buy anything you produce." If you have roughly a thousand true fans (also known as superfans), and you get your pricing right, you can make a living. A thousand true fans, each spending $100 a year on your products or services would give you a gross of $100,000 a year and, provided your expenses are not high, give you a reliable and sustainable basic income.

The keyword is "roughly". The number of fans and the revenue benchmark aren't meant to be an exact prescription. It's about setting a different framework for how we think about earnings as a creator.

> 1,000 true fans is an alternative path to success... Instead of trying to reach the narrow and unlikely peaks of platinum bestseller hits, blockbusters, and celebrity status, you can aim for direct connection with a thousand true fans.
>
> On your way, no matter how many fans you actually succeed in gaining, you'll be surrounded not by faddish infatuation, but by genuine and true appreciation. It's a much saner destiny to hope for. And you are much more likely to actually arrive there.
>
> — KEVIN KELLY

Kelly describes a pattern of concentric circles with keenest fans at the center, a wider circle of regular readers around them, a wider circle of mildly engaged readers around them, who may have read one of your books or bought something else from you. Around those one-off readers is the still wider circle of readers who have heard of you but not yet dipped in, and then the biggest circle: those in your niche who don't yet know you or your books.

You begin in the outer circle, cultivating an audience through advertising, social media and other methods, with the intention of converting some of them into subscribers, then some of those into buyers, and some of those into purchasers of higher-value products, such as premium print books, extra content, exclusive access, or direct interaction with the author, through patronage. You then segment your followers and offer tailored products and services to the different levels of fans at the varying price points in the different circles.

On the episode of the AskALLi podcast where Joanna Penn and I discussed this, she raised the concept of overlapping concentric circles.

> I have two very clear brands, Joanna Penn and J.F. Penn, and I definitely have people under my Joanna Penn brand who are amazing and do buy everything and are my patrons—all my books, all my courses, all my audiobooks and they listen to the

podcast. I don't think I have many people like that under J.F. Penn, because I have so many different series, which appeal to different readers.

Similarly, I am a true fan of Kristine Kathryn Rusch—but for her non-fiction, as Kris Rusch. I've read a couple of her novels, but she writes under all these different names and all these different genres and I've read some of them, but certainly not all. Whereas, with her non-fiction, I buy all her non-fiction, I'm a patron, I fly to America to see her speak.

Same with you Orna. I've read all your non-fiction, but I haven't read all your poetry. And so, what I would say for authors who write in multiple genres or series: understand that you can have different concentric circles, each built around pockets of true fans.[2]

— JOANNA PENN

In 2020, with Kelly's blessing, Li Jin, founder and Managing Partner at Atelier, an early-stage VC firm funding creator economy businesses, updated the thousand true fans theory. Jin argued that the rise in social media use, the impact of influencers, and the availability of new paid creator tools like Patreon, Podium and Substack, has shifted the threshold for success. Today, creators can effectively make more money from fewer fans.

Not 1,000 fans paying $100 a year, but 100 fans paying $1,000 a year.

Like Kelly, Jin points out that the revenue benchmarks of $1,000 or $100 per fan per year isn't meant to be an exact prescription. Also, that the 100 True Fans and 1,000 True Fans models aren't mutually exclusive. It's up to the creator to work out the model that best suits their offering and their fans.

To authors thinking solely about the traditional book buying business, the idea that 100 fans could provide a living for a creator might sound unlikely, even fanciful, but creator platforms like Substack, Podium, and Patreon show that the buyers are there.

Superfans

While a true fan is a reader who will buy everything you produce, a superfan is a reader who goes out and tells others all about you and your books. To have a whole team of fans pushing your book upon release is something that most successful indie author book launches rely on. More on this in Chapter 21 on book marketing.

A few of your fans will remain with you forever. Most will be around for a while, then they'll move on—and that's just as it should be. As you build your author platform you'll draw more readers into your sphere of influence.

YOUR AUTHOR PLATFORM

Writers can get very confused by this term which is widely used in publishing circles. They often don't understand how a good platform is built, or what it even *is*.

When considering whether or not to publish a book, a third-party publisher will do a review of the author's platform by asking three key questions: Who is this author? Who do they know? Who can they reach?

Your author platform is just that: the ability of you, as an author brand, to sell books. It is a composite of who you are, and who you can reach.

Your current platform measures your achievements to date in making your books and related projects matter to people. Growing your platform makes them matter more to more people.

Today, with technology like blogs, social media, and the ability to land in readers' email boxes at the click of a mouse, it's easier than ever for an author to establish a strong platform from a standing start. But your author platform is not just, as so many marketing experts now suggest, your social media presence. Your author platform is *anything* that helps your books reach an audience.

Any *project* (e.g. a PR campaign or ebook promotion) or ongoing *process* (e.g. your email newsletter or social media plan) that gives you or your books visibility or sales strengthens your author platform.

Social media provides one way to build a platform, but there are many other ways—connections to literary influencers like reviewers, podcasters, and bloggers, traditional media and PR, positioning on bestseller lists, winning awards, and more.

If you don't want to use social media, you'll need to decide what you *are* going to use. And if you do decide to use social media for business purposes, you'll need to understand that it is very different to using it for personal purposes. Chatting to your family, friends and even your readers about your weekend away isn't likely to build your platform.

When you set up for publishing as outlined in this book, you'll set up four pillars to uphold your author platform:

1. your **branding and book marketing**
2. your degree of **influence or authority**
3. the engagement of your **readers and fans**
4. your **book promotions**

You'll find each step on the reader journey—discovery, deliberation, deal, reading and endorsement—represents a touchpoint, an opportunity for the connection and good interaction that, over time, builds and grows your platform. This creative approach encompasses every aspect of your publishing—your book design, book descriptions, categories and keywords, comparable authors, reader magnets, and other content.

Our platform organically develops as we go about our business, as we make great books, share our work, and develop our relationships.

Dedicate yourself to your writing and publishing tasks with the intention of showing what you do, and how and why you do it, together with engaging and communicating with readers, influencers and media, and you'll find that your author platform builds itself.

---

1. https://kk.org/thetechnium/1000-true-fans/
2. https://kk.org/thetechnium/1000-true-fans/-podcast

14

METADATA: CATEGORIES AND KEYWORDS

How readers discover books has completely changed in the past decade. Pre-digital, the intention was to get your book into bookstores and have it placed in the front, and then get lots of author interviews and book reviews in relevant mass media outlets. The biggest authors got the biggest treatment, with their books appearing everywhere all at once, including TV ads and billboards.

This kind of campaign is aimed at the mass-market. The publisher knows the readers for this particular book are out there somewhere. A general message is dispatched to as many people as possible in the hope that the right reader will see the message and take action: go to the bookstore and ask for the book, or at least recognize it when they're in there browsing.

While all that still goes on in the book business, we now have a far more accurate and cost-effective route to our readers, through niche marketing—focusing on a smaller group with precision.

Niche markets addressing special interests are often seen as too unprofitable to be of interest to third-party publishers, and it is in these overlooked niches where many indie authors prosper. Over the past years, we've seen indie authors create whole new genres that have subsequently gone mainstream, like the *Fifty Shades* series of S&M erotica for middle-class women. (Who knew?)

For any publisher, niche marketing is about drilling down through the genre of the book, to its category, then its niche and sub-niches. You target your marketing at that small sub-niche, knowing it contains the rightest of right readers for your book.

Core to this is a familiarity with your book's metadata.

METADATA

Metadata is a publishing term for all the bibliographic information about your book—its title, author name, book description, ISBN, publisher name, publication date, and price. It also includes the marketing metadata, the categories and keywords that a reader or a book buyer is likely to type into search engines when looking for your book.

On publication, the data you select automatically feeds into various systems, publishing catalogues and stock lists, and is passed on to the rest of the trade, readers and other book buyers. Good metadata connects your book to its prospective readers. In digital publishing, metadata is fondly referred to as your book's "sales force."

Optimizing Your Metadata

- **Genre:** Choose two to three specific categories. Review the BISAC (Book Industry Standards and Communications) subject code (see below) to choose the best genre for your book.
- **Keywords:** Choose seven keywords—words or phrases designed to attract the right reader to your book (see brainstorming keywords below). Incorporate these keywords throughout your metadata: in the description and contributor biography.
- **Book Description:** Ideally 200 to 600 words.

- **Format:** Most specific description of your binding, such as mass-market paperback or ebook. Be sure to use one ISBN per format to keep formats distinct.
- **Review Quotes:** Ideally seven positive review quotes, from industry sources, publications, and relevant people such as other authors or reputable bloggers.
- **Audience Code:** Choose the appropriate audience code—general/adult, juvenile (for ages 0-11), or YA (for ages 12-17)—and align the audience code with subject code.
- **Age and Grade:** If you choose a juvenile or YA audience code, pick an age range and/or a grade range to target—use a two-year age or grade range for children and a four-year age or grade range for YA.
- **Title:** Ideally the title is fewer than 80 characters long, including subtitle, so that it's optimized for mobile viewing. Be careful not to misspell the title or alter it in any way from how it appears on your book cover.
- **Series:** Record your series name and number, again in fewer than 80 characters. Also ensure the spelling and any special characters you've used are consistent with the rest of the books (if it's a series).
- **Author:** Use all the names from the cover or title page, and be consistent with spellings, middle initials, full stops, etc. If you use your middle initial or a hyphen, spell it exactly the same way everywhere.
- **Author Bio(s):** Ideally between 50 and 250 words for each contributor. Don't use external links such as blogs and author websites but do incorporate some of your keywords.
- **Awards:** Has this book won any contests, awards, or prizes? When it does, make sure you add these to the book's metadata.

CATEGORIES AND KEYWORDS

Two aspects of metadata that demand more attention are categories and keywords. Many authors find choosing these hard—because it *is* hard. Books are complex creations. Each one brings together disparate elements in a unique mix. Book categorization splits open this act of integration in order to label the parts—genre, category, niche, keywords. It's only ever partially successful, and it can take time for a publisher to establish confidence around a new book's keywords.

It's important to match the content of your book with reader expectations and the promise of what your book will deliver.

Genres and Categories

The three macro-genres of fiction, non-fiction, and poetry are the top-level categorization of books. For most books, that part is easy—but even at this high-level, we get blends, from biographical fiction to political poetry.

Then comes genre. Different book classification systems approach this differently and none is wholly satisfactory. Libraries around the world follow the Dewey Decimal Classification (DDC) system, which gives the following top-level genre classifications:

- 000 – Computer Science, Information, and General Works
- 100 – Philosophy and Psychology
- 200 – Religion
- 300 – Social Sciences
- 400 – Language
- 500 – Science
- 600 – Technology
- 700 – Arts and Recreation
- 800 – Literature
- 900 – History and Geography

The online book retailers use different systems. Apple Books, Barnes & Noble, and IngramSpark use BISAC, while Kobo and KDP use their own. Amazon's is based on BISAC. BISAC codes are maintained by the US Book Industry Study Group (BISG), which you can find at bisg.org.

Book categories are subject to change, especially in recent years as author publishing invents new categories and niches that were neglected by third-party publishing in pre-digital days. BISG keeps an up-to-date listing, which is regularly revised and can be found at bisg. org/page/bisacedition.

This is a useful page if you are trying to work out categories and keywords for your book. You might not want to put your book in a box or a genre or a category, but you have to. That's how the publishing platforms organize themselves, and you'll have to choose a category and keywords to upload your book.

Many authors resist categorization, but it's a fundamental of book publishing. Every reader has expectations of their genre. If you don't meet those, they will be disappointed, and you'll get poor reviews.

You might not think this applies to you if you write literary fiction, particularly if you want to write fiction that transcends categorization, but from a publishing perspective, LitFic is just another genre. It gets disproportionate attention in the publishing and media circles, as those are the books that people who work in those fields like to read themselves. But in terms of the more democratic, digital online bookstores and blogs, categorization still works in exactly the same way.

KDP allows a publisher to choose two categories and seven keywords, some other platforms allow more, and others fewer. Not every online store supports keywords.

Amazon provides the following advice for choosing the best categories, and this is good advice that can be applied to all online retailers:

- **Pick the most accurate categories.** Make sure the categories you've picked best describe the subject matter of your book.
- **Pick the most specific categories.** It's better to choose more specific categories instead of more general categories. Customers looking for very specific topics will more easily find your book, and your book will be displayed in more general categories as well (for example, a book in the "FICTION > Fantasy > Historical" category will also show up in searches for general fiction and general fantasy books).

You should only select a "General" category if your book is actually a general book about a broad topic.

- **Ensure categories you choose are not redundant.** Since your book will be displayed in a variety of searches by choosing even a single category, you shouldn't place it in both a category and any of that category's sub-categories (for example, selecting both "FICTION > Fantasy > Historical" and "FICTION > Fantasy"). Even selecting just one specific, accurate category is preferable to selecting an inaccurate category just to have a second category listed.
- **Search other titles that are similar to yours.** You can then find the categories assigned to those titles by scrolling down the book's detail page to "Look for Similar Items by Category" at the bottom.

The number and kinds of categories and sub-categories in the Kindle Store have increased dramatically in recent years, and methods of getting a book into the correct categories and sub-categories have expanded, with keywords becoming ever more important.

Readers are sectioning off into narrower niches and genres, it seems. That is very good for us as writers who want to reach readers, as smaller niches are easier to target.

If you're struggling with deciding on your categories, then looking at other writers who write books like yours can really help. Check what categories they are in. Spend some time exploring whether your book fits there and check other possible options. And then create a list of categories for your book.

If you can't find a description that best represents your book—and this is happening as indie authors mine previously undiscovered micro-niches—you can suggest a new code to BISG through a contact form on their website.

Keywords and Key Phrases

The words and phrases that people type into search engines to find what they're looking for are often called keywords, or more accurately key phrases. This is an aspect of metadata that authors can find difficult. A starting point is to visit each online bookstore and start typing a word you think people would use to find your book. (Be sure you are in the book section for that store.) Do books like yours show up? This can be a tedious and confounding task but taking time to get this right is profoundly important.

There are two useful (paid) tools that can help. Dave Chesson's Publisher Rocket saves time and frustration by generating keywords and key phrases, and isolating categories for your book: Publisherrocket.com.

Publisher Rocket also allows you to see your potential competitors, including their book cover, list price, and number of pages, as well as their daily and monthly earnings on Amazon. By understanding what works for your competitors, you can create book titles, subtitles, and descriptions that convert better and sell more books, even if you don't intend to use Amazon as your primary outlet. How to use the information you gather about such "comp authors" is covered more fully in Chapter 21 about book marketing.

A second useful tool is K-lytics, k-lytics.com, a market-intelligence service for books, offering reasonably priced genre reports full of recommendations around categories, comp authors, keywords, and more.

Decisions, Decisions

These tools are wonderful, but at the end of all the research and exploration, you'll still have… ahem!… key decisions to make around keywords and key phrases, and nothing can shortcut the process of fully understanding your book's positioning and placement in the marketplace. It is a critical marketing step that will underwrite other aspects of your marketing.

Brainstorm all the keywords and phrases that apply, and then select the best. You can test Google, Amazon, Yahoo, and other search engines to get ideas by starting to type a keyword into the search bar and seeing what other keywords start to auto-populate. These are the most popular search terms for this aspect of your book's appeal.

Amazon, because it is an online bookstore, is the most useful search engine for this. You start your search typing in YA, but other words such as "YA books for teen boys", "fantasy", "romance", "YA books for less than five dollars", or something entirely unexpected shows up. Score! Note the keyword ideas and include anything particularly relevant in your book metadata.

For example, you can include the period or era in which your novel takes place. An example would be Second World War and World War II.

You could also use keyword phrases that describe your protagonist or another character in your book. Some examples are "divorced mom", "stay-at-home dad", "teenage drama", and "immigrant experience."

TRY THIS: Brainstorming Keywords. *Use these questions to brainstorm useful and relevant keyword selections for your fiction, non-fiction, or poetry books.*

__Genre:__ There will be a metadata field for your genre, but you can include secondary genres in your keywords, e.g. I write historical fiction which can include sci-fi, biography, romance, literary fiction, or something else.

__Categories:__ What is the top-level category of your book? e.g. Fiction: Historical; e.g. Non-fiction: Business; e.g. Poetry: Inspirational

__Subcategories:__ What is the next level down? e.g. Fiction: Historical Mystery; e.g. Non-fiction: Business Leadership; e.g. Poetry: Inspirational Non-religious

__Niche:__ What is the next level down again? e.g. Fiction: Irish Historical Mystery; e.g. Non-fiction: Business Leadership for Coaches; e.g. Poetry: Urdu Inspirational Non-religious

__Bonus Features:__ Any extras you'd like the reader to know about? e.g. Fiction: map of setting, family tree; e.g. Non-fiction: glossary, resource pack; e.g. Poetry: photographs

__Reader Notes:__ Is there anything extra you'd like the reader to know? e.g. Fiction: part of a trilogy but can be read as a standalone; e.g. Non-

fiction: draws on the work of a particular theorist; e.g. Poetry: the poetic tradition of the book

Story Type or Style: *e.g. Fiction: biographical multiple narratives; e.g. Non-fiction: Scholarly; e.g. Poetry: Epic*

Purpose: *e.g. Fiction: A story for the first day of school; e.g. Non-fiction: For coursework; e.g. Poetry: Consolation for the bereaved*

Update your keywords whenever you come across newer, more relevant options, or if your book's status changes, e.g. you win an award. Refreshing your metadata—trying new options—is rewarded by publishing platforms, especially if you are hooking in with current trends.

Every writing category and niche has avid fans who are hungry for their idea of a good book. Dive deep and do whatever you need to do to find them.

15

COPYRIGHT AND DIGITAL RIGHTS MANAGEMENT

C opyrights are legal rights that attach to certain types of intellectual property, granted under law to authors of creative works. Copyright is a passive right, which provides the framework that allows the book business to happen. You may never need to pursue it, but you need to know it exists and what it permits.

Copyright law, policy, and practice is fundamental to an author's ability to publish and trade in books, create successful author-businesses, and earn an income from their work. Independent authors, who are both writers and publishers, and who actively manage their own publishing rights, need to understand the importance of copyright and how to assert their rights in the digital age.

Copyright does not protect ideas but the expression of ideas. Protection exists from the moment a work is created in a fixed, tangible form, and authors do not have to apply for or file for copyright, though in some territories, notably the US, registration of the work with a copyright office is necessary in the event that you want to bring a case against an infringer. Registration can also prove useful in the case of disputed rights with Amazon or other publishing platforms.

In the main, the assertion of copyright with the appropriate copyright page in your published book is sufficient to assert your rights. Each of our books actually represents several sets of rights, each of which should be licensed separately and selectively. Indie author options are often presented as a binary choice between exclusively licensing all publishing rights to one trade (traditional) publisher or exclusively self-publishing.

When it comes to licensing those rights, ALLi recommends the principle we call *selective rights licensing*.

That's not so much the hybrid author option of licensing all rights on some books to the trade while self-publishing others. Instead of automatically licensing all rights to a book, the indie author offers only the right the publisher is seeking to exploit—the right to produce an audiobook, for example, or to translate the work, or release a print edition in a particular territory.

More on this and on how to limit the territory and format and term of a contract and pitch rights buyers in Chapter 23.

Publishing contracts from established and respected rights buyers, including corporate publishers, are usually less than ideal for indie authors, particularly when it comes to exclusivity. In the self-publishing sector, many services—often the ones advertising at the top of internet searches—also offer problematic contracts and agreements. A particular danger are "publishers" that are really exploitative vanity operations, often using the word "hybrid" as a cover.

WRITING A COPYRIGHT PAGE

The copyright page is a page found in most books, traditionally in the front matter, but now often in the back matter of the book. It indicates the copyright status of the book and is referred to by interested parties for information about the publisher. It may also include cataloging data for librarians. It declares the copyright status e.g. "all rights reserved", or "creative commons license".

This page doesn't assert your copyright, it is purely informational. What it does is announce to interested parties that the work is under copyright, that you are the owner, and how you want your work to be reproduced or replicated.

A copyright page has one or more of three elements:

1. a copyright notice,
2. a rights reservation statement
3. a disclaimer

Feel free to cut and paste anything below, entering your own details, as appropriate.

1. The Copyright Notice

This declares to readers that you are the owner of the copyright. It has four components itself:

1. The copyright symbol: ©
2. The word "copyright": Since the copyright symbol isn't recognized in some countries, reiterate it as a word so that there's no confusion.
3. The copyright owner's name: Your name or pen name.
4. The year of publication: Take note that this is the year you publish the work (not the year that you first created it).

Together, it will give you the copyright notice, as you'll find on this book:

Copyright © Orna A Ross, ALLIANCE OF INDEPENDENT AUTHORS 2023.

Because this book is a 3rd edition, that's also noted, together with the date of the first edition, 2018 and second edition, 2021.

Copyright © Orna A Ross, ALLIANCE OF INDEPENDENT AUTHORS 2023, 2nd edition.

First edition, 2018.

Second edition, 2021.

2. The Rights Reservation Statement

This statement informs the reader that rights are reserved under the copyright notice and should be respected.

The classic statement, which you'll see in most third-party publisher's books, reads something like:

> *All rights reserved. No part of this book may be reproduced in any form or by any electronic or mechanical means, including information storage and retrieval systems, without permission in writing from the publisher and copyright holder, except in the case of brief quotations embodied in critical articles and reviews.*

But given that the statement just reiterates the rights already granted by copyright protection and publishing contracts, others now feel this is overkill and prefer a shorter formulation. Something as simple as the following is sufficient:

> *All rights reserved.*

You will also see (on this book, among many others):

> *All rights reserved. The moral rights of the author have been asserted.*

The author's moral rights are a feature of British law. This highlights the fact that there is no international copyright legislation. Different countries have different laws, and, for example, the US and many other countries don't recognize the distinction of moral rights.

The Berne Convention of 1886 is an attempt to get over these differences, an international agreement that mandated several aspects of modern copyright law, agreed to by all countries that are party to the Convention (fifty-one parties, including the US and UK, to date). They agree to mutually recognize the copyrights held by each other's citizens—so the Convention provides for moral rights—the right to claim authorship of the work and to object to any mutilation, deformation or other modification of the work that would be prejudicial to the author's honor or reputation.

3. The Disclaimer

Disclaimers are not a full protection against being sued but they are widely used in book publishing. Here are some standard disclaimers, if your book requires one (not all books do).

- *For Fiction: This is a work of fiction. Any resemblance to actual persons, living or dead, events, or locales is entirely coincidental.*
- *For Creative Non-fiction: This is a work of creative non-fiction. Some parts have been fictionalized to varying degrees, for various purposes, with some names, dates, places, events, and details changed, invented, and altered for literary effect or to protect the privacy of the people involved.*
- *For Memoir: The events and conversations in this book are accurate to the best of the author's ability, although some names and details have been changed to protect the privacy of others.*

PLAGIARISM AND PIRACY

Plagiarism and piracy are both offences to author copyright, but they differ in legal standing. **Piracy** is the unlawful distribution of an author's books and the most common form of content theft. Digital publishing enables the cheap and easy copying of book files and raises constant questions about piracy for indie authors.

Plagiarism is when a writer repurposes another's work as their own. This can be unintentional (as when a non-fiction writer fails to properly credit a quoted passage); it can be coincidental (as when two writers independently develop similar plots); or it can be deliberate theft.

Piracy is an infringement on the commercial rights of the author. Plagiarism is an ethical failure that may not fit the legal definition of copyright infringement. As a result, incidents of plagiarism may fail to meet the legal requirements of a copyright infringement suit—and often go unpunished.

While you might assume that piracy is always a bad thing, studies indicate that piracy actually increases sales, both of ebooks and other media. Monty Python increased sales by 23,000% (yes, you read that right) by releasing free videos on YouTube.

Paolo Coelho is probably the most famous writer to take this approach to piracy, having gone so far as to call on pirates to please help themselves. Ever since a pirated Russian edition of *The Alchemist* was posted online in 1999, he has been a supporter of illegal downloads, provocatively calling piracy "a new and interesting system to promote the arts", and entering a partnership with The Pirate Bay— a website that's currently blocked, "pursuant to orders of the High Court."

You may not want to be quite so radical. We asked ALLi members how they felt about piracy and plagiarism. Out of 107 responses:

- 48% regard piracy and plagiarism as theft but feel that in most cases "pirates" probably haven't got their books.
- 22% ignore issues of piracy and plagiarism.
- 17% ignore pirates but do pursue plagiarists.
- 5% chase down perpetrators.
- 5% are glad to have reached a level where someone thinks their work is worth stealing.
- 2% pay a professional anti-piracy service to send takedown notices.

It's worth noting that much of the work that appears to be piracy isn't. If you key your book title into a search engine you may well find, on the very first page of search results, somebody handing out illegal copies of your work, for free. Most or all of these websites don't actually have your content. These operations are what are known as "phishing" sites, fronts for malware distribution, credit card scams, identity theft, affiliate link schemes, and more. They have software that gathers titles, covers, and descriptions from Amazon or other retailers and are using your book as bait, either free or at a ludicrously low-cost, "all you can eat" subscription fee.

When a cheapskate or idle browser wanders into this sticky corner of the World Wide Web, they discover the real price. Instead of a nice book for free, what they get is a malfunctioning computer, a decimated credit score and worse.

One popular con is the "recurring billing" scam. The site supposedly offers a free trial but requires users to enter their credit card information. "You can cancel at any time," the site promises. The victim cancels but finds that they're still being billed each month without their consent, and the website operator is unreachable.

DO THIS: Avoid Pirate Websites. *Do not click through to any pirate websites to confirm whether or not your books are there. To do so puts your computer at risk.*

DIGITAL RIGHTS MANAGEMENT

An important question you'll be asked by publishing platforms is whether or not you wish to apply DRM (Digital Rights Management) to your book. DRM is the use of various digital copy protection technologies to prevent ebook piracy, not by going after those who engage in piracy, but by preventing all readers from copying and sharing files.

Bestselling science fiction author, Cory Doctorow, is an activist in favor of liberalizing copyright laws and a proponent of the Creative Commons organization. The title of one of his most popular books says it all: *Why Authors Should Give Their Work Away, Stop Sweating Copyright and Focus on Building a Community of Readers.*

Practicing what he preaches, getting one of Doctorow's ebooks is as simple as going to his website and clicking a download button, yet he also sells millions of books, on and offline. Clearly, the availability of free copies doesn't hurt his sales.

ALLi's principle of non-exclusivity means making your work easily accessible to as many readers as possible, in as many formats and territories as possible. DRM goes against that. Treating all readers as potential pirates doesn't make you too popular. While it might seem reasonable to you as the author, a reader who has paid for a book may be frustrated to find they cannot lend it to their friend, as they can a physical book.

Given that DRM can be cracked easily by anyone who knows how, and that there are also free tools to remove DRM codes readily available online, many authors and publishers doubt that it is worth irritating readers who may well have come across your book without setting out to pirate. For all these reasons ALLi's advice is to choose "No DRM".

Takedown Notices

If most pirate sites don't have the books they claim to, is it worth trying to stop them?

Chasing down pirates that most likely aren't infringing on your copyright or cutting into your sales is wasteful. It's time and effort better spent on writing, editing, refining your marketing, polishing your book descriptions, or a hundred other activities that contribute in a more meaningful way to your prosperity.

On the other hand, many authors feel that having their name associated with a scam could harm their brand, even if their books are not being pirated.

And then there are situations where work has indeed been pirated, and a thief or a con artist has uploaded, and is trading in an author's hard work. We have seen this happen to a number of members, who have had their books translated, turned into courses and many other violations of their copyright.

If one of your books has been pirated, i.e. somebody is charging money for it, and you are not of the mindset that piracy helps build your author platform, DMCA takedown notice is your first port of call. DMCA stands for Digital Millennium Copyright Act, a US law that requires internet service providers to remove infringing content.

A DMCA takedown notice can be a cost-effective and quick way to remove material that infringes your copyright, giving you some power to protect your rights if that is what you wish to do. At the same time, the DMCA takedown mechanism has certain safeguards in place to protect the rights of those who have a right to publish material that is not infringing. This is important, as copyright law protects the rights of readers, researchers, and information dissemination also.

Technically, DMCA law only has jurisdiction over companies operating in the US, but notices filed from around the world are regularly acted on. The US law covers Google, Microsoft, and Yahoo!, which collectively account for 96.3% of English-language internet searches. And the DMCA-like legislation has spread to other territories, like the EUCD in the European Union and Bill C-11 in Canada. Many governments have now enacted laws making compromising DRM illegal (even if no copyright infringement took place).

Your first port of call is to attempt to contact the owner of the website. You can do this by either using the contact details on their site or using a specific host searching engine like HostingChecker.com.

Unless the owner of the website has paid for privacy, then the original email address setting up the website will be noted there. Failing that, the contact details for the host of the website will be available. You can visit the host's website and use their contact form or use the email address provided through the search. If this fails, then the last piece of contact information on these searches will be the registrar email and again, you can use this to reach out.

A takedown notice should be addressed to the Online Service Provider (OSP) and ask them to remove or block the offending pages. A takedown notice has no set formula but should contain the following:

1. Your name.
2. Identification of the work that has been infringed (or a representative list of such works) with titles and URLs.
3. Identification of the material that is infringing and which you wish to have taken down or blocked, with enough

information to allow the OSP to locate the material e.g. a link to the offending page.

4. A screenshot of the infringement.

5. If you have already attempted to contact the owner of the website, provide proof or evidence of this.

6. A statement that you have "a good faith belief that use of the material in the manner complained of is not authorized by the copyright owner, its agent, or the law."

7. Your signature as the copyright holder.

8. Ways for the OSP to contact you, such as an address, phone number, email address.

9. It's also important you state that you have the right to submit the DMCA because you are the owner of the IP/copyright.

ALLi has two books that explain more about the value of your copyright and intellectual property, available for purchase in all formats. Members enjoy free access to the ebooks.

How Authors License Publishing Rights *explains how to approach rights buyers and how to pitch and close a rights deal:* Selfpublishingadvice.org/rightsbook

Our campaign book, **The Copyright Bill of Rights**, *builds on the work of previous copyright activists from the viewpoint of self-publishing authors.* SelfpublishingAdvice.org/billofrights

PART V

THE CRAFT OF PUBLISHING

In this section we look more closely at the seven processes of publishing, all of which have to be mastered if you are to become a good publisher: editorial, design, production, distribution, marketing, promotion and rights licensing.

Together these seven processes comprise the three elements of publishing: book making, supply, and sales.

While focusing mainly on principles and best practices, the section also describes the main ebook, audiobook and print book services that underwrite SelfPub3.

16

THE SEVEN PROCESSES OF PUBLISHING

While each book is a unique publishing project with its own creative and commercial imperatives, every manuscript is put through a standardized procedure on its way from writer to reader. This is the craft of publishing and it has three elements: book making, book supply and book sales.

These three elements can be further broken down into seven processes: editorial, design, production, distribution, marketing, promotion and rights licensing.

Book making: putting the book together in various formats; electronic (ebook), audio (audiobook) and print (print book). Book making relies on the publishing processes of *editorial, design, and production*.

Book supply: ensuring a wide range of book distributors and retailers, libraries and archives stock the book, know which kind of reader it's aimed at, and where to place it on their physical or virtual shelves. Book supply relies on the publishing processes of *distribution and marketing*.

Book sales: pricing and promoting the book, and licensing its associated publishing rights, so it reaches as many readers as possible. Bookselling relies on the publishing processes of *promotion and rights management.*

Digital tech and tools have revolutionized publishing in the last decade and there are now more ways to make, supply and sell books than ever before, but these fundamental elements of publishing never change.

Whether a book is published by its own author or by a huge, corporate conglomerate, a good publisher engages all three publishing elements, and takes responsibility for the outcomes of all seven processes of publishing.

PUBLISHING ELEMENT 1: BOOK MAKING

- **Process 1: Editorial**: The first process in publishing is editorial: revising, amending, rearranging and improving the words and flow of a manuscript, aiming for clarity, simplicity, brevity, and artistic effect.
- **Process 2: Design**: The second process in publishing is book design: configuring the cover and interior text to consolidate the content, style, format, and sequence of the book into a coherent visual unit.
- **Process 3: Production**: The third process in publishing is book production: assembling the book in audio, electronic, or print format.

PUBLISHING ELEMENT 2: BOOK SUPPLY

- **Process 4: Distribution and Sales**: The fourth process in publishing is book distribution: circulating the book through channels that make it available to readers for purchase.

- **Process 5: Marketing**: The fifth process in publishing is book marketing: ongoing, repeatable activity which generates awareness of a book and its author among book distributors, retailers and readers. Marketing positions you as an author, and your books, to be what the publishing business calls "discoverable"—which means you can be easily found by readers who are searching for a book like yours. Marketing covers ongoing activity like tending to your website, your regular social media activity, growing and communicating with your email list.

PUBLISHING ELEMENT 3: BOOK SALES

- **Process 6: Promotion**: The sixth process in publishing is book promotion: concentrated sales-driven activity behind a particular book for a particular period of time. Promotion is consumer centered. It takes one book and brings it to its target readers, with enticement to buy. This publishing process includes advertising, price promotions, online and live book tours, PR and media coverage, and more.
- **Process 7: Selective rights licensing**: The seventh process in publishing is rights licensing: assigning or granting the right to a third party to exploit a book's content or characters in exchange for royalties (a percentage of sales revenue).

For a creative self-publisher, each of these seven processes expresses your vision, clarifies your offering to the reader, strengthens your author platform and grows your business.

Deepening our awareness of the challenges in each process of publishing and improving your skills in each: that's how we become better publishers with each book we write, produce and sell.

The following seven chapters consider each process of publishing in turn. These are necessarily brief, a summary of what you most need to know.

Two ALLi resources supplement this information. Both are available for purchase in multiple formats in our bookstore:

Selfpublishingadvice.org/bookshop/. Members enjoy free access to the ebooks.

To help you make good decisions in choosing services, see **Choose the Best Self-Publishing Services: ALLi's Guide to Assembling Your Tools and Your Team** *by head of ALLi's watchdog desk, John Doppler: SelfpublishingAdvice.org/choosethebest*

For answers to common questions about book distribution, see **150 Self-Publishing Questions Answered: ALLi's Writing, Publishing, & Book Marketing Tips** *by Outreach Manager Michael La Ronn:* SelfpublishingAdvice.org/books/150

When it comes to applying the knowledge, every author is different, with different creative needs, intentions, goals, and constraints. If you're stuck, or not moving as fast as you would like, my creative planning program for authors and poets may help: SelfPublishingAdvice.org/planning

17

BOOK EDITORIAL

PUBLISHING PROCESS ONE

E ditorial is the process of turning raw typescript into publishable text. A good book is a complex, intricate cultural form and a large undertaking that requires close attention if we want to put the reader at ease, and ensure our words deliver the impact and influence we seek.

The editorial process touches every aspect of the words in a book, from the big picture stuff like character development in a novel, structure in a non-fiction book, thematic links in poetry books, down to a spelling mistake in a single word—and everything in between.

Editing has a number of phases. Ideally, you self-edit first. Then you use beta readers to give you general feedback and pick up gross errors. Then you bring in the professionals: developmental editors, copyeditors, and proofreaders.

The more ambitious your project, and the earlier you are in your writing development, the more editorial feedback you need.

Good editing is labor-intensive. You can use editing software like ProWritingAid or Grammarly to help, but it still takes human input—often that of several humans, each reading and correcting the full manuscript. This makes it expensive, in terms of time and money, and so beginner self-publishers are inclined to minimize its importance and give it a skip. More experienced authors too, sometimes.

In third-party publishing, every manuscript is brought through a number of rounds of editing (see below for more on these). Experienced authors welcome this process that improves on their own efforts, knowing there is lots about their book that they don't see when they've just finished, as they are far too close to the words and the sentiments.

There is a movement in certain corners of the indie world that emulates software creators by putting out what's known as **minimally viable product**—effectively a raw manuscript that has had little or no editing. Books are not software, best refined by users. Some readers may be forgiving, especially if you're a talented storyteller or you're imparting great information or inspiration, but this approach to publishing is bad manners towards your readers, marking you out as an amateur, and leading to poor reviews that reduce your ratings.

Ensuring that your book is well edited is vitally important to its success. At ALLi, we recommend that every book receives at least two rounds of professional editing: a developmental/copyedit followed by a copyedit/proofread, and ideally these shouldn't be done by the same person.

The ideal is three rounds: developmental, copyedit, and proofread.

Each of these processes is different and even if someone is trained to do both, it's best to have a fresh pair of eyes for different stages.

This does represent an investment upfront, that you may find challenging. You will recoup this, and move into profit, if your book is good and you market it well.

If you absolutely can't afford professional editing, you will need to invest much time, and call on your writer friends for help. Whatever you do, don't be one of those indies who skip over the editing. Even if you are a skilled or professional editor yourself, it's not recommended that you edit your own book. Nor should you send it to a friend who is a journalist or teacher who fancies themselves as an eagle-eyed grammar guru. A qualified editor, who has completed certified training approved by one of the editor associations, and who carries good recommendations and testimonials from other authors and publishers is what's needed.

CONSIDER THIS: *No author, not even the most experienced, is beyond the need for editing. Not a single one. Not the very best, at the top of their game. And not you either.*

Sooner or later, if you persist in publishing, you're going to realize the need for editors. Make it sooner. ALLi recommends that you hire the best editorial assistance you can afford and that you take great care and a sufficient amount of time to find the right editors and develop a good relationship, work flow and process with them.

It benefits you both if it can be a long-term relationship, a creative marriage. So choose an editor like you would choose a spouse!

And give yourself sufficient time for the editing process, first self-editing, then working with an editor. It's common among beginner authors to want to get this stage over as quickly as possible to get the book out. This is understandable. It is also a mistake.

When we open ourselves to creative collaboration with beta-readers and editors, we not only greatly improve this book, but we learn a lot and hone creative skills that we can take into the next. Take the time that's necessary.

AUTHOR EDITING

For author-publishers, editing is a stage in both the writing process and the publishing process. There are three different stages here and it's important not to confuse them.

1. The deepening and development stage of the writing process (redrafting and rewriting your early drafts).
2. The correction and clarification stage of the writing process (self-editing your final draft).

3. The editing done as part of the publishing process by an editor (professional editing after you've done all you can).

All this editorial work is what separates professional authors from the amateurs.

Self-Editing

Rewriting and self-editing are part of your job as a writer, and not substitutes for professional editing. Doing as much self-editing as you can will reduce your editorial bill substantially, however it must be done to satisfaction before editors will agree to edit your book.

Before you outsource to professional editors, there's much you can do on your own, perhaps with the help of a book coach or mentor, or with the help of other authors, and your readers too, once you've acquired some fans.

The better a manuscript you can deliver to your editor, the more value you will get from the editorial process.

TRY THIS: Your Editing Goals

Once you've got your finished draft to hand, f-r-e-e-write your hopes and aspirations for the editorial process. What would you most like to achieve in your self-editing pass? What elements do you instinctively feel are underwritten, or might need more work? Which are you proudest of and think will need the least work?

Then write about what you'd specifically like to achieve with your beta-readers, and your professional editors? What would a great outcome look like?

DO THIS: Share Your Goals

Share your creative intentions for your book with your beta-readers and all your editors.

Beta Reading

Beta reading happens when you feel like you've done as much self-editing as you possibly can. You then step back from the manuscript and seek feedback from some trusted others (beta-readers).

They offer you their comments, observations and suggestions for improvement before you send the manuscript to your professional editor.

Your beta-readers could be trusted authors or publishing friends, or recruited readers, or perhaps family or friends. The main qualifications are that they are well read in your genre. There is not much point giving your YA lesbian mermaid romance to your Booker-prize loving uncle (it happened!). Also, encourage them to give you an honest assessment. This exercise isn't about self-congratulation or creating an echo chamber, it's about honest feedback.

You want articulate people, who can convey what they thought clearly, but are not prescriptive and who focus on the big picture. In fiction, this might be major issues around plot, character, pacing and voice. In non-fiction, the feedback might be about argument, structure and voice. You don't, at beta-reader stage, need detailed feedback about word choice and sentence structure. That comes later, from the professional editor(s).

How many beta-readers do you need? As many as you can get. The wider the range of opinions you receive, the better.

Beta Reading Step by Step

1. Give your betas a tidy manuscript, with as few errors as possible.
2. Be specific about the kind of advice/opinion you want. Brief them about particular issues that are troubling you. ("Does the argument hold together; did I lose it in the middle?" "Do you find the protagonist sympathetic, or just pathetic?")
3. If you are sourcing beta-readers from the internet you can recruit them via your blog, social media or even create a

mailing list. You can also find beta-readers by putting out a request in the ALLi private members forum on Facebook.

4. Provide each beta-reader with a copy of your manuscript in their preferred format. If there's something particular you'd like a reader to comment on, be sure to ask, but this isn't essential.

5. Set a deadline for your beta-reading to be completed by; two weeks is a good ball-park.

6. Wait until you have all the replies in and sit down to read them all together.

7. If you find yourself feeling closed, step back and observe your own resistance. It's a defense mechanism, your mind and body trying to protect you from a perceived attack. Take a moment to center yourself and clear your mind by following your breath—then remind yourself that you are using this feedback to learn and grow as a writer and publisher. Observe until you can consciously see those defensive thoughts and feelings as they rise and leave you. Use this awareness as a tool to consciously open back up to learning and growth.

8. Remember you are the creative director of this book. You won't be taking on board every single comment. Discard any outlier opinions or those that seem wrong to you. What you're looking for is clues as to how "most people" would rate your book. If the majority, or a significant minority, of your readers hone in on one facet of your book, that's what you want to focus on for revision.

9. Incorporate desirable changes into your next pass.

10. Send a thank-you to all your beta-readers, include them in your acknowledgements page and send them a copy of the book when it is published.

PROFESSIONAL EDITING

Once the beta phase is over, your book is no doubt better than it was. Now it's time to bring in the professionals and make it really shine.

Beta-readers are not a substitute for professional editing. However well-intentioned or perceptive they are, they bring biases. Perhaps they dislike happy endings, or dark humor, or screwball comedy, and those are the very qualities on which you pride yourself. Professional editors are objective, by training, by professional development, and by experience, repeatedly working with a huge variety of books and authors.

Every edit is a learning opportunity, but it can be hard to hear feedback, especially when we're starting out. Never take it personally, and never get personal about it. It's an opinion about your book, not about you.

Developmental editing

This involves evaluating the book with specific focus on coherence, structure and tone. A good developmental editor will pay particular attention to what the book is trying to convey, and how best to relay that within the confines of the author's writing style and genre.

A good developmental editor will evaluate:

Fiction and Narrative Non-fiction

- Character Development.
- Plot.
- Settings.
- Story flow and pacing.
- Scene openings and scene endings.
- Climactic satisfaction and denouement.

Practical Non-fiction

- Tone of voice.
- Overall coherence.
- Inconsistencies in logic and arguments.
- Ambiguous or underdeveloped logic or arguments.
- Climactic explanation or conclusion.
- Further reading and resources.

All:

- Structure and balance.
- Flow and pace.
- Story—overall arc and subplot arcs for fiction. Storytelling use and relevance in non-fiction and poetry.
- Word choices.
- Inconsistencies.
- Unwarranted repetition.
- Optimal word count—for the genre, and per chapter and per scene (fiction), per point (non-fiction), and per stanza (poetry).

This sort of edit works at the level of the whole book. It identifies structural and story issues and mistakes, and offers a variety of solutions, developing and refining your voice and style choices, ensuring you have said what you meant to say fully and completely and that the overall book is in balance.

When you receive your feedback, evaluate it before you get to work. Use your discretion, as creative director, to discern which you'll address and which you'll ignore. If you disagree with a development note, sit with it before dismissing it outright. More often than not, there may be a grain of truth in the editor's response, even if the suggestion is not ideal.

Whether for fiction or non-fiction, developmental editing is a deeply creative process and at the end of it you should feel you've been given a range of suggestions that help improve the story or the information you're trying to convey.

Developmental editing takes time and, depending on the condition of the manuscript, and the experience of the author, can take anywhere from a few weeks to many months to complete.

Copyediting

Once your manuscript content is in good shape, the next editorial level is the copyedit. A copyeditor broadly works at the paragraph level and copyediting is the process of making the text flow well from sentence to sentence to eliminate little errors that can trip a reader up and pull them out of your carefully constructed world or argument.

Precisely what is covered by copyediting varies from editor to editor, but you should expect them to check for:

- Unclear, repeated or confusing passages, including use of jargon.
- Clichés or stale phrasing.
- Over or under description or explication.
- Repeated sentences or words.
- Run-on sentences.
- Passive or weak sentence structure.
- In stories, telling versus showing. In non-fiction, preaching or lecturing instead of examples or exercises.
- Too many, or unnecessary, adverbs or adjectives.
- Stylistic mistakes, e.g. purple prose, or too many sentences or paragraphs structured in similar ways, inappropriate vocabulary, tense shifts.
- Inconsistent spellings (US versus Canada versus UK).
- Inconsistent hyphens, punctuation or capitalization.
- Language errors including punctuation, grammar and spelling.

The copyeditor also ensures your manuscript is internally consistent and accurate. They will watch for mistakes and factual errors and will ask you questions about your intention and meaning. In a novel, a copyeditor might comment on the narrative pacing and point out inconsistencies in character motivation, description, story facts and setting.

A copyeditor will also watch for linguistic issues like odd phrasing, faulty parallelisms, point of view issues and clumsy use of alliteration, metaphor or similes. This latter type of editing is a subset of copyediting called line-editing (or sometimes "stylistic editing").

A soft copyedit focuses on these objective changes, whereas a hard copyedit also includes more subjective issues like the use of filter words in close point of view, or the use of too many adverbs, or over-elaborate dialog tags.

However, a copyedit is not a detailed proofread, as the manuscript at this stage is still not finally set. You might be left with many questions to answer, so allow time for this.

Proofreading

The last phase in the editing process involves checking again for errors in spelling or punctuation, typos, repeated words and other human slips, such as copy/paste mistakes. It's also the very last look at your typescript before it goes into the production process. If headings and subheadings are used, these will be checked for consistency.

Proofreading is about presentation, not subject matter. Mistakes like a character having blue eyes in chapter one and brown eyes in chapter twenty should have been picked up in copyediting, but this is the last chance to pick up errors that might have been missed, or even introduced, at earlier stages.

HIRING AN EDITOR: STEP BY STEP

Choose an editor who has experience in your genre or specializes in your book topic. Don't pick a travel editor for your romance book.

Also, find out what others have said about their work. Get a list of work they've edited before and check it out. Check their LinkedIn and check out the works they've edited along with any reviews.

Evaluate any testimonials; talk directly to the author, do not take comments on an editor's website at face value.

Next, ask them to do a sample edit of your manuscript. Most editors will do a sample edit on a few pages so you can get a sense of their approach. The relationship is also important. Do a face-to-face interview, on an online video call or in person.

When you get your manuscript back from the editor, it will generally be in MS Word with track changes enabled, so you can see the work they've done. Make sure to check over the errors they spotted. It's a great way to learn the mistakes that you most regularly make so you can improve upon them next time.

Address all the notes they've made. Delve back into your draft and implement as many or as few of the suggestions as necessary. Use your discretion, as creative director, to discern which of the notes you'll address and which to ignore or adapt.

If you disagree with a development note, sit with it before dismissing it. Even if you don't agree with their verdict or solution, if they've noticed a problem with something it probably needs more attention from you.

Costs and Comeback

Because each editing job is unique it's impossible to say in advance what an editing job will cost. Editors can give an indicative range of pricing, a per word or per hour rate, but they'll need to see a sample to give an exact quote.

ALLi partner members are required to give such indicative pricing on their websites. You can also find price ranges from the Chartered Institute of Editors and Proofreaders and ALLi Partner Member Reedsy.com.

If you feel a beta-reader or editor has let you down, or been unprofessional, don't rant and argue and tell them they're idiots who know nothing about writing. Say thank you for the feedback or the work, and quietly drop them off your list.

18

BOOK DESIGN
PUBLISHING PROCESS TWO

G etting a first look at your first book cover is one of the most exciting moments in an author's life. It's often the first time your book feels real. The cover is the first thing the reader sees, the first thing that grabs their interest and draws them to pick up your book. So you want a cover that communicates to the reader what the book is about, and makes it stand out visually for the right reasons.

It's important that whoever is designing the book understands what your reader expects and what is usual in your genre, niche and micro-niche.

Unless you are yourself a book designer, ideally you need to hire one. At ALLi, we encourage indie authors to focus time and attention on the work that only we can do (writing and building our author platform), and to hire other publishing professionals for the rest, wherever possible.

If you get the cover right, your sales can improve dramatically. If you get it wrong, it doesn't matter how good your book is. It's likely to be ignored. According to tests conducted by the book promotion company BookBub, a book's cover alone can make a 30% difference to whether it gets clicked on a listing or not. This is not something you want to skimp on.

You can get away with pre-made covers, many indie authors do (see below), but whatever way you choose, make the cover the centerpiece of your book's production and marketing efforts, and give this important element of your book the time, money and attention it deserves.

TRY THIS: Your Dream Cover: *Take a few blank pages and sketch the dream cover for your current project. Make brief notes first or engage in a quick f-r-e-e writing exercise.*

This task isn't about drawing skills, it is about exploration and discovery. If you have a very strong vision already, try some alternatives. You might surprise yourself with the results.

DO THIS: Genre Conventions: *Look at your genre on Amazon. Examine the book covers in the top ten, choose your favorites and f-r-e-e-write your answers to the following questions.*

What features do they share?

Which book covers do you like and why?

Especially, study the covers that you like.

What stood out for you?

Which elements encapsulate the genre and mood of the books?

What impression would these covers make on your right reader?

BOOK COVER ELEMENTS

Book covers work best when the cover communicates, in shorthand, the experience the reader can expect to have. The ideal cover synchs with genre expectations but has a unique and attractive emotional resonance.

The basic book cover formula is a single intriguing image, and an easy-to-read title and author name. Any book cover has five basic elements:

1. Title.

2. Subtitle, tagline, series statement, or testimonial/blurb—a short, catchy sentence to pique the reader's interest. The tagline will also help a designer catch the soul and spirit of your book. You might have testimonials from readers of this book or your previous titles.
3. Author name.
4. Foreground.
5. Background.

When you understand the cover elements, you can address each one with your designer, and you can make more informed decisions when looking at other books in your genre. Do all the covers in your genre have a city in the background, or a lone woman in the foreground, for example?

If you figure out the commonalities in your genre for each cover element, you can make sure your cover matches, or departs from, what's currently working in your genre—from a position of intentional choice.

BRIEFING A BOOK DESIGNER

Identify your target audience: This is the first rule in marketing, business and self-publishing. Before you even consider hiring a designer, do proper research on your ideal reader for this book. A good idea is to create an audience persona and analyze its needs and expectations. Start with demographics. Answer questions like:

- What age are your potential readers? Gender? Ethnicity? Sexual orientation? Occupation?
- What's their income level and what type are they? The well-off can be more "posh" than "dosh", or vice versa, for example.
- What education level do they read at?

Next, dig into psychographics: your readers' interests, activities, and opinions.

- What values are my potential readers looking for in the book?
- What life challenges might they be dealing with?
- What's their cultural background?
- How about their desires, fears, and needs?

Once you've got your answers to these questions, compress the information. Don't share all that with your designer, summarize it into key ideas. Provide references and examples. Go onto Pinterest, Instagram or Google, and see what catches your attention. Make screenshots and notes and attach them for the designer to see.

Give as much detail as possible. Share your tastes and ideas. Pay attention to all the things you'd like to see on the cover and describe them as clearly as possible. Be clear and precise with the designer about the message you want to deliver, the spirit of your book, any plot elements or characters you'd like to see on the cover, and the setting. Explain too, any colors, fonts and images you'd rather avoid.

- **Genre:** you absolutely must specify the book genre. Representing the genre well is one of the primary responsibilities of a great book cover. If you are writing in a less common niche, include a description of its main characteristics to your designer. If your book is a combination of a few genres, explain what's going on.
- **Description:** give the designer your blurb and some commentary to explain the plot, setting, historical timeframe and characters (especially noting their appearance, outfit, gender and behavior patterns).
- **Back cover information:** tagline, blurb, author bio and testimonials.
- **Author brand details:** e.g. logo, color palette, fonts, specific graphic elements.
- **What kind of cover(s) you'll require:** paperback, hardback, dust jacket or ebook.
- **Images Sourcing and Attribution:** when taking images from the web, use licensed images from paid libraries, e.g., iStock

or Getty Images. To save on costs, you can use free libraries such as Wikimedia Commons and give credit as their guidelines require. Unsplash is a great resource that many indie authors use.

- **Use high-resolution images:** images must have a resolution of at least 300 DPI for print.

Start talking to your designer in plenty of time and communicate regularly. Give constructive feedback. Don't be afraid to say if you don't like something. Designers are professionals and understand there will be changes to their initial concepts.

Many quote for a set number of changes, but keep going if you need to, asking for revisions until you are completely satisfied. Some authors also want to test options for their cover design (known as A/B testing) in their newsletters or on social media. Just ensure that you have a clear cost quotation in advance, citing the number of rounds included, so there are no surprises.

Pre-Mades

Many designers make pre-made book covers and sell them for a smaller fee than when a cover is commissioned. These are *not* cover templates, used over and again, which can cause embarrassment if another author in your genre chooses the same one. When you buy a pre-made, you provide your book details and the designer puts them on the book, and then removes it from sale. Pre-mades are a cost-effective alternative for standalone books.

The thing is: quality varies. Some are poor, but some are very good.

Pre-mades are a respectable choice for an author on a budget, but pre-mades aren't designed for your book, so it may be difficult to find one that matches the spirit of what you're trying to achieve. And if your book is the first in a series, check whether the designer offers enough options to complete your series.

Book Cover Checklist

Once you have a possible design, evaluate the following elements.

Is it clear? A simple design is almost always better.

Examine the two elements of foreground and background and how they are layered.

Can we discern the title and author name easily? How does it treat the subtitle, tagline or series statement and any testimonials?

Does the cover work at thumbnail size? This doesn't mean all the elements have to be legible, but it must attract and intrigue. Reduce to thumbnail size and consider. If it's a mush, it needs more work.

If the cover is for a print book, is the trim size right?

Are the typefaces appropriate for your genre? Is the mix of typography right? There should be no more than three and ideally just two typefaces on your cover: one for the title, often decorative; a different typeface for the author name (supporting the title font, without drawing attention from it) and any strapline.

How does the cover reflect what your book is about? Is it genre appropriate? Here are some possible tones for different genres:

- Non-fiction: authoritative or friendly.
- Memoir: nostalgic or dark.
- Thriller: mysterious or violent.
- Science fiction: other-worldly or technological.
- Romance: cozy or steamy.
- Young women's fiction: fashionable fun or inspirational.

Seek feedback, but make sure your commenters are experienced in assessing covers. Friends and family are likely to love what you show them, because they love you. They don't understand what a cover needs to do and they are likely not your target audience.

ALLi members can share covers on the member forum to get expert feedback. If you have several variations, you could use a service like PickFu to carry out split tests on cover designs (and also book titles), to assess which cover might be more appealing to your target readers.

A big advantage with self-publishing is that it is easy to change a book's cover. If, once your book is published, you find that sales aren't taking off in spite of great reviews, reconsider your book's cover design. It is never too late to change it.

First time out, cover design can be daunting, but you get better at knowing what works for your readers as you go along.

You now have a clean text and a compelling cover. Wonderful—but book design goes beyond the jacket. It's about creating your reader's entire experience, from the moment they are first attracted to your book, to the very last word.

Book design encompasses the chapter headings, ornamental breaks, handling of paragraphs and quotations, and much more. We draw together the design of these disparate elements in the third stage in the publishing process, production.

19

BOOK PRODUCTION
PUBLISHING PROCESS THREE

This chapter focuses on the general processes of book production. You can find the latest advances on tools and tech on our self-publishing advice blog.

Before digital publishing, book production always required an interior designer and typesetter who arranged and formatted the text to be visually pleasing and well balanced. In those days, producing a book meant assembling physical covers and pages. And the core format was print.

Today, indie authors use digital tools to produce books in three formats: ebook, print book and audiobook. For most indie authors the core format is ebook because it is easiest, cheapest, and quickest to produce.

Software has reduced the need for interior designers, but if you have complex needs, such as illustrations, graphics or charts, you'll still need to work with a formatter. But do check your tech options, especially if you're writing a text-only book like a novel.

If this is all new to you, don't be daunted. Most of the options are good, and it takes trial and error to see which one suits you best. Self-publishing is very much a learning-by-doing exercise, and you learn an enormous amount in the production of your first book.

How much time you spend on production depends on how creative you want to get. You can express your creativity with font choices, page design, illustrations—and there's plenty of room for that too.

I'm pretty practical about production, most of the time. The book you're reading was written on Scrivener and designed using Vellum, a software program for Mac. These two softwares are sufficient for all my production needs for my standard books. I mostly keep my creativity for the writing rather than the publishing. Every so often, though, I like to do something that's more complex and needs other human hands.

In 2015, I produced *Secret Rose*, a special hardback gift book for a WB Yeats anniversary in replica of his 1890s original. More recently, I worked with a young artist, Miki Lowe, and designer, Jane Dixon-Smith, to make the series of creative business workbooks and planners that accompany this book. And I'm about to start work on a premium gift edition poetry book with AI illustrations. Fun, fun, fun.

CONSIDER THIS: Your Production Process: *What approach do you take to production? Fast and easy? Slow and crafty? A mix?*
What do you dearly love to make?

Which Format First?

If this is your first time publishing (and if you are not using Vellum.pub, which produces electronic and print formats simultaneously), start with an ebook, as that will set you up fastest for sales. Once you've mastered ebook production, and sold some books, you'll have much of the materials and skills you need to produce print and audio, which are more time-consuming and expensive.

The sales process across the three formats is similar, so once you've proven to yourself that you can make and sell ebooks, reinvest some of your profits into making a print and audiobook edition as soon as you can afford to. This also gives you a chance to make sure you have fixed any errors that may have found their way into the ebook, before committing to these more permanent formats.

Although with print-on-demand, also known as POD, it's possible to make changes after publication, as you'll see, it is more complex and with audio, even more so.

The assumption here is that you are like most indie authors, and most of your income will be generated by online sales of ebooks and audiobooks on your own website and on platforms such as Amazon or Apple. However, there are other models for distribution and sales and you may have quite different plans, in which case, of course, you will be guided by your needs.

We all have our preferred reading format. Many older authors, in particular, are romantic about print. They love the feel, the smell, and the weight of a print book in their hands. But a good publisher knows that this personal preference is irrelevant. The job is to get books into as many formats as possible so that readers can have their own preferred format, not ours.

And, from our point of view as publishers, each format also serves as a discovery tool for our other formats.

ALLi, therefore, recommends that you publish in as many formats as you can. Obviously, this will be time and money dependent, but having many formats is the ultimate goal.

EBOOK PRODUCTION FOR AUTHORS

When producing an ebook there are two types of layouts to choose from, fixed or reflowable. A fixed-layout ebook acts more like a print book, but a reflowable layout allows the reader a lot more control over how they view the file.

The key point to keep in mind is that reflowable text in an ebook behaves differently to a print book. There are natural expectations that come with reading print books, like rarely hyphenated words and a linear reading experience that are not replicated in most ebooks.

Some of the common features that are alterable on an e-reader or app are:

- font style (changing the type to a serif or sans serif font)
- text size (this can create a lot of hyphenated words)
- reading orientation (portrait or landscape)
- leading (the space between the lines of text)
- margins
- justification (whether or not to space words to fit columns)
- page-turn or scrolling
- theme (white, sepia, night-mode, etc.)
- auto-hyphenation
- single-page or two-page view

The availability of the above options depends on the device or app. Your esthetic intentions may or may not be maintained once the reader has their hands on your reflowable ebook.

Many writers prepare their work in Microsoft Word or Mac Pages and then have it converted into one of the publishing formats welcomed by the major ebook publishers.

This process is called **formatting**.

It may be very simple if your book is straightforward prose like a novel, or more complex if you have illustrations, charts or other specialized layout needs. You may also wish to add design flourishes such as drop capitals at the start of a chapter.

Authors have a wealth of options for creating ebooks. Smashwords, one of the earliest distributors of ebooks, once made a list of the various book-creation tools authors use, and it included a wide variety: Adobe InDesign®, Apache OpenOffice, Atlantis, Calibre, ePubMaker at Project Gutenberg, HTML, Jutoh, LibreOffice, Nisus Writer Pro, Scrivener, Sigil, Writer2ePub, and more. The two big favorites in the indie author sector are Vellum (for Mac Users) and Atticus (which is as yet new and a little buggy).

Each produces good results, so the choice is down to personal use and preference.

EBOOK FORMATS

We speak of ebooks as a single format but there are actually several. Here, in alphabetical order, are those most commonly used at present.

The two most important are those used for distribution: EPUB and KPF (Kindle Package Format) for the Kindle. While retailers like Apple, Barnes & Noble, Kobo and others use EPUB for distribution, the Kindle file is Amazon's proprietary ebook format. It's exclusively sold through Amazon and can only be viewed on Kindle devices or the Kindle app.

EPUB

EPUB (short for "electronic publication") is now the most widely used ebook format, and the industry standard, supported across all platforms. All e-readers—Apple iOS, Barnes & Noble's Nook, Adobe Digital Editions, Kindle, Aldiko on Android and nearly 300 others—support EPUB files (suffix .EPUB).

The EPUB format is "open standard." That means it is free and publicly available. There are specific rules for its usage maintained by a global trade and standards organization, W3.org. The EPUB format has been through three iterations and all agree that EPUB 3 is a major advance for illustrated and complex books.

EPUB was built from the intersection of internet technologies and print books. Books made special demands that didn't apply to web pages. We expect to be able to read ebooks while offline, to be able to save them, keep them and share them, and to be able to buy and sell them. Books, even in electronic format, offer a kind of permanence we don't typically expect of websites.

The Book Industry Study Group endorses EPUB 3 as the format of choice for ebooks and is encouraging the global publishing industry to adopt and promote this single standard. ALLi supports this call and encourages it as the preferred option for indie authors.

Recognizing EPUB format: *EPUB documents take the extension .epub.*

Kindle

Kindle File Format is a proprietary ebook file format created by Amazon that can be downloaded and read on devices like smartphones, tablets, computers, or e-readers that have Amazon's Kindle app.

Recognizing Kindle format: *Kindle documents generally take the extension .azw*

Microsoft Word

Commonly called "Word", this is the most used word processing software in the world. Word does not generally display well on ebook platforms—the formatting often goes awry, though it is improving all the time, and is now more widely accepted. However, Word is commonly used to create documents for converting to ebook formats. It is also, because of its "Track Changes" function, the format that your editor is likely to require, and use, for editing purposes.

Recognizing Word format: *Word documents take the extension .doc or .docx.*

Pages

Pages is Apple's equivalent of Word.

Recognizing Pages format: *Pages documents take the extension .pages*

PDF

PDF from Adobe (portable document format) preserves the original layout of any text, drawings, multimedia, video, 3D maps, full-color graphics and photos, so that it is difficult to subsequently edit the file, without special software. PDF files are viewable on reading devices, but do not allow some of the versatile functions such as changing the font size. PDFs come into their own during the production of print books.

Recognizing PDF format: *PDF documents take the extension .pdf*

Mobi

The Mobipocket ebook format is now being retired. It was another cross-platform, open standard format, and was best known as the favored format for Amazon's KDP (Kindle Direct Publishing).

Recognizing Mobi format: *Mobi documents took the .mobi extension*

PRINT BOOK PRODUCTION FOR AUTHORS

The majority of readers still read in print, sometimes in addition to digital alternatives like ebook and audio, sometimes exclusively.

Although print books typically yield a much smaller margin than ebooks, publishing in print enables you to satisfy readers who prefer that format, and thereby grow your fanbase and income. Print-on-demand makes that relatively easy and affordable for you, though your reader will pay more for a POD book published by a micro-publisher (you!) than they would for a corporately-published book in the bookstore.

The layout of the inner pages is an important aspect of book design. Your cover designer might be able to do this for you, or you can hire another service, or you can use one of the software options to generate the files you need, like Vellum (Mac only, limited design options) or Scrivener (more complex, but more flexible). Template page designs, which are available on most self-publishing platforms, can also be used if you do not mind the effort involved and the cookie-cutter designs.

Your layout is exported as a PDF, which is then uploaded by the printer or self-publishing service.

Once you have your PDF, there are two ways that books can be printed: print-on-demand or a print run.

Print-on-Demand (POD)

Print-on-demand was introduced in the 1990s and ignited the era of SelfPub1. It allows authors, and other publishers, to produce a single copy, or a short print run (say, ten, twenty or fifty), instead of hundreds. I've always thought the process should be called "print-on-request", but it's too late now.

There are two large print-on-demand distributors for authors: KDP Print (formerly CreateSpace) and IngramSpark (formerly Lightning Source). When a reader orders a copy of your book from the sales outlets serviced by either of them (Amazon's worldwide stores for KDP Print, and brick-and-mortar bookstores and libraries for IngramSpark), the order is sent to a printer which prints and assembles your book there and then, and ships it directly to the reader. This "just-in-time" production system saves us from having to:

- Keep expensive inventory.
- Store stock against future orders.
- Fulfil orders as they come in.

The platform funds the production, bills the customer, takes their cut for production and distribution, and then pays you the rest as publisher's compensation (often wrongly called "royalties").

Some authors believe IngramSpark offers better quality; others prefer KDP Print. Opinions can be quite heated. Having surveyed thousands of titles over the years, our conclusions is that the interior print quality of black-and-white books is similar between the two services.

It's also worth noting that the quality of print-on-demand books is improving all the time.

Interior Options

One key decision you have to make, regardless of which service you use, is *trim size*. This describes the dimensions of the book, such as 6 x 9 inches or 5.5 x 8.5 inches. Both KDP Print and IngramSpark offer all the industry-standard trim sizes, and some variations. We recommend you stick to standard trim sizes, unless you have a very good reason to do otherwise. The standard sizes are easier to work with across the platforms and give you more choices with distribution channels.

For non-fiction and business books, 6 x 9 inches is the most common size, and for fiction and poetry the usual size is 5.5 x 8.5 inches. A bigger trim size gives you bigger pages, obviously, so your book will be slimmer—another factor to bear in mind. A slimmer book costs you less to print, but if your book is less than 40,000 words, 6 x 9 inches can feel unsubstantial. If you're working with a designer, they can advise you on the optimum size.

Both KDP and IngramSpark offer black-and-white and color interiors. Color print-on-demand is usually two or three times more expensive than black-and-white, even if you haven't used color on very many pages, so think carefully about whether color is essential in your book. Of course, it is for many—children's picture books, for example, or premium gift books.

When you choose black-and-white printing, you also get a choice of paper: bright white, cream/off-white or groundwood. Cream paper is generally slightly thicker, and paper thickness can change the spine calculations for your cover, so decide your choice of paper before creating your cover. White paper can look odd for fiction and narrative non-fiction.

Consignment Print Run

Before print-on-demand became cheaply available, a print run was the only option for publishers, and many still use it because it's cheaper per book. The minimum order for a print run used to be 250, ideally 500 to make it worthwhile. Now printers will provide as few as 50 books, at reasonable cost.

The bigger the print run, the lower the unit price, but only once all the books are sold. A thousand books for $2,000 gives you a book that costs $2 when you've sold every copy. If you sell only a few, you've paid hundreds of dollars per copy sold. Print runs are, therefore, riskier than POD and before ordering a print run you should have a solid marketing and distribution plan in place e.g. an agreed special sales deal, or a regular speaking gig where books are sold at the back of the room.

Every week at ALLi, we hear of self-publishers who've spent

thousands of dollars to print books that languish in their garage, to eventually be sent to the landfill.

AUDIOBOOK PRODUCTION FOR AUTHORS

Audiobook production is the process by which your written book is narrated and recorded. The market for audiobooks is growing steadily. The first heavy consumers of audio were only older females and those with impaired vision or difficulty reading, but now there is a growing young audience who listen on their phones and other devices. And, of course, listening in the car is huge. In the UK, audiobook sales increased by 38% in 2018 and some time-strapped people now "read" only in audio.

For some indie authors, audio is now the second format of choice. They produce ebooks first, then audio, then print. Audio is less well established than print or ebooks, so there is less competition in this sector. Genres that are particularly popular in audio, like business books, may even benefit from being produced in audio first.

The process of making an audiobook is more complex, expensive and demanding than producing a print book or ebook, so most authors wait until they have a clear marketing plan and already know how to sell books.

Amazon, again, is a huge player in the production of audiobooks. According to IBISWorld, Amazon's Audible controls over one-third of the audiobook market. Compare this to 5.1% for Penguin Random House, for example, or 3.9% for HarperCollins.

ACX.com is Amazon Audible's marketplace and self-publishing platform, "where authors, literary agents, publishers, and other rights holders can connect with narrators, engineers, recording studios, and other producers capable of producing a finished audiobook," and is a tool wide open to authors.

You can choose from two royalty models: payment upfront, or what they call "royalty share", though strictly speaking these are commissions, not royalties, where narrators get a percentage of each sale.

ACX offers exclusive and non-exclusive options, with different royalty rates, and, as ever, ALLi recommends that if you want to maximize your income over the long term, you should definitely work with Amazon, yes, but on a non-exclusive basis.

Audible promises authors 40% commission on each book sold, but this is 40% of what's left after the retailer has taken their share. Tim McConnehey, founder and owner of collaborative publisher, Izzard Ink Publishing, laid out the economics on the ALLi blog,[1] based on having an exclusive agreement with ACX on an audiobook that retails for $24.95.

Right from the top, the retailer gets $6.08, or about 24.37 percent. After that, $13.48 goes to ACX, or about 54.3 percent. Only $5.39, or 21.6 percent, goes back to the author. And in some cases, it can be even less than that... ACX also offers different compensation based on how each book was sold.

In our example, *à la carte* sales on Amazon or iTunes would pay $9.98 to the author, Audible sales to non-members would pay $6.98, and sales to Audible members would pay just $5.19. And there's no way to predict what proportion of these will make up your overall sales.

Without an exclusive agreement with ACX that prevents you from selling your book elsewhere, you'll make even less— $3.37 in our example.

Moreover, authors don't decide the price of their book through ACX, which means it's impossible to accurately calculate what kind of return you can expect. By leveraging their nearly exclusive control over the industry and distribution channels, Audible is effectively fixing prices.

— TIM MCCONNEHEY, FOR THE SELF-PUBLISHING
ADVICE BLOG

In recent years, other players have entered the audiobook market and are offering publishers and authors more control over product and revenue. Findaway Voices, recently taken over by Spotify, not only offers discounts and allows authors to set prices, but it pays authors a higher percentage from many retailers.

While ACX only sells through Amazon, Audible, and Apple, Findaway covers those retailers and dozens more, including Google, Scribd, Audiobooks.com, Walmart and Nook.

Check out ALLi's Self-Publishing Services Directory for other good audiobook production and distribution options. We also recommend *Audio for Authors* by ALLi Enterprise Advisor, Joanna Penn, who has been, for a long time, an audiobooks pioneer.

Narration

If you decide to make an audiobook, your first big decision is whether you are going to narrate the book yourself. It's more common for authors to perform their own audiobook in non-fiction than in fiction. The various characters, dialog, voice ages, accents and modes of description require a professionally trained voice actor. Nothing is worse than the sound of an author who doesn't understand voice projection, reading page after page of their own work, not realizing that they are deadening their own prose. Readers do like to hear the writer's voice—but only if the writer does it well.

Doing it well also means a soundproofed place with good recording equipment and software. No, your phone earbuds are not good enough. The equipment and software are not expensive. By far the biggest investment is **time**—time to narrate your book and time to edit your files in post-production.

Audible estimates the average narrator reads 9,400 words per hour, so a 70,000-word novel would take approximately 7.5 finished hours. Budget about 2.5 times the length of the finished audiobook for total recording time needed, to allow for breaks and retakes.

After you've finished, you will need to listen to the entire book and fix or re-record parts. This process will likely take three to four times the length of the fully recorded audiobook. Then you need to prepare the files for upload.

So, for an audiobook of 70,000 words, you can budget an additional twenty to thirty hours of post-production work, but rates are not standard as different channels have different models of sales and subscription.

Many authors are now using AI narration for their audiobooks. This reduces costs considerably but many listeners report that the voices are still too machine-like, though they are improving all the time. It's now even possible to have your AI voice double narrate your book. At time of writing, Audible and other major audiobook distributors do not accept AI narrated books.

Hiring a Narrator

Most authors choose to hire a professional narrator. To do so, create an account at one of the audiobook publishers or production companies, such as ACX or Findaway, and find a narrator (sometimes called a producer) by listening to their auditions. When you find someone you like, you agree how much they will get paid for each finished hour of the audiobook. They record and upload the audiobook, which you then approve.

OTHER FORMATS

In addition to the three core formats of ebook, print book and audiobook, your books can also generate translations, films, TV programs, merchandise and many other formats. These are traditionally called subsidiary rights and are given a separate section in a publishing contract. These will be covered in Chapter 23 "Selective Rights Licensing", the seventh step in the publishing process. Here it's worth saying that as technology advances, we authors will increasingly be able to handle the production and distribution of more such formats ourselves. With advancements in software and AI, creating audiobooks and multimedia content, for example, grows ever more affordable and accessible.

1. SelfPublishingAdvice.org/economics-of-audiobooks

20

BOOK DISTRIBUTION
PUBLISHING PROCESS FOUR

Distribution is the process of making your book available for purchase. It is your supply system—how you make your books available to book wholesalers and retailers in various formats.

We are fortunate as authors today to have excellent distribution options across the three book formats of ebook, print and audio, but getting your distribution channels set up across these three formats can be confusing to begin with.

Distribution takes you on a big learning curve and every single indie author finds it challenging at first. When you're tearing your hair out with the tech and tools, hold in mind that you are not just getting tasks done. You are learning by doing. The first time is the hardest. Second time out, it all feels far easier. Third time out, it has become just a series of tasks. You may tweak a bit, but you know your way around the platforms, and your process is established. You shouldn't need to think about it again, unless you decide to make changes e.g. move from KDP exclusive to publishing wide.

At that point, major congratulations are due for mastering the nuts and bolts of book production and distribution. Going forward, you'll hardly think about this and can expend your energies on the core challenges: writing and marketing.

PUBLISHERS AND PLATFORMS

If it's your first time to produce and distribute a book, you may find yourself confused by the different parties involved in book distribution: publishers, platforms, wholesalers, distributors, retailers. Let's clarify under two headings: Business to Business (B2B) and Business to Consumers (B2C).

Business to Business: B2B

- a **publisher** is a business that invests in a book with the intention of making a profit. You, the author, are the publisher unless you choose to license your publishing rights to a third party.
- a **platform** is a digital service provided by a company for production, distribution or sales, or all three.
- wholesalers, distributors, bookstores (including online stores), ebook aggregators, and libraries are **distribution channels**.
- the companies or platforms that publishers, including self-publishing authors, use for production, printing, distribution, marketing and so on, are all **publishing services**, hired by the publisher either through an upfront fee or a percentage commission on sales. Some publishing services like IngramSpark and Kobo Writing Life are also distributor channels, through their global business partnerships.

Business to Consumers: B2C

- All of the above are B2B (business to business) companies. Businesses that sell books to readers (B2C: business to consumer), are **retailers,** and include physical bookstores, online bookshops and author websites.

- Some platforms like Amazon KDP, Apple Books, and Google Play are self-publishing services *and* retailers, with their own **online retail stores** where readers can purchase books.

DISTRIBUTION FOR AUTHORS: EBOOK, PRINT, AUDIO

As previously explained, ALLi's guiding policy for the most effective distribution plan is to be in as many formats as you can—ebook, print and audio—and in as many stores as you can, while making your own website the core of your bookselling operation.

Below are the categories of sales channels and stores that you need to know about, however you decide to publish or distribute.

- **Major global distributor-retailers who both distribute and sell** e.g. Amazon, Apple, Google Play, Kobo, Barnes & Noble.
- **ebook aggregators:** e.g. Draft2Digital, PublishDrive, Smashwords, StreetLib. Aggregators allow you to upload your book onto one single dashboard which then automatically distributes it to multiple distributors and retailers. Through aggregators, we get access to channels that authors cannot approach directly, e.g. Scribd, a digital subscription service deducts a further percentage. Each aggregator has pros and cons and some indies—including me—use a variety of them in combination e.g. Draft2Digital is very strong in the US and provides a universal book link that helps readers find and buy your books wherever they're sold online—a handy, timesaving tool. PublishDrive, based in the US and Hungary, offers AI tools to help you make the most of Amazon ads and a royalty management facility if you have books with multiple contributors. PublishDrive has a good reach in Hungary, Romania, and China. StreetLib, based in Italy and founded in 2006, has the widest global access and has been a pioneer

in many respects, e.g. it was the first aggregator to introduce audio distribution and production, the first to connect with Nordic players like Storytel, the only aggregator offering print-on-demand access to Italian bookstores, the only aggregator offering podcasting revenue opportunities, and the first aggregator to partner with online reading sites.

- **Reader subscription services:** e.g. Amazon's KU and Audible, Kobo Plus, Scribd, Bookmate, Storytel, 24symbols. As with every other form of entertainment, books are now being made available by subscription services that charge readers a monthly fee for unlimited titles. Subscription services give readers a huge library for the price of one book.
- **Library providers:** e.g. OverDrive, Bibliotheca, Hoopla, Mackin, ODILO. Just in the US, there are roughly 135 million potential readers yearly who you can reach if you distribute to libraries. In the US and Europe, there are roughly 160 million people you can reach by using OverDrive services.
- **Regional services:** e.g. Tolino (Germany), DiBook (Slovakia/Hungary), BookBaby (US). If you are a native English-speaker you might not be aware of how many people outside of your home country read in English. In Europe, those who are not native speakers but read in English tend to be avid readers, often English majors or teachers.
- **Print distributors:** Most notably Amazon KDP Print and IngramSpark.

Each of these distributors (except ACX) is an ALLi Partner Member. All (except PublishDrive) charge you by commission payment at the point of sale. They don't get paid until you get paid.

DISTRIBUTION RECOMMENDATIONS

ALLi's distribution recommendations are based on the approach that is most likely to succeed in creating a sustainable publishing business, over time. It is not a quick-and-easy approach. Many authors choose other options, most notably those who publish exclusively to Amazon.

Lots of authors, particularly those who publish wide, get admin help with their distribution tasks, to leave them free for writing and marketing. If you do this, ensure that all dashboards are in your author name and that the payments go directly to your bank account, not that of an intermediary service or agent.

ALLi Recommendations: Ebook Distribution

To avail of the best financial return on the widest possible distribution of you ebooks, time permitting, ALLi recommends that you upload directly to the ebook Big Five (Amazon's KDP, Apple Books, Barnes & Noble, Google Play, and Kobo Writing Life), and use one or more ebook aggregators to cover the rest of the world.

The benefits of uploading directly to the big retailers include faster payments, up-to-date sales figures (important for measuring the effectiveness of marketing), more direct control of metadata (particularly categories and keywords which are important for discoverability), and the ability to manipulate pricing quickly and easily (important for promotion).

However, each of the ebook retailers has different dashboards and requirements, so going direct can be time-consuming, especially if you have a lot of titles.

Aggregators like PublishDrive, Draft2Digital and StreetLib will take a cut for handling the different outlets for you, but they will save you time. Time is a key consideration for indie authors. As writers, especially if we have day jobs and other commitments, our writing time must be protected.

It's also worth noting that not everyone *can* go direct, even if they want. The US and UK are best served, but options vary widely around the world. Apple famously requires self-publishers to use a Mac to upload, which is inconvenient for authors who use other devices.

Even if you use all of the Big Five distributors, it makes sense to also use an aggregator distributor. They will reach parts of the world you can't reach any other way. Although at the moment, these other markets are smaller and account for a negligible proportion of sales, they help to increase your visibility and the set-up takes very little time. More promisingly, they are also growing much more rapidly than the more mature North American and UK markets. There is an advantage to being there first.

If you use those five for your ebooks, together with Amazon KDP Print and IngramSpark for print as described above, and ACX and Findaway Voices, Author's Republic, Soundwise or similar for audio, you have covered the channels that account for 97% of ebook, print book and audiobook sales around the world and maximized your income potential from your books.

Stress on *potential*! Distribution alone rarely sells books, except in very nascent markets. Books must be marketed and promoted to sell. Marketing and promotion (see the next two chapters) are as fundamental to the publishing process as editorial and design.

ALLi Recommendations: Print Distribution

Amazon KDP and IngramSpark (IS) are the two most influential players in the self-publishing arena and warrant a closer look in this chapter.

Amazon controls book sales to more readers than any other single entity in the world, including the largest publishing houses. The company sells about half of trade-published books and an estimated 70% of self-published books (the latter is harder to quantify as not all self-published books show up on current data measures—e.g. those sold directly by authors to readers, and those sold through unregistered global retailers).

According to Codex Group, Amazon now accounts for over 35% of all unit sales of books, 77% of online sales of new print or ebooks, and 80% of ebooks overall in the US. Amazon has also set up its own, traditionally curated imprints. For print and ebook these are: 47North, Amazon Crossing, Amazon Crossing Kids, Montlake Romance, Skyscape, Lake Union Publishing, Little A, Amazon Original Stories, Topple Books, Amazon Publishing, Jet City Comics, Grand Harbor Press, Waterfall Press, Thomas & Mercer, Amazon

Encore and Two Lions. For audiobooks: Audio Studio and Brilliance Audio.

What makes Amazon so powerful in publishing (as in other retail sectors) is not just how many books it sells, but how much it knows about its readers and other consumers. This gives Amazon an unassailable position for online book sales in ebook, print and audio. Amazon also offers the largest ebook subscription service in the world, KU, which is still expanding as part of their Prime program. It rewards authors and publishers who make their content exclusive to the Amazon platform.

From an author's perspective, access to KU is had by being part of KDP Select, the Amazon exclusivity program for indie publishers. If you sign up to this, you cannot publish your ebook version on any other website for ninety days (though you can then decide whether to renew or cancel the arrangement). In return, you are included in KU, Amazon's subscription model, the Kindle Owners' Lending Library, and, from the KDP Select Global fund, paid based on how frequently your book is borrowed.

KDP Select authors have access to other promotional tools for the length of their enrollment. For example, you can offer books free to readers for up to five days during that period or receive higher commissions in certain countries (e.g. India and Brazil). You get other promotional tools like a Kindle Countdown Deal (currently available only on the Amazon.com and UK stores).

Before Amazon was in the self-publishing sector, there was Lightning Source (now Ingram Content Group), a huge operation that has print facilities, distribution centers and sales offices in the US, Australia, the UK, France, Germany, and, soon, the Middle East. It was Ingram that underwrote **SelfPub1** in the 1990s, setting the industry standard for print-on-demand.

Ingram began as a wholesale company in the US, warehousing books for publishers so that stores and libraries could purchase through one vendor. It now provides distribution to 220 countries and territories.

In 2013, it reinforced its importance to new publishing with the launch of IngramSpark, making it a preferred print distributor for indie authors and other small publishers. Although Amazon KDP also does print-on-demand through KDP Print, IngramSpark is the dominant supplier to most bookstore and library accounts around the world, many of whom are uncomfortable stocking Amazon-supplied books.

IngramSpark carries far more print titles than Amazon. And, unlike Amazon, it can ship books in an anonymous box to anybody in the world, making it appear to come from any client, rather than from the company. So many publishers, booksellers, authors, and other direct-sellers use IngramSpark for their print book fulfilment.

There are other large print-on-demand companies around the world, but they have no wholesaling or retailing network.

IngramSpark also serves as an aggregator for ebook distribution, but its reach for ebooks is not as wide and its terms not as favorable as other aggregators like PublishDrive, StreetLib or Draft2Digital. It is IngramSpark's print operation that makes it so valuable to authors and ALLi recommends IS only for print.

KDP Print and IngramSpark are the giants of print-on-demand self-publishing, and are well-positioned to keep growing, as the industry morphs and changes.

IngramSpark or Amazon for Print? Both?

If you want to reach most readers and maximize income, ALLi recommends publishing your print books simultaneously on both KDP Print and IngramSpark. Both platforms fulfill print orders in pretty much the same way, so why both, you may wonder? Isn't that a needless duplication of effort?

Short answer: no. Each offers different benefits—and you want the best of both worlds. Publishing through KDP automatically includes you on Amazon's storefront in all the territories it serves with print (an extensive list, if not quite as long as the list of territories served by ebooks). And at terms that are more favorable than for other booksellers. KDP Print does not charge a distribution fee and only charges you commission when someone buys your book.

So why bother with IngramSpark? IngramSpark does not have a

storefront itself, but its distribution catalog reaches beyond the internet to brick-and-mortar bookstores and libraries. These outlets are unlikely to order stock from Amazon, because most bookstores see them as competition and the discounts are not commercially viable.

A brief word about distribution to bookshops. This is often tricky for indie authors. Although IngramSpark will distribute to bookstores, it's difficult for authors to offer competitive terms and price, because of the higher unit cost of print-on-demand. Although bookstores might place one-off orders for customers, indies usually find that publicizing to bookshops is highly time-consuming for very little financial reward, compared to selling direct to readers online.

Still, IngramSpark distributes to Amazon. So why not publish exclusively through IngramSpark? Because Amazon favors KDP Print books by displaying an "out-of-stock" notice against IngramSpark-only books, or by warning the purchaser that the book might not be delivered for weeks or months. This is usually wildly pessimistic. In reality, the delay is likely to be only as long as it takes Amazon to send the order across to IngramSpark for fulfillment. (Amazon is also IngramSpark's biggest customer, using its print services to fulfill much of its own book orders.)

Amazon says its priority is to provide the best customer experience —and here the customer in question is the reader, not the author. They'd rather give a too-long lead-time that leaves the customer pleasantly surprised when the book turns up "early" than risk upsetting them with an unsatisfactory delay.

In short: If you upload your print book to KDP Print, Amazon will always list it as in stock. If you also upload to IngramSpark, it is available through their catalog to thousands of bookstores around the world for one-off orders, and also to libraries. Both is best.

This is not as complex as it might sound. You set up an account on each store and upload pretty much the same files and metadata to each. There are slightly different requirements for cover artwork and interiors, but it's just a question of tweaking the original rather than reinventing it.

ALLi Recommendations: Audiobook Distribution

The global audiobook market is expected to grow from $3.3 billion to $15 billion by 2027. For some years, Amazon's ACX (Audiobook Creative Exchange) the self-serve production and distribution service for Audible, was the only audiobook publishing option available to indie authors, and it is still one of the most widely used distribution services, but that is changing rapidly.

It's relatively easy to compare the different levels of royalties offered by the leading audiobook distributors for *à la carte* sales—i.e., when a listener buys the audiobook at full price through one of the major retailers.

But such sales only represent a small part of audiobook income on most of the major distributors, where subscription services and library sales already pre-dominate and are growing faster. There are several distributors operating several different models e.g. cost per checkout, credit-based subscriptions, revenue pools. You need to have some understanding of these models to understand your audiobook payment statements.

Subscription services

- **Credit-based subscription:** listeners pay a monthly subscription fee to get "credits," which they can redeem against audiobooks. Authors earn the same royalty as an *à la carte* sale when their audiobook is purchased using credits.
- **Unlimited subscription:** listeners pay a monthly subscription fee to listen to as many audiobooks as they want. Authors earn the same royalty as an à *la carte* sale when a subscriber listens to 15% or more of their audiobook.
- **Revenue pool share subscription:** listeners pay a monthly subscription fee, contributing to a total "revenue pool". Authors receive a percentage of that revenue pool based on their pro-rata share of total listening time.

Audiobook Creation Exchange (ACX)

ACX offers authors exclusive and non-exclusive options for distribution to three outlets: Audible, Amazon and Apple Books (previously iTunes).

1. Exclusive to ACX. This option prevents you from distributing or selling your audiobook through any other channel—whether that's another retailer, a subscription service, directly on your website, or even in physical CD form. In exchange for your exclusivity, ACX pays a percentage payment of 40% of the list price.

2. Non-exclusive. This allows you to distribute your audiobook elsewhere in any form you want but your percentage payment will only be 25% of the list price on ACX.

If you choose to produce your audiobook under ACX's royalty-share with a narrator option, you will automatically be enrolled in the exclusivity option—and will not be able to get out of it unless you "buy out" your narrator.

Under advocacy pressure, ACX changed its terms to allow authors who own the full rights to their audiobook to get out of exclusivity after 90 days. This doesn't apply to books produced under their royalty-share agreement.

There are still many outstanding issues with ACX, including a lack of control around pricing. ACX provides the following guideline of the pricing you can expect on Audible, depending on the length of your audiobook, though some books deviate from this.

- < 1 hour: under $7
- 1 - 3 hours: $7 - $10
- 3 - 5 hours: $10 - $20
- 5 - 10 hours: $15 - $25
- 10 - 20 hours: $20 - $30
- 20+ hours: $25 - 35

Whether you're exclusive or not, there's one crucial element you can't control on ACX: the price of your audiobook. Some retailers change the price you set for your books at their discretion, but pay the commission you would've received before the discount. Only Audible frequently discounts its books, without any reference to the publisher or any compensation. The typical discount is 30% but it can be more.

ALLi strongly recommends audiobook authors not to take up ACX's exclusivity program.

Firstly, the compensation mechanism is extremely opaque. Payment spreadsheets have few data points and it's impossible to know if you've been paid correctly. ACX also charges authors for returns, even when they are not true returns (where the reader has consumed 10%, or less, of the book), and even where the company has itself encouraged the listener to "exchange" the book, after reading.

To add insult to injury, they were doing this secretly, until outed by an enterprising indie author Susan May, who started a campaign (Audiblegate.com) to alert other authors, narrators and rights holders to what was going on.

ACX reports at that time didn't even show a returns column, even though ACX was charging all returns received, for a full 365 days after purchase, to the author—while encouraging readers to return an audiobook when finished and download another.

On straight sales, authors earn 28% of list price for exclusive titles, and just over 17% for non-exclusive titles.

Things get more complicated when listeners use one of their monthly credits to buy a title. Then Audible calculates what it calls an "Allocation Factor" to discount the list price before paying the publisher the agreed 40% (exclusive) or 25% (non-exclusive).

The calculation is supposed to be determined based on the volume of membership sales and the list prices of books purchased with credits and various other complex additions and subtractions, including, supposedly, returns in this figure (as Audible charges for a book returned within 7 days of purchase, this would be double dipping).

In the course of the Audiblegate campaign, ACX admitted that it is not performing this Allocation Factor calculation, instead uniformly setting it at 52%. This is better for authors, they say, but they do not provide enough data for authors to check whether that is true.

The end result is that authors receive just 20.8% or 13% of list price for any book sold on the Audible platform through membership credits.

ACX has since made some changes to its dashboard and vowed to document "returns" and payment deductions. However, getting a clear picture of orders, returns, and final royalties is still a long way off.

ALLi recently downgraded ACX/Audible's rating to "caution" due to mishandling of author payments on the platform, and continued lack of transparency, accountability or recompense. Many authors are currently moving away from ACX, despite it having the largest cohort of listeners, and exploring other distributors as opportunities expand.

Libraries, Kobo and Wide Audiobook Distribution

Many other audiobook distributors offer authors a strong alternative to ACX and a greater reach into the many audiobook retailers, subscription services, and libraries around the world.

With wide audiobook distributors, you can choose your own retail price—which all non-Amazon retailers will respect. This opens price promotion opportunities, free first-in-series or prequels, and other discounting possibilities.

It also opens up Chirp, a sister site to the popular ebook discounting platform, BookBub, which offers similar discount marketing emails for audiobooks, handpicking selected audiobook deals and promoting them to a growing list of listeners.

While often overlooked, libraries can play a big role in audiobook discoverability and revenue. In the USA and UK, libraries purchase a license to lend an audiobook to a maximum of one patron at a time. Publishers are paid every time a library patron borrows the audiobook, with the pay per checkout depending on which distributor the library uses (Hoopla and Overdrive are two of the most popular), the length of the audiobook, and its library price—which is usually more than the RRP (the recommended retail price).

Uploading your book to Kobo Writing Life distributes audiobooks to a network of publishing and library partners, including Bol (NL), Booktopia (AUS), Indigo (CA), Overdrive (library distributors), and Walmart (US), as well as putting it directly on sale at Rakuten Kobo.

To maximize your income from audiobooks over the long term and across the world, ALLi recommends using Kobo to distribute directly to their retail partners, and ACX for Amazon, Apple and Audible, then using the aggregators for the rest.

Aggregators: Findaway Voices, ListenUp, Author's Republic

Findaway Voices (now part of Spotify) is one of the leading audiobook aggregators, with a distribution network that reaches over 170 countries around the world. The platform also offers a royalty-share option with narrators, Voices Share, and other audiobook creation tools through Voices Marketplace. And they offer seamless integration with the ebook aggregator Draft2Digital, so you can carry over your metadata from there, if you use that service.

Findaway Voices pays authors 80% of the income received from their distribution partners. That income can vary greatly depending on the partner's retail model (straight sale vs. subscription service vs. library). Most non-Amazon major retailers pay between 40% and 50% of list price. After Findaway's distribution cut, this represents a net payment to the creator of 32%-40% of list price.

For sales through Amazon or Audible, Findaway receives 25% of the list price, giving the author 80% of that 25% (equivalent of half of an exclusive sale through ACX).

Listen Up and Author's Republic have both been around for longer than Findaway Voices, running a similar business model but with slight differences in reach, services and payment models. ListenUp charges a $149-$199 upfront fee per title for distribution—which they waive for titles produced through ListenUp. Author's Republic don't offer audiobook creation services, focussing exclusively on distribution. They accept submissions from anywhere in the world, so they are a good option for authors in countries not supported by other major distributors. ACX is not yet functioning in Australia, for example.

Author's Republic take a larger commission on sales—30% so you receive 28%-35% of list price on most non-Amazon store sales, and 17.5% on Amazon/Audible sales—but as an ALLi Partner Member they are open to matching competitor rates for some ALLi members (depending on your books, catalog etc.). If you're interested in using this provider, it's worth asking.

PublishDrive

At time of writing, PublishDrive is the only aggregator offering ebook and print-on-demand distribution as well as audio, which has the advantage of allowing authors to control all of their different distribution needs from one place. Another advantage is their access to CNEP Reading, the leading library content provider in China.

Their business model is subscription based. PublishDrive charges publishers a monthly fee and then pays over 100% of income received. The fee depends on the number of titles distributed, with each format (ebook, print, audio) counting as a separate title.

PublishDrive works with Findaway to reach many outlets, and publisher income varies, depending on whether they are distributing directly to an outlet or partnering with Findaway. Your income on the partnered outlets will be the same as through Findaway (minus your subscription fee).

Soundcloud, Soundwise & BookFunnel

Authors who want to sell audiobooks directly, and build a listenership on their own websites, need an audio hosting tool. Two of the best are BookFunnel and Soundwise. Both provide audio hosting and are more content creation tools than retail services.

Soundcloud began as a home for musicians and is like a YouTube for audio. It's a good place to create and offer samples of your work for listeners to try out, or to create advance copies to send to your street teams or reviewers. Listeners can leave feedback and star ratings.

Soundwise is a much more authorcentric platform, which can similarly be used for hosting and listener feedback, but also offering promo codes, analytics, and a payment facility, if you need one. A direct-to-consumer platform like Soundwise is a great tool to experiment with marketing strategies to optimize your funnel for future sales, as you have full access to analytics.

OPTIMISING AUDIOBOOK DISTRIBUTION

Should you sell through a large platform like Audible, go wide, or sell more directly using a tool like Soundwise or BookFunnel? The answer is the same as for ebooks and print: not either-or, but all. Or as close to all as your time and money resources allow. The advantages of non-exclusivity and building your own direct platforms applies to audiobooks, just as with ebooks.

Once you've made a product, the more territories and platforms you use for distribution, the better. Again, your own website should be the hub of the enterprise, unless you are using an algorithm marketing strategy to drive your book up a platform's charts. Whether you use ACX or not, you should always prioritize building your own audience and email lists. Allow Audible and/or Spotify to stream your work but include a call-to-action in your book that directs listeners to your full catalogue on your website—perhaps bundled at a discount, and using Soundwise or BookFunnel to host and deliver that bundle.

You can create shorter, free audiobooks to distribute via Soundwise to build your email lists, while publishing full-length audiobooks on all platforms.

Use ACX to sell individual audiobooks, but use Soundwise or BookFunnel to sell audiobook bundles, or your audiobook plus "add-ons" at a higher price e.g. audiobooks with additional content, audio-and-print bundles, extra chapters, blooper reel tracks.

Go creative!

Whatever retailers and distributors you use, experimenting with different marketing strategies to optimize your sales funnel for future sales is key.

The specifics of audiobooks are beyond the scope of this book. ALLi has a guide on audiobooks which you can read at: Selfpublishingadvice.org/self-publishing-audiobooks

21

BOOK MARKETING
PUBLISHING PROCESS FIVE

Book marketing and promotion are often confused, or spoken of together, but they are not the same thing. Marketing is letting the right readers know that you exist, as a writer, that your books exist, and what sort of books they are. Promotion is a focused sales push.

Marketing centers on what the book publishing business calls "discoverability" or "findability"—ensuring that you and your books can be found by the right readers and that the promise you're making to them is clear. It embraces your author platform, your covers, your descriptions, your review requests, your email lists, your reader funnels, and physical assets like bookmarks and postcards.

You might refresh your marketing look and feel, periodically, and you're always tweaking here and there, but essentially the marketing keeps on rolling along, taking in each new reader and each new book. The process is similar for most authors and the aim is to standardize and automate your marketing processes as much as possible, delegating certain tasks to technology, tools and assistants.

Book promotion, by contrast, kicks in around a particular book and a particular point in time. It's a push that has a start and an end date and there are countless kinds of promotions, including book launches, virtual or real-life book tours, advertising and other purchased promotions, and book-specific activities. Promotions are non-standard. They vary widely from author to author, book to book, genre to genre. Book promotions are limited only by your imagination, time, and money.

Marketing is passive selling and promotion is active selling.

Both book marketing and promotion are huge topics, and ALLi has a specific guidebook on this huge area that you must master, Book 3 in our Publishing Guides for Indie Authors Series: *Reach More Readers, Sell More Books.* Here, we'll take a top-level view that emphasizes the importance of creativity in every aspect of the process.

The creative approach to marketing is to see it as another channel for your personal passion and mission. That's the approach that underlies these two chapters—connecting your **raison d'être** as a writer with how you make your books visible to readers.

THE RIGHT READER

Marketing is your promise to your reader. It answers the reader's implicit question whenever they meet a new writer or book: would I like this? Is it for me? If your marketing is properly set up, they'll quickly be able to answer that question. And you'll easily be able to know if somebody is the right reader for one of your books.

My son is currently reading through one of those "100 books to read before you die" lists and was excited to read *The Girl with the Dragon Tattoo,* as so many of his friends had loved the book. As he read it, he was completely baffled as to how this book which so many other people loved–it has sold over seven million copies–had left him utterly underwhelmed. "You just weren't the right reader," I said.

Newsflash: not everyone is going to like your book. No matter how well you've done your job as a writer, readers will enjoy it to varying degrees. Some will be indifferent, and some will actively dislike it. And that's okay.

If I ask a successful indie author who their book is for, they are able to describe them with laser-like precision in terms of age, gender, demographic, values, and touchpoints. If I ask a new author, the most common answer is "pretty much everyone." Or: "It's not for any particular demographic." Or: "I don't know, I didn't write it with a reader in mind."

If you've fallen into this camp up to now, that's ok, but it's time to start thinking about your genre, niche, and micro-niche if you want to attract readers. While it might seem like a nice idea to appeal to as many people as possible, going broad and marketing to everyone doesn't mean more sales. The opposite is true. Going narrow and niche is where you score.

The "right reader principle" is this: aim your book obviously and exclusively at fans of your micro-niche. Market in a way that attracts those who are most likely to be most attracted and forget everyone else. If you do this, other readers do actually find their way to you, drawn in by clear messaging and attractive, focused branding. Ironically, when you aim your marketing more widely in the hopes of attracting "pretty much everyone", what happens in practice is that the reader doesn't know what kind of book it is, so they take a pass, even those who would have loved it.

When the right reader principle is adopted, it permeates all you do: your social media, book descriptions and covers, front and end matter. It helps you point ads at the right ad-sets, attract readers into your email and newsletter lists, choose images for your website. And it helps you choose the right category and keywords for your books.

By getting to know your books from the reader's perspective, you can tease out your book's potential points of difference, uniqueness, and value for the reader. Once you crack this and find your niche and micro-niche, you've found your fanbase, and their long-lasting loyalty becomes the core of your author business.

Enshrine that core principle of engaging the right readers, and only the right readers, in everything you do as an author and publisher and creative business owner.

CONSIDER THIS: Who Cares? *Step back and ask yourself what attracts a reader to you as an author.*
What need do your books fulfill?

Who might be interested?

What makes your work so compelling or entertaining that a buyer would choose yours over a comparable book or another author in your field?

Understanding your readers at a granular level can be invaluable in shaping your marketing approach and even your writing. By listing your readers' personal and psychological habits, you can to get a clearer picture of their needs and how to meet them with your books.

DO THIS: List Your Readers' Outer Attributes:

Age

Gender

Sexuality

Race / Ethnicity / Nationality

Education level

Occupation

Hobbies and interests

Class: Aristo, high, middle, or low income? Unemployed?

Urban or rural?

Married or single?

Parent or childfree?

Spiritual or religious affiliations?

Generation: Boomer? Gen X, Y, or Z?

Who do they live with: parents, partners, kids, alone?

Where do they holiday?

Attitude to health and fitness?

Describe their lifestyle.

DO THIS: List Your Readers' Inner Attributes:

- *Family history*
- *Childhood*

- *Current important relationships.*
- *Beliefs, goals and values.*
- *Any noteworthy attitudes?*
- *What occasions, feasts, celebrations are important to them?*
- *Pet peeves or irritations?*
- *Political leanings?*
- *Fears, worries, and frustrations?*
- *Secrets or fantasies?*
- *Anything you want to add?*

DO THIS: List Your Readers' Reading Attributes:

- *What outcome do they most want from reading? Information, education, entertainment, inspiration? Romance, adventure, thrills, shock, awe? To laugh, cry, be scared? To learn, transform, grow?*
- *Emotion or intellect?*
- *Mac or PC?*
- *Amazon or Apple?*
- *Favorite format: ebook, print book, audiobook?*
- *Favorite device: reader, phone, print books only?*
- *Any buying patterns?*
- *How price sensitive are they?*
- *Types of books they read (other than the type you write)?*

The answers to these questions need to be more than guesswork. Take time to consider them, then see if you can find evidence that backs or contradicts your hunches.

If you currently have an email list, even if it's small, poll your readers and ask them to complete a survey to better understand what they need and want from you. Ask questions: in your emails, in comments on your own blog, or in the comments of other's. Join a forum, book club or Goodreads group that discusses your topic or genre. Learn from comparable authors.

Your relationship with the right readers is an ongoing refinement and should deepen over time.

CREATIVE BOOK MARKETING

Once you know who your right reader is, then you can begin to market to them. The creative approach to marketing is to see this less as a commercial task and more in terms of deepening that relationship. Your book marketing becomes another channel for your personal passion and mission, as personal and individual and important to you as your writing.

That's the approach that underlies these two chapters about marketing and promotion—connecting your *raison d'être* as a writer with how you make your books visible to readers and offer them for sale.

So many indie authors say, "I love writing but I hate marketing." But in these digital days marketing *is* writing. How you attract a reader's attention is through good words, good images and good storytelling in your book descriptions, your advertising blurbs, your social media, and wherever your book is found online.

This is where your creativity comes in. Every day, we see indie authors who take the very *un*creative approach of going out on social media full of, "buy my book, buy it now, please buy my book, please promote me, please follow me, please like me, please review".

It's understandable. By the time you get to the marketing phase, you've spent months, maybe even years, on your book. You've worked harder than you knew you could and now you've got a book to sell. It's so exciting! Except nobody else is all that excited.

A decade ago, publishing a book was a big deal. Not so much anymore. As the bar for publication has fallen, the number of people publishing has risen and these days, using artificial intelligence, even machines can produce passable books.

To most readers, you're just another person they don't know, who's trying to sell them something.

Reader attention is *earned* these days. First you must understand your books' value, then you must communicate that value in creative and exciting ways, to those who are most likely to be interested.

Book marketing is best when it is personal and there are many ways to do it well. You don't have to do anything that doesn't appeal to you, but you *do* have to do *something*. Books, even great books, don't sell themselves.

Approaches to book marketing can be divided into three categories.

1. **ACCESS Marketing and Promotion**, already mentioned in Chapter 13 "Readers, Fans, and Superfans", my step-by-step approach to developing a relationship with the right readers.
2. **Algorithm Marketing and Promotion.** Using advertising and other methods to harness the power of algorithms to give your book exposure and sales.
3. **Influencer Marketing and Promotion.** Working with other literary and media influencers e.g. agents, authors, booksellers, critics, journalists, librarians, publishers, reviewers, social media accounts.

ACCESS Marketing

ACCESS marketing is a way of creating and mindfully nurturing your relationships with the right readers, so that you lead them through the reader journey you want them to take and encourage them to move from being readers to fans, and maybe even superfans.

ACCESS marketing revolves around content. You attract interest with media and social media content. You hold interest with content on your website. You attract more interest with a reader magnet which you offer in exchange for *access* to readers' direct contact details, and their permission to contact them.

ACCESS stands for attracting, captivating, connecting with, engaging, subscribing, and satisfying the right readers for your books. When they've followed you through that sequence, selling books to them is easy. They have come to know, like and trust you and will be keen to read your book.

- **Attract** – find readers through social media and advertising activity online—blog, podcast, video, ads—that use carefully chosen words and images designed to hook the right readers. Craft this content to be unique and exceptional, offering real value that aligns with the value offered in your books.

- **Captivate** – release captivating content on a schedule that suits your writing process, keeps existing followers interested, and attracts newcomers.
- **Connect** – offer a channel by which followers can connect with you and perhaps also with each other e.g. email, Facebook group.
- **Engage** – make this channel meaningful by starting and nurturing valuable conversations that are aligned with the values that attracted these readers to your channel, and with the values you offer in your books.
- **Subscribe** – invite these and other potential followers to sign up to receive some free content (often called a "reader magnet") in exchange for regular communications from you. Make it clear what they will receive from you.
- **Satisfy** – Value your readers' contact details. Contact them as promised and when you do, offer even more value. Aim to make your communications exciting and delightful. Immerse your subscribers in the world of your books.

Once these ACCESS marketing steps are completed well, selling books or other products or services to this group is no great effort. If you've done the job well, readers are asking, "when is the next book out?" and, "what else can I buy from you?"

Sometimes, from discovery to purchase is the act of a moment. They see your book on your website or in-store, like the cover and description, and—click!—they buy. More often, it takes time. They see you on social media and "like" what you're saying for weeks, months, or even years before they wander across to your website and have a browse. They get distracted and wander off, but there you are, popping up on social media again, saying or showing something else they like. They are attracted again—this time signing up for your reader magnet.

You send them your newsletter each month and then, one day, when invited, they finally get around to buying a book.

ACCESS marketing sounds like it's very time-consuming but with automation tools and regular output of content, you're set up in such a way that all of this can be easily fitted into the challenges of writing and producing books.

Nurtured mindfully, this access to your readers can be the basis of a lifelong relationship that is hugely fulfilling for both you and your readers. You can offer your subscribers other premium products and services, as well as books. Some of them will become superfans, who spread the word about your books, review your books on publication day, and influence others to buy.

INFLUENCER MARKETING

Some authors formalize this influence into reader teams like an **ARC (Advance Review Copy) Team**, a group of readers who receive a copy of your book in advance of launch and leave a review, or a **street team**, a subsection of your ARC readers who not only post a review but are gung-ho about your book to everyone who'll listen.

These readers are ready with their reviews on launch day, turn up to your book party, post updates on their social media sites, and help you to push sales any way they can. These true superfans are very precious to an author.

In addition to readers, many other people can act as influencers on your behalf: booksellers, critics, librarians, literary event organizers, social media mavens. Covering them all is outside the scope of this book (see ALLi's marketing book for more). What's important here is to recognize what gives a writer influence: ideas, skills, and relationships. Of the three, the most important is relationships. Your author platform is, essentially, about other people.

One other group of influencers warrants particular mention: other authors, those whose book are comparable to yours and with whom you share a readership.

Comps

Comparable authors and books, or "comps" for short, aren't necessarily those you choose to read yourself. They will likely be in your genre and category, but your point of comparison might be style of writing (e.g. literary, didactic, lyrical, fast-paced), setting (e.g. Irish fiction) or theme.

Any notable aspect of your writing can provide a point of comparison between you and other authors, between your books and other books.

To find your comp authors and titles, you need to set aside the view that your book is completely unique, and your voice is nothing like anyone else's. You may already know some writers who are comparable, or you may not have a clue. It doesn't matter. You can easily find them. The important thing is being willing to do the work on this, to drill down into what makes your books appealing to readers.

The information you glean about comp authors will inform and improve your decisions about every aspect of marketing—cover design, titles, subtitles, pricing, back cover copy, blurbs, and testimonials. And, most of all, advertising, as you can use comp author names as keywords in your ad targeting.

Finding and leveraging comparable authors has long been at the center of thriller writer Mark Dawson's strategy, and he has built not just a seven-figure publishing business but an education platform on the concept. "My books are often compared in their genre to Lee Child, so one of the things that I do on Facebook is to serve ads just to people who know or like Lee Child—fans of Lee Child's fan page, fans of the Jack Reacher fan page, and so on."

In a similar way, find an author in your genre whose books are comparable to yours. This is not just about ads. Knowing your comp authors is key to all aspects of marketing and promotion. They have the readership that you want. They can tell you what those readers like and enjoy, what stories they want to hear, what words and images work well when attracting them.

You find your comp authors by asking yourself questions: Who are the best known/most successful authors in my genre, niche or micro-niche? In what ways am I like these authors? In what ways are my books like theirs?

DO THIS: Comparable Authors' Emails. *Sign up for ten newsletters from authors in your genre and sub-genre. Which approaches do you like? Which don't you like? Why?*

Compare your marketing materials to your comps. Make notes for upgrades and improvements.

Do this: Find the Emotion. *As you read your comp authors' reviews, you'll come across words and phrases that convey the connection and emotions that the readers value. Look for the words that convey emotion, write them down.*

DO THIS: Note the Reviewers. *As you read comp book descriptions and reviews, keep your eyes open for balanced and insightful reviews; you can add the reviewers to your shortlist and approach them for a review when your book is ready.*

Thinking about comp authors brings us back around to the right reader principle and the source of the true creative connection between you and your reader. Reading is an act of such deep exchange between two minds, such a pure distillation of memory, hopes, dreams, goals, ideas and insights, melded in imaginative sympathy.

In the highly competitive creator economy, it's not enough to write and produce a good book. Every reader is wading through noise. You need to rise up from that noise in some way, to get their attention.

Marketing and promotion will continue to be key processes—not just for publishing a book successfully, but for the alternative earning options in the developing creator economy. Every successful author in the creator economy must become a hype artist as well as an artist.

This might conjure images of loud, aggressive promoters, but hype is not about volume and noise; it's about resonance and connection.

The hype artist is not just promoting for the sake of sales but is deeply passionate about what they're selling, genuinely believing in its value and wishing to share it with as many people as possible.

They understand the pulse of the market, the nuances of readers' preferences, and, most importantly, the essence of the work they're promoting. They skillfully amplify the work so that it reaches those who would most benefit from and appreciate it.

Michael Schein, founder of MicroFame Media and author of *The Hype Handbook and How to Create an Atmosphere of Curiosity and Intrigue*, defines hype as any activities that generate an emotional reaction from your readers which lead them to buy. Igniting and engaging your readers in ways that excite and delight them is a skill and, like all skills, it can be learned. "People are getting better at tuning out the self-serving messages they are bombarded with all day long," he says. "We need to promote our work in ways that make it stand out, that ignite emotions."

To break through, Schein advises that you don't just go through the motions but aim to "sell your message with the skill of a master". Develop your own unique style, around your books, that links with what's within them.

Keep looking at what others are doing in the same field but don't get lost in the crowd. Readers respond to uniqueness.

What's different about your books, about your brand?

Exaggerate that appeal.

TRY THIS: List five ways you could:
be more contrarian
exaggerate your appeal
attract more attention from people that matter
create a reader community that is super engaged
create an atmosphere of curiosity and intrigue around your books
create a step-by-step author manifesto, a rallying cry to your readers

---

Book marketing is a complex skill-set that takes time to learn. Yes, occasionally a book breaks through for reasons unknown but for most of us, it's about experimenting and learning and growing, as we respond to reader feedback.

For most authors, success is not just about racking up profits, but about becoming profitable while also feeding the creative passion that fires their writing. The cradle within which this happens is the relationship with the reader. Creative self-publishing invites you to bring all your creativity into that relationship, by understanding and sharing the creative imperatives that inspired you to write your books.

22

BOOK PROMOTION
PUBLISHING PROCESS SIX

T hese days, if you don't promote your books, you're unlikely to sell them. Marketing is essential, but often it is not enough to move the needle on sales. Promotion is key. This chapter is an overview of some of the most common promotion strategies used by indie authors at the time of writing, starting with pricing, and including advertising and ebook and audiobook promotion sites.

PRICING

Pricing is a key promotional tool. This is where indie authors can gain a competitive advantage over trade-published books especially in ebook and audio.

Ebook Pricing

For ebooks, the general sweet spot for indie authors is between $2.99 and $9.99, the price point where Amazon offers a 70% royalty for self-published writers. For all price points under $2.99 and over $9.99, Amazon's royalty is only 35%.

Some retailers such as Kobo are more generous with their payouts on books priced above $9.99, so you should take that into consideration if you have a book that you feel may be worth a higher price.

On the other hand, many traditionally published books are priced north of $9.99, so you'll make your book more attractive by comparison if you price it slightly lower.

Most books fall between $2.99 and $5.99, however box sets and omnibuses are priced more toward $9.99. But do experiment to find the best price point.

Many indies price the first book in a series lower, as a loss leader. It's not uncommon to see the first book at $2.99, and sequels at $3.99 or higher. There's also perma-free pricing, where you offer book one for free. At the time of this writing, Amazon doesn't allow free pricing, except in its Kindle Select Program, and then only for five days each quarter. But if you set your book's price on other retailers to free, Amazon will price-match. It is believed by many that Amazon suppresses the visibility of free books.

And finally, let's talk about the $0.99-$2.99 price range. These are bargain, discount prices to be used as promotional price points. A lot of writers post their first books for 99 cents because a number of Kindle readers routinely buy only 99-cent books. Another popular price point is $2.99, the minimum price for which you receive 70% sales commission.

Print Pricing

Print books are a different matter. First your cover price—what the reader pays—must be higher than your print cost or you won't make a profit. Also, stores will expect a discount, so your cover price still has to make you a profit with that discount. This generally puts your price somewhere between $10 and $20. Do some research. Don't go to a bookstore and see how they're pricing books in your genre and expect to hit those prices in POD. They have economies of scale that you can't compete against.

You can and should charge more for your print books than ebooks. Your costs are higher, and readers will pay more for paperbacks.

Higher-priced paperbacks also make your ebook look cheaper, and therefore more attractive, by comparison.

Audiobook Pricing

For audiobooks, the pricing depends on where you publish. As we saw in the distribution chapter, you cannot change your pricing on Audible audiobooks. Pricing there is based on the length of your audiobook. When distributing through other audiobook retailers and your own website, you set the price.

A higher price can say "quality" to some readers, and I have had the experience of selling more when I raised prices and we've had other members report the same.

There are readers who like expensive, lovely things. You have to test to identify what works best for your books and may find a difference between books. Look at other books in your genre that are at the top of the charts. That's direct evidence of what readers are willing to pay.

Don't be afraid to experiment with pricing on all your formats. Sometimes, breaking the rules can work. Be flexible and be open to trying different things.

Another consideration is currency conversions. In your sales dashboard, you set your price in one currency, and the platform converts it to the others. But this can result in weird prices—€2.84, for instance. It looks more professional if you round up to 2.99 in the major international currencies (pounds, euros, yen, pesos, US, Canadian, and Australian dollars, etc.). It will also probably convert better to sales. This is known as "pretty pricing".

ADVERTISING

Book advertising is a complicated business. It's very easy for authors to be lured into bad advertising "opportunities". Meta and Amazon ads have become very popular with authors in recent years (see below) and can definitely help us find new readers and grow our readership.

Whatever advertising platform we use, we need to keep ROI in the front of our mind. It's easy to spend a lot of money with poor outcomes. Emotional investment in our books can lead us to make poor decisions, which is why vanity publishers can persuade authors to part with large sums for dubious value, but we're all vulnerable. There are many platforms, some briefly surveyed here. All require you to be vigilant.

The first distinction when considering advertising is between ads in print media—newspapers, magazines, catalogues—and digital ads, which are served on social media platforms, online bookstores, and search engines. The big advantage of digital advertising is its ability to track results and iterate from what we learn from the ad.

Digital advertising allows you to know the cost per click on your ad, the cost per conversion (a signup to your newsletter or the sale of a book), and gives you a much clearer indication of return on investment (ROI) than print. This doesn't mean digital necessarily delivers higher ROI, though, just that it's easier to measure. So do think laterally about your book and whether a targeted print ad might work.

Digital advertising campaigns are often presented by marketing agencies and those selling how-to-advertise courses as "set-and-forget". In fact, they need more time and attention than a print ad. A successful digital ad campaign needs to find the right target audience, track the ad to learn from responses, optimize the content and design, and perfect the budgeting, bidding and pacing.

However, digital advertising offers a sophisticated and efficient promotional method, and many authors have found it well worth the time and effort. As far as we can tell, all the indie authors who are heading up the bestseller lists are using digital advertising.

Some of the platforms that are most popular with authors are:

- **Amazon advertising:** rolled out in 2017 in the US, increasingly available around the world, and one of the most effective advertising options for authors.
- **Facebook/Instagram (Meta) advertising:** globally available, easy to test and scale and allows very specific targeting. You can specify fans of other authors, age groups, employers, job titles, locations and interests.

- **BookBub email list promotion:** another constantly improving option and with less competition from other authors than on Facebook or Amazon.
- **Other social media advertising:** though Facebook is arguably the best social media advertising platform, some authors are finding success on Twitter, LinkedIn and YouTube, where there is less competition. Consider where your readers are found online and think about whether your book advertisement might do well there.
- **Search and other digital advertising:** there are many other types of digital advertising platforms you can consider, like search advertising (Google AdWords), banner ads on websites, display network advertising and so on. None of these has, as yet, widely paid off for indie authors, but always consider whether your niche makes you an exception. It's much easier to stand out when you're not in a crowded marketplace.

When thinking about digital ads think about:

1. **Placement:** where do the ads show up?
2. **Targeting:** how can I decide whom the ads get shown to?
3. **Cost:** when am I being charged? What is the minimum I need to invest? What budget can I afford? What is optimal? Most platforms start low, and you scale up as you succeed.
4. **Analytics:** how do I know if my ads are working or not?

Meta ads

At the most basic level, authors can use Facebook and Instagram ads to find readers who have an interest in books similar to theirs. For as little as $5 a day, you can deliver your ads to different 'sets' of audiences to learn more about what appeals to readers of books like yours.

BookBub Ads

BookBub has built genre-based passionate communities of book-lovers. It sends out millions of genre-targeted emails every day, to readers keen to buy books. Authors can apply to be featured in these emails (which we'll cover below), but BookBub also runs an advertising platform where you can target readers, with complete control over your ad design, spend and timing. BookBub ads are good for creating a campaign around a specific book promotion.

You can target fans of similar authors to reach new readers and your ads reach not only their followers, but any readers who have shown an interest in their books on the platform.

BookBub provides a good self-serve portal that makes it easy to check real-time results and test different ad images, copy or targeting. There are nuanced targeting options, such as retailer preferences or author interests, that let you reach only the most relevant readers. And you can tailor each ad image to that particular audience's tastes.

Amazon Advertising

As well as these special promotions in KDP Select, Amazon has an advertising platform, Amazon Marketing Services (AMS), which it has been consistently improving and growing. It is straightforward to use with clear reporting that allows you to advertise your books in an environment where readers are searching for and purchasing books. It's like standing in a bookshop, hovering around your genre shelf with a book brochure and placing it under the prospective buyer's nose.

Like any advertising platform, AMS brings challenges and a learning curve. Success depends on data analysis and iteration: applying what you've learned from the analysis.

Amazon ads come in two types: sponsored or product display. For sponsored product ads, you can start advertising for as low as $2 a day. For product display ads, you need to set up a "lifetime cost" per campaign (the minimum is $100). Many authors report that it's hard to get AMS to spend the full budget, especially at first.

1. AMS Sponsored Product Advertising

These ads show up on search result listings and other books' product pages.

You create your ad and set a budget, then you have another choice to make: manual or automatic targeting? With auto targeting, you let Amazon choose which readers see your ad. Obviously, Amazon has plenty of user data on which to base its choices. Auto targeting can work very well if you have clearly defined your niche, especially for non-fiction, and your metadata is well set up.

With manual targeting, you select keywords, and Amazon will run your ad when people search for those keywords. If you choose manual targeting, make sure you start off trying a huge variety of keywords. Most authors setting out on AMS use ten or twenty keywords but when you start, you should test **upwards of 300** keywords, aiming to keep those that work, eliminating those that don't.

Think about your right readers: what they like to read, what they are likely to search for. Search by title, author name, genre or by ASIN (Amazon identification number).

You only pay per click, so you can be highly experimental with keyword targeting. If a keyword isn't relevant, people won't click, and you won't pay anything.

Target your genres and subgenres in every way you can think of.

2. AMS Product Display ads

These ads show up right next to the description on another book's product page, and on the Kindle "home" screen and screensaver. There are also two targeting options: by interest or by product. "Interest" is a matter of selecting one or several Amazon categories or subcategories. "Product" means selecting which exact titles you want your ad to display beside.

Measuring the Success of Your Ads

First off, you need to be patient. Amazon takes seven days to attribute a sale to your ads, which means your campaign has to run for a week before you even start to get results. You need to calculate your **conversion rate**—what proportion of your ad views led to a book sale. Two useful metrics for this are the click-through-rate (the percentage of people who were shown the ad, and who clicked through to the sales page) and the click-to-sale rate (the percentage of those who clicked through, and actually bought the book).

AMS gives you a chart for monitoring how well your advertisements are performing. The chart breaks down five factors.

1. **Impressions:** How often your advertisement shows up in searches. The higher, the better.
2. **Clicks:** How often a consumer clicks on your ad. Remember, you pay Amazon per click. More is good... if they're converting into sales!
3. **Spend:** The money you've spent on the campaign.
4. **Sales:** The money you've made off the campaign.
5. **ACoS:** Advertising Cost of Sale.

The most important metric is that last one, ACoS. This measures the amount you spent on a campaign relative to the sales you earned directly from that campaign. It is expressed as a percentage: spend/sales.

ACoS is the metric you're testing for when you analyze the performance of a keyword. You want to get it down as low as you can.

One important thing to note about this metric: Amazon's sales figure is based on the **retail price** of your book, not the **commission** they are paying you. To get the real value of an ad, you need to do your own calculation: spend/commission.

If your ACoS is over seventy, you're definitely **losing** money. Why? On Amazon, a book priced between $2.99 and $9.99 makes 70% of each sale, so your ad only starts to make you money if ACoS is lower than 70%. If your book is priced below $2.99 or above $9.99, it pays 35%

author commission, so you're only making money if ACoS is lower than 35%.

An ideal ACoS is around 20–25%. If it's higher, look for ways to optimize your campaign. Identify keywords that work and create different campaigns for them. Cull those that don't. Scale up what works.

The overall conclusion from watching a great number of authors experiment with ads is that you **can** get a positive return on your investment by paying close attention and modifying your ads to scale up. The success comes down to targeting—showing ads for your book to readers who are likely to be interested, and then having a good book page when they click through. Manual targeting is the trickiest part of AMS, and record keeping is essential. Test and evaluate consistently and use a spreadsheet to keep track of your keywords and their conversion stats.

Everyone who succeeds at AMS talks about two things: doing the work (constantly testing and iterating) and not giving up too soon. Like all advertising and promotion, Amazon ads are hard work and ALLi members report varying results. Many authors who use the platform struggle to get enough clicks and conversions to make it worth the effort, so they give up.

Having said that, while ads work for many authors, if you're not willing to put in the time, or if you hate the thought of ads, you'll only waste time and money trying. Choose a different promo method.

OTHER AMAZON PROMOTIONS

Amazon has the widest reach of all the self-publishing platforms. Amazon promotions give you access to targeted readers, but also another benefit—sales and page-reads (in the subscription program) will register in Amazon's bestseller charts. This spurs Amazon's algorithm to recommend your book to other readers with similar tastes.

KDP Select

To enroll into this program, you must give Amazon exclusive distribution rights to your ebook for a ninety-day period. Discounting is known to be very effective in improving visibility and sales, and for any five days during a KDP Select period, you can offer your book for free or set up a Kindle Countdown Deal. Moreover, any book sales generated under this program will fetch you Amazon's highest royalty rate of 70%.

Choosing KDP Select also enters your book into KU, the subscription service that pays authors for the number of pages read.

A look at the Kindle bestsellers shows many of the best-performing books come from KU. It is said that Amazon gives preferential treatment to KU titles, but perhaps this is simply because a KU borrow counts as a normal sale or download, so it is easier for KU titles to climb the charts.

The major publishing houses don't publish their books through the KU program, so the competition within the KU program (which includes the books listed in the Kindle Countdown Deal charts and elsewhere) is other indie or small press titles.

OTHER PROMOTION SITES

Running your own email list is arguably the single most important aspect of an author-publisher's business. This section is about paying to access other people's carefully curated lists. Examples are Freebooksy, Fussy Librarian, and the market leader BookBub (for ebooks) and Chirp (for audiobooks).

BookBub began life as an email advertising platform and this "featured deal" service on BookBub is still one of the best ways to sell a lot of books in a short time. However, it's not cheap and does not produce the same ROI as it did in the past.

Many authors shy away from BookBub because of the cost, but many others continue to find the investment worthwhile. BookBub promotions can drive a spike in sales that can last even after the promotion ends. Those with books in a series benefit most, as readers who enjoy the advertised book want more.

Other good sites that cost less but also yield less return include BookGorilla, The Fussy Librarian, Pixel of Ink, Booksends, Freebooksy/Bargain Booksy, eReaderIQ. All are popular, and all receive repeat business from authors.

ALLi has a comparison of ebook promotion sites here: SelfpublishingAdvice.org/ebook-discovery-book-promo-services-review.

After conducting this in-depth comparison of the main book promotion sites, ALLi's Watchdog, John Doppler, came to the following conclusions:

For free books, **BookBub** remains the gold standard for ebook discovery services. Its gargantuan membership places it in a weight class of its own, and it is arguably the most popular of the services in our roster. That popularity also makes it one of the most difficult services to enter; high demand and increasing interest from traditional publishers leads to heavy competition for relatively few slots. But if the steep price tag is within your means and you can secure a spot in their schedule, BookBub offers a solid return on your investment.

For paid books (particularly books priced at $2.99 and over), the clear champion is **The Fussy Librarian**. Fussy Librarian has a much smaller membership, but its correspondingly lower fees do not vary with the price of the book. With superior cost-per-thousand impressions (CPM) for higher-priced books and the best CPM across nearly every fiction category, Fussy Librarian presents an outstanding value for a surprisingly low price.

Bargain Booksy ranks moderately well in fiction genres, particularly in the higher price brackets. However, where it really shines is in non-fiction categories, where it sits at the top of most rankings. **Freebooksy** does not fare quite as well as its sister site, generally resting in the lower half of its genres. The popular categories of mystery, cozy mystery and thrillers are a notable exception.

BookGorilla performs erratically overall, offering moderate value in most categories, and bafflingly uncompetitive pricing in others. BookGorilla is a good investment in categories like mystery and thriller, but compare pricing and consider alternative sub-genres to obtain the best value.

Robin Reads represents fair-to-poor value in its categories, with the median CPM weighing in at over $1. Robin Reads' best category is mystery, placing fourth out of the six companies represented in that genre.

Booksends/eReaderIQ are listed jointly here, as their shared membership and uniformly high price consistently place last in the rankings—sometimes with a CPM as much as ten times higher than the closest competitor. There are more cost-effective options for promoting your books.

The above is a general guide only. It is impossible to know how your book would perform without testing it, and well worth making a small investment to find out.

AUTHOR COLLABORATION

Authors with similar audiences might group together to promote their books, perhaps collaborating in a paid box set of titles or offering a spread of free titles in return for mailing list sign-ups. Platforms like BookFunnel and Prolific Works (formerly InstaFreebie) make such collaborations easy.

PROMO STACKING

Every so often, time and budget allowing, do a big drive on one book, promoting through an orchestrated sequence of multiple coordinated marketing campaigns within a set time frame. This is known as "promo stacking", and your goal is to increase the sales and rank of a specific book or series.

The timeframe for a promo stack is short, typically four to seven days, and it involves driving your book every way you know: email campaign to your list, featured deals on other email promotion sites, ads on Facebook or Amazon or BookBub or all three, and features on book promotion platforms.

Promo stacking can really drive a book forward and sometimes results in a permanent rise in sales rank.

PROMOTING AUDIOBOOKS

Audiobooks are sold by promoting them to readers who like their books in audio. That might sound obvious, but sometimes authors assume their ebook or print marketing will automatically cover their audio too. Not so.

- **Have you optimized your audiobook cover?** Audiobook covers aren't rectangles like ebooks but square in shape. So you'll need to tweak your ebook covers to ensure the title of the book and the author's name are clearly visible. Ensure you've got your audiobook wrapped up well before you present it to your reader.
- **Do you talk about your audiobooks with your email subscribers?** You can use your email list to announce or tease new audiobook releases and also remind your listeners about your backlist audio titles.
- **Do you distribute copies of your audiobooks to reviewers?** Like ebooks, audiobooks can be safely distributed using services like BookFunnel. You could share advanced copies of audiobooks with a review team or with reviewers / influencers who promote books.
- **Creating audiograms** is a fun way of drawing your readers in. Audiograms contain a snippet of the audiobook (a few seconds of recording), and a static book cover with some

animated elements in it. Just like when you listen to music on Spotify and the album cover is animated.

- **Creating boxsets** is a great way to expand your reach. Author anthologies, i.e. compiled audiobooks from other authors are a great way to reach listeners who enjoy the sort of books you write. Authors of a similar sub-genre/trope compile their work into anthologies, and each markets it to their own audiences. No matter how rapidly we publish, we cannot meet reader demand. It takes so much longer to write and publish a book than to buy and read it. Comparable authors don't compete with other authors as much as work as a team to jointly satisfy readers who like books like ours.

- **Podcasting** is a good way to spread the word. Podcast listeners are consuming content in audio format, so are more likely to listen to audiobooks. If you are on a podcast or host your own, you can build a community of listeners who will easily transition to your audiobooks.

Promoting audiobooks largely depends on the method you've chosen to distribute them i.e. distributing exclusively with Audible versus selling wide (direct, through retailers, or with the help of an aggregator like Findaway Voices).

Your chosen method of distribution can be based on the number of audiobooks you have and whether you've used a royalty share method with the narrator. But if you distribute wide, you've probably heard of or use Findaway Voices.

- **Findaway Voices,** which is now owned by Spotify, allows authors to find narrators to create audiobooks as well as reach audiobook retailers. They don't demand exclusivity and authors can price their own books. Their dashboard has a promotions tab where authors can set up a special price for the duration of their promotion. Findaway Voices will then communicate this price and the duration of the price change to retailers.

- **Using in-house promotions:** Kobo Writing Life also offers promotions for audiobooks, including those books in sales on Kobo's storefront, e.g. their Audiobook Daily Deal program. Authors can submit their audiobooks to this program, and KWL selects one audiobook each day to be featured as the Audiobook Daily Deal at a discounted price for a limited time. Working in tandem with Kobo's merchandising and marketing team, they also help you set up email marketing campaigns, social media promotions, and dedicated audiobook landing pages on Kobo's website.

After you've set up promotional pricing, you must let listeners know about the promotion you're running.

You can use services like the giant newsletter deals website mentioned in the ebook section, BookBub. In the audio world, they call themselves Chirp. If you are already signed up as a BookBub partner, you have access to it. And if you haven't, you can sign up for both services on Chirp. You can then apply to enlist your audiobook for a promotion deal. If selected, they will let the people signed up on their category specific email list know about your book and special offer.

Another such service is Audio Thicket by Written Word Media which sends out emails promoting audiobooks deals. They are Audible centred but their email list is also based on sub-genres, helping you target specific readers.

One Thing A Day

Structure your book promotion so you do one thing a day to sell more books. Devise tasks that are achievable in a realistic time frame. Just like you can exercise effectively in just fifteen minutes per day or learn to write your book in fifteen-minute increments, so too can you promote your books in small increments of time.

What could you do in fifteen minutes? It might be tweaking some of your ACCESS marketing autoresponders or newsletters, or refining your Amazon Author Central entry, or connecting into your

Goodreads group but make sure you are also making room for actual promotion tasks, i.e. something that sells more books.

You might research and pitch a book influencer; apply for a promotion on an ebook discovery site, set up a new ad or asset on Facebook or Instagram.

Doing one thing a day will make you productive in your promotion and drive momentum. When you do small promotional tasks frequently, it takes less energy than when you approach it as this huge thing that goes against your creative grain.

You're building your skills as a book promoter and as you do, you begin to actively enjoy it.

In Part VI "Creative Business Planning", I offer you a planning method that makes this very doable. Taking time to make a plan means you don't waste time figuring out what promotional task to do each day. You can just dive in and do it.

23

SELECTIVE RIGHTS LICENSING
PUBLISHING PROCESS SEVEN

W hile indie authors, like all publishers, focus on book sales as their core business activity, there is a seventh process of publishing: rights licensing and management. A book is just one of the formats that can be generated from your words. Each of your books actually represents several sets of potential rights which can be traded by license: film, TV, international editions, translations, stage adaptations, merchandising and more.

As no individual author can directly exploit all these publishing possibilities, most use other publishers and rights buyers to maximize the return on their intellectual property (IP). Rights licensing and management affords self-publishers some excellent opportunities—if we are aware of the inherent value of our publishing rights and have a strategy and implementation method to exploit them.

If your publishing business is up and running, working with an agent or assistant to pitch and negotiate good rights deals can provide a nice additional income stream. Trading in publishing and production rights generally only opens up after you've achieved significant sales success or have some other significant value to offer a rights buyer e.g. a prestigious award.

If you're on your first book or two, for now all you need is awareness of some core principles, so you don't tie yourself into a dud deal, and you are properly set up to make good rights deals when the time arrives. Without such understanding, you can be seduced by offers from publishers, other rights buyers and even self-publishing services that can sound great but actually offer very little—or may even be damaging.

Licensing rights is an administration-heavy task but one that increasing numbers of author-publishers are choosing to do for themselves. It is also possible to hire an agent or sub-agent to assist with this publishing process.

RIGHTS FACTORS FOR INDIE AUTHORS

This chapter covers three key factors for self-publishing authors who are considering rights licensing.

1. the laws of copyright
2. the principle of non-exclusivity
3. the practice of selective rights licensing

At the end of the chapter, you'll find a list of places where you can learn more, including ALLi's specific guide to this topic, *How Authors License Publishing Rights: ALLi's Guide to Working with Publishers, Producers and Others*. This book is available for purchase in all formats at: Selfpublishingadvice.org/rights-licensing/. Members enjoy free access to the ebook. There is also information about ALLi's dedicated literary agent, who works with us to maximize rights opportunities for our members.

1. Copyright Law for Self-Publishers

Copyright used to be a publisher's right, but previous generations of creator activists secured it as a creator's right. Authors now have the power of copyright law on their side, but every day disempower themselves by naively signing away their rights, or not exploiting them.

What a rights buyer purchases from you is a license to publish or produce, and such licenses may be exclusive or non-exclusive. They may be limited to a particular use or claim all uses (e.g. editorial, noncommercial, educational). They may cover an individual format or all formats (e.g. print, ebook, audio, web, film, TV). They may be for an agreed term or for the term of copyright (author's life + seventy years). They may be for a specific territory—or all territories (world rights).

Licensing all rights to one buyer, without due consideration, is an expensive mistake we've seen too many authors make. The savvy author thoroughly researches agreements before signing to verify what rights they are being asked to give away. They never want to assign **all rights** to a third party. Instead they employ **selective rights licensing** (see below) whereby rights deals with publishers are just part of being a successful independent author.

More on copyright in Chapter 15 and in ALLi's *Copyright Bill of Rights* campaign book.

2. The Principle of Non-Exclusivity

As we saw in Chapter 11, exclusivity in publishing means limiting your publishing to a single outlet and in third-party publishing, exclusivity is the default option. Self-publishing platforms like Amazon KDP, Apple Books, or IngramSpark adopts a more liberal approach. By default, these platforms aren't exclusive. They operate more as collaborators than controllers, distributing and sometimes selling the authors' creations, and earning a commission for these services.

Amazon however carves its own exclusivity niche. The allure of exclusivity via Kindle Direct Publishing Select for ebooks and the ACX exclusivity option for audiobooks is enhanced payments, a slot in their often lucrative subscription programs, and a suite of marketing tools.

Choosing this path can help your work to shine on Amazon's KDP, but only there. You are excluding all other ebook platforms, even your own website.

Amazon's Kindle Unlimited (KU) has been a boon for many authors, offering a vast audience and the potential for significant earnings. The success stories are numerous, and for some, KU has been a life-changer. However, the fluctuating algorithms, changing rules around page reads, category adjustments and account closures can impact an author's revenue overnight.

Amazon is a tech and retail giant with a primary allegiance to its bottom line and shareholders. While they have created a platform that has been immensely beneficial to writers, they can—and do—also make moves that are not always in authors' best interests. All of this emphasizes the importance of diversification in the publishing world, as in all kinds of business and investment.

Opting for exclusivity, whether through traditional publishing contracts or platforms like KDP Select, undeniably limits one's reach. While it might be the right path for a time, or for a particular book, it is a risky strategy. Spreading distribution across various platforms and channels not only reduces the risk of sudden income drops due to changes on a single platform, but also increases visibility and reach across different reader bases.

Given the dynamics of the creator economy, more authors and author groups are encouraging a non-exclusive approach, which aligns with the ethos of the modern creator, emphasizing flexibility, adaptability, and a direct connection with readers.

There might be situations where exclusivity offers benefits that align with an author's specific goals, such as a particularly lucrative deal, a strategic partnership, or special promotional opportunities. While you may have good reasons for going exclusive, do not make the choice to cut off multiple territories and opportunities without due consideration.

SELECTIVE RIGHTS LICENSING

Discoverability—having your books available for readers to find—is key to building a long-term, sustainable business as an indie author. As we've seen, one of the greatest benefits of self-publishing is the ability to reach customers all across the globe, in a variety of formats. Beware of any contract—with a third-party publisher, self-publishing service, or other rights buyer—that signs those benefits away.

As a general rule of thumb, the savvy author attempts to negotiate each publishing right individually, making separate decisions based on market size, reach of the publisher, and potential value, all the while aiming to limit term, territory and format.

This is **selective rights licensing.**

Publishing contract terms are built around acquiring final draft manuscripts from authors who have no publishing skills. If you've published successfully already, the rights buyer is benefitting from your existing readership and publishing experience and needs to offer terms that are better than those offered to a novice writer. They need to be open to splitting ebook, print book and audio rights, as often the ebook and audio rights are too lucrative, or potentially lucrative, for the indie author to give up. And ideally, they need to be more open to author input into marketing, metadata and other publishing decisions.

Selectively licensing your publishing rights gives you a tremendous advantage over authors who have signed all rights exclusive to a single third-party publisher. It's common to see publisher contracts claiming world English-language rights and all subsidiary rights, including valuable ebook rights, in return for low royalties and a paltry advance, or even no advance at all. Some add the insult of a very long rights term, in extreme cases, the life of copyright, to the injury of poor terms and conditions.

Licensing is the term to use, always, in discussions with rights buyers. They may speak of "granting" or "assigning" rights, but what indie authors want to do is license non-exclusively and selectively, rather than hand across the whole suite of rights to a buyer who has no real plan—which is what most publishing contracts are set up for.

Consider each clause separately. For example:

- Transferring **reproduction, distribution, public display, or public performance rights** is likely to prohibit you from sharing your work with readers, institutions, libraries or other repositories.

- Transferring **distribution** rights is likely to prohibit you from making your books available on your own website.
- Transferring **the right to make derivative works** is likely to prohibit you from creating follow-up or related works.

Your starting position is that the license is limited, exclusive to the rights buyer only for publication in a specific format or formats (e.g. print), within a specific territory or territories (e.g. US only), and for a specific term (e.g. five years).

It's understandable that publishers want as many rights as possible. Publishing is unpredictable so they're working on the "just in case" principle, acquiring all rights just in case a book takes off. You should hold the rights for the same reason. Rights buyers will push hard to acquire world ebook rights, audiobook rights and print rights. Authors should hold hard to limit the format, territory and term. These three concepts (format, territory, term) are the rights mantra to hold in your head.

And your attitude in negotiations should be: "Use it or lose it". Your aim is to limit licenses to publishers who have the wherewithal and strategy to exploit those particular rights.

Of course, if the deal is right, it may make sense to also give over the publication of core English language ebook, print or audio rights. International bestselling author JD Barker explains how this works in practice for the successful indie author.

I consider all options for each book and I go with whatever makes the most business sense for a particular title... Some of my titles are with traditional publishers, others are indie published through my own small press... I have several books that are indie published in some territories and traditionally [trade] published in others.

— JD BARKER

RIGHTS LICENSING: GUIDING PRINCIPLES

1. Understand the Contract

Take the time to understand publishing agreements and contracts. Even if you plan on engaging an agent or attorney to negotiate on your behalf, you need to understand contract terminology in order to have intelligent conversations with them and with producers, publishers and other rights buyers. ALLi offers various services that can assist its members, including contract review and a dedicated literary agent for those in a position to license rights.

2. Capitalize on as Many Rights as Possible

As you get your work into more retail outlets, regions, formats and languages, you'll build a stronger foundation for generating long-term income. The challenge is finding the best way to take advantage of all these options. Can you do it yourself or should you sell rights to publishers and producers? The most successful authors do some of both.

3. Limit the Term, Territory and Formats

Limit the rights you sell to those who have the wherewithal to exploit them and generate income. Undoubtedly, this creates tension in any contract negotiation. As the author, you want to license as few rights as possible, while the buyer wants to acquire as many rights as possible. This is healthy business tension and not something to avoid, as so many authors do.

It's a negotiation. Publishers, agents and producers expect to negotiate, and they respect those who enter the negotiation as an equal trading partner. This is not the time to be a grateful artist, seeking validation. There's a place for that, but it's not when negotiating the terms on which you will license your invaluable intellectual property.

4. Delete Onerous Clauses

Publishers talk about standard contracts but there is no such thing. Don't be afraid to strike out clauses. For example, an indie author should never sign this nasty agreement to license "all formats existing now and to be created for the term of copyright" that is popping up in contracts all over at the moment.

5. Specify granular rights

As the creator economy expands, each right becomes more precious. So specify clearly what is and is not being licensed e.g. human narration for audio, retaining AI narration.

6. Do your Research

Research the market climate and potential partners and imagine the rights potential for each title. Identify priority markets and key titles to sell. Watch out for offers from overseas "publishers" in countries that are not adequately covered by copyright agreements, where piracy is rife, and payment unlikely.

7. Have a Strategy and an Implementation Plan

Set up a database to record details of your titles, submissions and sales, and details of what you've sold to rights buyers. The database should enable you not just to keep track but to note points about specific rights buyers, learnings from negotiations, and your general strategy and implementation plan for rights. For example, how many buyers will you pitch each month? What territories do you want to sell into? How much money are you receiving in different territories? Can you expand that? What about moving into different formats like TV or film?

For more about licensing your rights, see **How Authors License Publishing Rights: ALLi's Guide to Working with Publishers, Producers and Others**: *Selfpublishingadvice.org/rightsbook*

See also **The Copyright Bill of Rights** *which sets out eight fundamental rights that self-publishing authors need to know to best avail of their economic and moral rights in digital publishing:* SelfpublishingAdvice.org/billofrights

PART VI

CREATIVE BUSINESS PLANNING FOR AUTHORS

In this section you are invited to think about your publishing business in depth and to a try a particular kind of creative business planning that has worked well for me and many other authors. Designed to manifest your personal definition of success, your plan promotes and measures your productivity, platform, profits, and personal satisfaction.

We'll also explore how executing your creative business plans will bring you up against fear, resistance, and block, and how to harness them into creative flow to create a balanced and integrated author publishing business.

Each of us working in this way will unfold a more diverse, more accessible, and more equitable publishing landscape—and, I hopefully suggest—even a better world.

24

CREATIVE PLANNING FOR PROFIT

At the start this book, I said I would distinguish between proven techniques and tools, ALLi's best practice recommendations, and my own approaches and opinions. I'd now like to offer you my own method for planning a profitable, passion-powered, self-publishing business.

When I started self-publishing, I brought little by way of planning to my publishing life. I had just a f-r-e-e-writing notebook and a to-do list. As a writer with a third-party publisher, that had served me fine but as a self-publisher, it wasn't enough. I now had too many different kinds of tasks, drawing on different kinds of skills. I'd go to sleep ticking tasks off my list and wake up remembering something I'd forgotten. The to-do list never got any smaller, and I never seemed to have enough time for everything.

Ticking tasks off lists is satisfying when a job has a clear beginning and end, but for an indie author, our work is never done. The next book, the next promo, the next campaign is always looming as soon as this one is finished. As we add new ideas and think up new projects, the to-do list grows on the other side. We're left with little sense of accomplishment, except on big milestones that don't happen too often: finishing the first or final draft, publishing the book, hitting a list.

When my list failed to cope with the multi-layered nature of writing and publishing, I tried various time management and planning programs. Many actually stopped me in my creative tracks. They were too linear and goal-directed for me. The business language and vocabulary were too hard-edged, too goal-driven, too simplistic, and took no account of the fluid, nebulous, and unexpected aspects of the creative process.

For all the talk of innovation in the workplace, the financial and business worlds still run on very conventional frameworks and those of us who run passion-powered enterprises find much business advice does not apply to our situation. Conventional business, for example, wants to outsource or delegate production, but this is often the most interesting part of the business for creative business owners. It is the reason we're in this business in the first place. A business model or method that delegates the writing is not for me and, I suspect, not for you either.

I'm in the publishing business because it's the best way for me to make a living from my writing. Book writing and book production is the last thing I want to outsource. As creative writers and publishers, we want (need) to make money, yes, but we also want to make our mark. We want to make meaning. At the same time, it's easy to push your creative passion all the way into work addiction and burnout, without ever seeing a profit.

My publishing plan had to hold these two—money and meaning—in fine balance. It had to care about the process as well as product, about *how* I do things as well as what gets done. It had to bring everything together in a way that made me feel good about myself and my work, day by day, no matter where I was in the process.

It also had to account for more than just the writing productivity that had been the central concern before I started self-publishing. Getting our writing done is vital, of course, but it's only one strand of success for an indie author who is a publisher as well as a writer.

GO CREATIVE! BUSINESS PLANNING FOR AUTHORS

Some time ago, I formalized this personal approach to creative business into a shareable program: *Go Creative! Business Planning for Authors and Poets*. The program takes a holistic approach that embraces the creative and the commercial equally and recognizes that self-publishing authors must develop three very different skillsets, which I call **maker, manager,** and **marketeer.**

In short, this program integrates all the different aspects of the indie author's job—production and placement, promotion and sales, profits and pleasure—into one well-honed creative enterprise.

Rather than relying on received wisdom or what works for others, *Go Creative! Business Planning for Authors* begins where you are right now and fosters flow through a program of self-awareness and self-support that puts creative balance at its heart.

By following this guided process—doing the exercises, filling in the plans, taking the associated actions—you are following a time-honored and scientifically endorsed creative process. One in which your destination is profit and progress in the future, yes, but also passion and pleasure right here, right now. And one in which your measures of success are your own self-chosen, self-defined metrics.

The big advantage of planning for me is that it enables me to relax. Knowing all aspects of my writing and publishing are receiving attention across time, I can focus on the one task I'm supposed to be doing right now.

When creative business planning becomes part of your everyday work, your days have a soothing structure that has taken charge of ensure what's most important right now is what's getting done. You get a sense of creative contentment, as you move towards what you enjoy, drop what you don't, and incrementally build your skills and your output

Quarterly Planning

Like most planning systems, the *Go Creative!* program begins with framing creative intentions and goals over the long term— typically a year, or maybe even five or ten years—then breaking these down into shorter-term intentions.

The system divides the year into four and plans around quarters. Each quarter is then divided into three months, each month into four weeks, each week into how ever many working days you want to incorporate, and each working day into hours—until you are clear about the tasks you have to do in the time available right here, right now.

Most businesses employ quarterly planning, for good reason. Planning for an entire year can give a false sense of unlimited time. Planning for as soon as possible (my favorite time-frame in the past!) creates unnecessary stress that doesn't get any done any faster. More haste, less speed, and all that.

When we embrace the quarter, we gift ourselves the chance to reassess, to reshape our plans in response to the unexpected, that always happens. The world of publishing and self-publishing is ever dynamic. By planning and reviewing each quarter, we can adapt and pivot with purpose.

As independent authors, our task is always to balance our creative dreams and visions with the practicalities of running a publishing business. Within a quarter, we can harmonize these dual roles, and find a structured rhythm that suits our moods and modes.

As indie authors, we wear many hats, as we shall address below. By mapping our quarter, we can best manage our time and energy, effectively attending to each role in a planned way and setting clear markers along our creative path.

As we review our progress, discover gaps, and if necessary, adjust our course – we gain clarity and confidence that grows us, as it grows our publishing business. That sense of progress itself becomes a spark that keeps the flame of motivation alive.

In my experience most authors are reluctant to plan but when they do, they quickly come to enjoy how planning harnesses their creative flow into the structure it needs, so they can steadily increase influence, impact, and income over time, enjoying each step of the way.

Planning Questions

The program is ongoing, and you can step into any plan at any point. It is set up around three planners: a starter plan, a quarterly review, and a monthly map. Each is centered on your own creativity, your own definition of success, and your personal passions as an author and publisher. Each encourages you to go deep and harness your creative capacity, so you can achieve more by doing less.

Four key questions ignite and drive the *Go Creative!* plan:

- Where am I now? Review.
- Where do I want to be? Intention.
- How am I going to get there? Explain, explore, experiment.
- How will I know I've arrived? Measure.

Where are you now? Begin with a review of the previous year. What unique value did you bring to readers? What is it about your books that make them valuable to another person? The value of fiction and poetry can be subtle, but valuable nonetheless. Are you on the right track? Do you want to keep on keeping on or to shake things up? Consider the strengths and weaknesses, opportunities and threats your author-business faces right now.

DO THIS: Comparable Authors: *Compile or update your list of comparable authors and think about your own work compared to theirs — not in any hierarchical way, but at the level of offering:*

What do they offer the engaged reader?

How does that compare to what you're offering?

What's not out there that you feel compelled to write?

What can you learn from their book descriptions, covers, and reviews?

What's new or trending in your genre?

Where do you want to be? What are your creative intentions for the year ahead? What goals will best feed your personal passion, mission, and values, at this time? What outcomes will be most likely to deliver the profit you'd like to make, the reach you'd like to have in your genre and niche? What processes will feed those outcomes while also nurturing you, so that your success can be sustainable?

How are you going to get there? What do you need to do in the next year to achieve what you want to achieve—not just in writing, but also in your publishing, in your author-business? Plan the tools and technology you'll use to achieve your goals as well as the publishing team you'll need to support you (editors, designers, formatters, assistants). Commit to investing in your books and your business, with an expectation of a return on that investment.

Think about the optimal blend of books and other products you can create to produce the most profit while most deeply satisfying your creative passions.

TRY THIS: Creative and Commercial Processes.

What creative conditions do you need to set up for yourself? How will you organize your time and space?

What practices will you adopt to further strengthen your strengths and mitigate your weaknesses?

Who do you need to help you? Editors? Designers? Marketers? Administration assistance? What about other resources?

How much time and money will you need to invest? What sort of return can you realistically expect?

Keep things as simple as possible while you plan how to optimally harness your time, money, and resources. Slow down and take it easy. Be realistic and be kind to yourself. Pushing, forcing, harassing ourselves—these usually have the opposite effect to what you intend. Little and often is the most creative way to go.

How will you know when you've arrived? You'll be measuring. You now have your particular, personal definition of success, passion, mission and purpose. And you also have the four key indicators of a healthy author-publishing business—productivity, platform, profits, and personal satisfaction—that we referred to back at the beginning of the book, in Chapter 3 "Your Definition of Success".

These are universal measures of success, common to all indie authors.

The creative business planning program ahead uses all four measures, and keeps bringing you back to them again and again, particularly to the fourth and most important measure—your CHQ. Your self-chosen, self-identified, self-assessed creative happiness.

The two outer measures—productivity and profit—tell us *how much* we're creating, while the two inner measures—purpose and personal satisfaction—connect us to *how* we're creating.

Measuring success as an indie author isn't just about sales numbers or recognition. It's a mix of tangible results and intangible satisfactions. The outer measures like productivity and profit are essential for sustainability and the inner measures of purpose and personal satisfaction are essential for creativity. Understanding and balancing these measures keeps us moving while ensuring we enjoy the ride.

It's good to have an end in mind, but in the end what counts most for a creative is how we travel.

———

25

PAY YOURSELF FIRST

Key to publishing success is setting up your enterprise up in such a way that you get paid, from the start. I'm talking here about the income that goes to you, as opposed to your business. You have separated your business and personal money into freestanding accounts, haven't you? If not, that is your first task as an effective publisher.

It's a legal requirement that all your income from your writing and publishing goes into one business account, from which you draw your own personal payment. The time to start paying yourself is not "when it becomes affordable", but as soon as you earn your very first dollars from publishing.

If you're like many authors, you may be thinking: "I can't pay myself until I have some money left over from my expenses." Not true. No matter how little you are earning, you need to start paying yourself first.

PAY YOURSELF FIRST

Pay yourself first (PYF) is a well-known financial practice recommended for personal as well as business money management—

paying money into your own bank account before you do any other spending. As a financial axiom, PYF was coined and circulated in the 1920s by indie author George Samuel Clason.

Clason mostly published maps and handbooks. His most successful work, for which he is still remembered a century on, was a series of financial self-help books with names like *Seven Cures for a Lean Purse* and *The Five Laws of Gold*. In these books, he used the power of story to deliver financial advice, through a collection of parables supposedly first spun 4,097 years before in ancient Babylon. In 1930, he collected his core parables into the self-published title: *The Richest Man in Babylon*[1], a book which has sold more than two million copies in 26 languages.

Arkad, the proclaimed richest man in Babylon, posited that paying yourself first was the quickest way to "start thy purse to fattening". Clason expressed the axiom in less Babylonian terms in an interview with his local newspaper: "Part of all you earn must be yours to keep" and recommended putting aside a percentage of income earned before paying anyone else.

When I first heard the PYF principle many moons ago, I was struggling financially, running a creative enterprise that had plenty of business but poor cashflow and low profits. Sadly, it was many years after I first heard the advice when I put these principles to work. I urge you now to set it up for yourself, as soon as you possibly can. It is core to your creative business success.

For an indie author running a self-publishing enterprise, PYF means dividing the money that arrives into your business (at the point of entry), taking care of tax obligations and diverting some of it into your a profit and personal bank account, immediately.

Most writers do it the other way round. Paying themselves any sort of a salary, never mind dividends and a pension plan, feels impossible. "I'll pay myself when I make enough money," they say, but their business expenses forever expand to fill the money available in their income account. Payday never dawns.

The conventional formula for working out your business profits is usually expressed as income minus expenses and taxes equals profit.

my business revenue
- [minus]
my business expenses and taxes
= [equals]
my profit, from which I take my salary

In this formulation, profit is what's left over after you take away the costs of running your business from your business income. From that profit, you then pay your salary, dividends and pension.

This is of course true, and it's fine for your accountant to think of it like this, but it creates problems for the creative business owner who lives by this formula. If you wait until you see what's left after all the expenses and taxes have been paid, you'll find there's never enough for you to receive a suitable salary, never mind see a profit. This is so common an experience for indie authors that I'd say it's inevitable, if you start from there.

So the invitation here is to begin by turning that formulation around.

my profit, from which I take my salary
= [equals]
my business revenue
- [minus]
my business expenses and taxes

It might seem to you that there's no difference and mathematically, yes, you're right, but everything changes when you think about ensuring there's enough profit to pay yourself first. It's our old friend creative intention at work.

YOUR PROFIT INTENTION

Before you take any action, get clear in your intention to run a profitable publishing business. Declare that you want to make a profit sufficient to pay yourself a salary, cover your tax bills (business and personal), and have enough money to comfortably cover your business expenses and grow its resources. That's what a successful business looks like.

The action that supports this intention is paying yourself first. It's like putting the oxygen mask on yourself first in an aeroplane, before you take care of a child or other dependent. If you're feeding money to your business before yourself, sooner or later you are going to find you've choked yourself off. Your business needs you to be in good shape if it is to survive and thrive.

My recommendation is that you have a primary revenue and expenses account (cashflow account) into which you put all your business income, from all sources. Much of this money is not yours. From it, you must pay taxes and expenses, for starters, but using the PYF method, the first person you pay is you.

Twice a month (I do it on the 5th and 20th), divide all income that arrived into your cashflow account four ways, allocating pre-decided percentages into:

- Your personal profit account
- Your tax account,
- Your salary account
- Your revenue/expenses account

You deposit the percentage of income that you've decided to allocate to each of the three accounts. In the PYF method, you start wherever you are right now. This is possible because you're not allocating fixed amounts, but percentages.

No matter how small a payment to you is, it can be divided by percentage. There is a saying in business circles: "If you can't manage £1,000, you won't be able to manage £10,000." Paying yourself first gets you into the habit of putting your money aside no matter how much or how little you're earning.

Next month, you'll do better. When you pay yourself first, you show yourself with a twice-monthly action that you mean business, rather than telling yourself what you want with words in your head.

Show don't tell has as much resonance here as it does in your book. You are giving your money attention, twice a month, and where attention goes, energy flows.

Too many authors give money attention only to bemoan their lack of it. Getting in the PYF habit instead will make all the difference between taking the actions that create a functioning business and running yourself into a wall.

Once you adopt the PYF method, you see how much your cashflow account *actually* has to cover your publishing expenses. The pressure to find the money for everything you need to pay out clarifies your business decisions. It's acting as-if, in a real and very practical way.

Bank Accounts

The PYF method requires you to have four separate bank accounts and to check in with these accounts twice a month, in order to allocate your percentages.

DO THIS: Set up or connect four bank accounts.

1. Revenue and Expenses (RevEX) Account. This account will see the most movement. Make it a business account that is separate from your personal income account, and keep it current for ease of money movement.

2. Salary Account:You already have a personal account, which you use for personal expenses. You pay your salary in there.

3. Tax Hold Account: Savings account for taxes only.

4. Profit Hold Account: Savings account for profit only (Dividends).

QUESTIONS ABOUT PYF

What Percentages Should I Pay Over?

As you build your business, it will go through various stages—startup, expansion, maturity, and sometimes maybe even a decline. Depending on the stage of your business and your personal circumstances, the size of the percentages you allocate will vary.

The biggest variable is whether you are fully dependent on your business income for survival. A lot of authors have day jobs or spouses who sponsor them. For those who don't, these questions are more acute. Good accounting software can help you work out how much you can afford to pay yourself. It can also help you keep track of expenses and calculate profit.

PYF isn't about gross amounts, it's about percentages. Set a target percentage to come out of whatever money you earn this month for allocation e.g. 40% RevEx, 30% salary, 15% profit, 15% tax. Depending on your tax allowances, that figure may need to be higher, in which case your salary and profit percentages would be reduced.

What's the Profit Account for?

Your profit is paid as dividend income, over and above your salary, and the percentage you allocate will depend on the stage of your business.

The difference between the salary you pay yourself, as a beginning author-publisher, and the salary you'd be entitled to on the open market is "sweat equity"—your investment of your time and energy into your author business. This makes you an investor in your business, and an investor expects a return on investment.

As your business grows and becomes more profitable, you will in time be able to take more money out of your business versus receiving a market-related salary. That's your reward for all your earlier efforts (your sweat equity) when you didn't take a market-related wage.

Why Every Two Weeks?

Why not monthly, or weekly, or as needed? By allocating your accounts and paying your invoices twice monthly you get the benefits of batching, which is more efficient. It also allows you to stay in touch with your accounts at a rate in which you can see what's really going on with cash flow.

It's the perfect balance between constant checking, which wastes time, and doing it too rarely to pick up on trends. I do mine on the 5th and 20th of each month, and the *Go Creative! Business Planning* PDFs use those dates too.

How Accurate Do I Have to Be?

Rough numbers are fine; round down to the nearest five. This is not accountancy. As a business owner, you will have an accountant, maybe also a bookkeeper, who will take care of the actual figures. What PYF is about is your relationship with money.

Can I Automate?

You can certainly automate a small percentage of your income to go automatically into your various accounts but the system is also designed to harness the power of intention and attention. You make the intention to pay yourself first, then you check in with your money twice a month and allocate the percentages you've agreed.

Whatever you need to do to scale up, become profitable, or increase cashflow will emerge. You will know what actions to take, simply because you checked in. Just doing that keeps you in touch with the money movement in your business and strengthens your relationship with money.

What do you mean by Relationship with Money?

So many authors are locked into a relationship with money that is draining and unhealthy. They don't feel good about their income or their money management.

It's not surprising. We've all been exposed to highly conflicting philosophies around wants and needs, wealth and money. On one hand, we have Western materialism, a culture that has turned every human impulse into a commodity. It has at its core a multi-billion advertising and entertainment industry entirely devoted to reinforcing and expanding our wants: "Just buy this new skirt/car/house/yacht/island and you'll be happy…"

This materialist culture is spreading across the planet, nudging aside traditional and religious definitions of wealth. Yet these religious notions still hold powerful sway, even in rampantly consumerist societies. Christianity, for example, has long denounced most desire as sinful: according to its teachings, it is easier for a camel to get through the eye of a needle than a rich man to get into heaven. Apparently, the "camel" came from an error made in translating from Hebrew and the correct translation is "rope", so the saying in fact is: it is easier for a rope to get through the eye of a needle than a rich man– or woman–to get into Heaven, but one word or the other, we get the message. Buddhist philosophy holds that attachment to our desires is the cause of all our suffering and that to be enlightened is to transcend wants.

As well as religious pronouncements, we have the evidence of the war, famine and environmental blight caused in our world by the untrammeled pursuit of money. We live within the historical legacy of previous generation's financial greed: colonization, slavery, religious and nationalist strife. We hear daily in our media news of financial corruption and fraud at home and abroad. We regularly see the effect of financial compromise in the faces and statements of our business "leaders" and politicians–and it's not a pretty sight.

Alongside all this, a new voice has recently added another contribution: New Age philosophies that claim we can have anything we desire, without limit, if we are open enough to that possibility.

That idea has great appeal because no matter what our priests or monks say about denial, self-sacrifice or attachment, no matter what we see or read of financial excesses or corruptions, it doesn't speak to that part of us that wants more.

The following are signs that your money relationship could be improved:

- You are nagged by money cares and worries.
- You have plenty of money but are obsessed with making more, without understanding why.
- You feel insecure about your future, with or without good reason.
- You are too caught up with earning a living to enjoy life.
- You lack true intimacy, spiritual connection, healthful activity, fun or creativity in your life.
- You are regularly time poor.
- You are troubled by unarticulated feelings of lack.
- You feel like you never have, and never will have, enough.

The more broke you are or the more financially vulnerable you feel, the more you need to do this money-relationship work.

Just as you have date nights with your spouse to keep the relationship in a happy place, investing time in your relationship with money pays real dividends in terms of two of your key success measures as an indie author: profit and personal happiness.

Why Am I Resisting?

When I propose PYF, the response I get most often from indie authors is: my business isn't profitable yet, I need to wait until I turn a profit. But that's the wrong way around. Your business will become profitable if you pay yourself first. An author business that doesn't have the pressure of needing to earn a salary will take ten years to succeed instead of two.

Like most things—healthy eating, regular exercise, daily meditation —PYF is very simple to do, but not always easy to follow. If you find months are going by without a check-in, you are in resistance and need to explore what's going on, at a deeper level.

As a creative, you can't eliminate resistance, it's part of the process, but you can acknowledge it and, when you see it for what it is, use various practices to dissolve it.

Begin planning and measuring your publishing profits with my Creative Business Planners for Authors, available for purchase in our bookstore: SelfPublishingAdvice.org/bookshop.

---

1. GS Clason. (1930) *The Richest Man in Babylon.*

26

GROWTH, RESISTANCE AND BLOCK

A s you plan your creative expansion and set about putting your plans into action, you will meet resistance. This is inevitable, part of the process, and not a personal weakness or a sign that you should give up.

When you're stretching yourself, aiming to do something new and different, something no one's ever made before, something that comes out of the core of who you are, part of us feels excited and expansive but another part feels fearful and resistant. Resistance held strongly, or for a long time, turns to block.

Self-publishing authors need to understand the dynamics of resistance, block, and flow as they are constantly playing out for us, sometimes in conflicting ways, in our publishing as well as our writing.

The Pain of Creative Block

The poet Samuel Taylor Coleridge gave us literature's most famous lines about writer's block when he confessed to his notebook the "indefinite, indescribable Terror" that was his everyday experience and its sorrowful, shameful outcome:

"... A whole year passed, with scarcely the fruits of a month—O Sorrow and Shame ... I have done nothing!"

When a friend, tiring of this artistic angst, tried to get him to rouse himself, and quit the opium to which he was becoming addicted, the poet gave his famous description of the psychic helplessness of the blocked creative:

Go bid a man paralytic in both arms rub them briskly together, and that will cure him. 'Alas!' he would reply: 'that I cannot move my arms is my complaint'.[1]

When we are in resistance, we are stopped by the tug-of-war between our creative expansive energy and our resistant, contractive energy. Sometimes, especially if we do a lot of busy-work, we may not even notice that we are in resistance and blocked.

Writing and Publishing Resistance

Creative resistance and block can manifest in subtle ways. Consider the following syndromes and see which, if any, apply to you.

Don't Know: You don't know what to write or publish next, or where you might even start. You probably spend a lot of time reading or watching other authors' successes but are unable to get moving on yours. You just don't know how to write a book, or if you have a completed manuscript, you don't know how to set about publishing it.

Can't-Get-Going: You *do* know what you want to do. You may even know your ideal readers and your personal definition of success, you may have even identified your micro-niche but, for some reason, you can't seem to get going. You look at those who are doing well in your genres or categories and wonder how they do it. How could you ever have this person's energy, that person's ingenuity? How could you dare to think you might come close to their achievement? The chasm between their gift and yours swallows all your hopes. You feel self-conscious, perhaps inadequate, or even unworthy.

Fizzled Out: You've had a success or two of which you are proud. It wasn't as good as you hoped, but not as bad as you feared, and you learned a lot for next time. Except next time isn't happening. You're stuck in the dawning realization of the challenges—the gap between where you are and where you want to be. Perhaps you're obsessing about the bits that didn't work. Perhaps conditions have changed, or you've hit a personal obstacle. Perhaps your creative intention was the first project, or getting your business started, and you never looked beyond that.

Stop/Start: You have fertile periods and long stretches where you produce very little. Ebb is, of course, the natural response to flow, but your downtime is not natural rhythm or good creative rest. It's a dry spell, and you're experiencing it not as replenishment but as exhaustion, indolence, procrastination, accompanied by Coleridge's "indefinite, indescribable" anxiety. Or else a sense of flatness. You might be working, but not well. You may have folders full of half-finished work. You may be spending your time on distractions, or the wrong work, or overworking something rather than getting it done. You may be wasting creative time on social media, or in front of the telly, or hitting the vodka or opium. One way or another, it's more stop than start.

Underdeveloped: You're producing books, but they are weak or incomplete. This is not down to neglecting the work. You might be driving yourself at a fierce pace, but there is a disjunction between the work produced and the original vision, an inability to go deep or open up. It might be a laziness of spirit, emotion, or intellect. You might need more craft skills. You might be copying others, second-guessing the market, or people pleasing. Whatever the cause, you're not achieving what you could and should, given your creative intentions, and you know it. The signs are the horrible queasiness you feel when you think about your work, poor sales, poor feedback, or poor reviews.

Shadow Career: You're spending a lot of time in another job that's closely related to writing and publishing. Maybe teaching, freelance writing or a desk job in a publishing house. You may have been drawn in by external rewards, like money, prestige or power, but haven't managed to balance the benefits with your passion projects and are dissatisfied or frustrated with your days.

Overloader: You've taken on too many commitments, or you have too many ideas fighting each other, or you're overwhelmed by incoming demands. You're bouncing around a thousand opportunities, options, and obligations, and heading for burnout from working too hard for too long. Deadlines pass, you let people (and yourself) down, stress and a nagging feeling of anxiety are your constant companions.

The self-publisher failing to produce or sell books feels every bit as disillusioned, disappointed, and despairing as Coleridge felt about his failure to produce poems. They too go about their days in the grip of an "indefinite, indescribable" fear. Everything feels like a struggle. They know there must be a better way but don't know how to find it. They come to bogus conclusions about the marketplace—"Self-published books don't sell". Or they blame themselves in ways that describe the problem as a personal, fatal flaw: "I'm no good at figures.", "I hate marketing.", "I can't master social media.", "I don't do data.", or "I'm a fool to have borrowed that money".

Some respond by putting *everything* into their work. They sacrifice personal life, press not just nose but heart and soul to the grindstone, and give it all they've got, thinking that if they work hard and hold out long enough, some day they'll cut a break that will wipe away the worry, the debt, the stress. Others slip into stasis. Production all but stops. In between are those who are spinning their wheels, reading all the blogs and books, trying one thing and then another, but producing rarely, in fits and starts.

As writing and publishing are a series of complex processes, you may have more than one kind of resistance or block, operating at the same time in different parts of your process.

None of this means you've made a mistake in wanting to be a successful self-publishing author—that you haven't "got what it takes", or that you're a has-been who's been left behind by tech or other advances. Every single one of us has been there. Creative blocks are a fundamental part of the creative process. Uncovering, understanding, and unlocking them is how we expand and grow.

Recognizing Resistance, Being With Block

When it comes to resistance and block, practical advice doesn't help. Drugs don't help, as Coleridge discovered. The tricks of your trade, the skills of your craft, the artistry of your art, none of these help. So, what does?

Some writers recommend discipline. In his book, *Turning Pro*, Steven Pressfield calls out resistance as the enemy of every creative.

"Resistance's goal is not to wound or disable," he says. Resistance aims to kill. "It will kill you like cancer… to achieve its agenda, which is to prevent you from actualizing your [creative] self."

Pressfield's books have been highly influential in creative circles and contain much wisdom, but his war metaphor is dangerous for many. Yes, there are times when getting things done is a matter of discipline but for every action, there is an equal and opposite reaction. Push and you get pushback. Whatever we try to suppress and control bounces back up, twice as strong. To fight resistance can strengthen and entrench it.

I prefer to work with the understanding that, as the Irish poet Mary O'Malley puts it, "what's in the way *is* the way".

What's in the way, more often than not, is some form of fear.

CREATIVE FEAR

Three particular fears that need to be understood by any indie author embarking on the business of succeeding as a publisher.

1. Fear of failure
2. Fear of success
3. Fear of the creative process itself—also known as fear of change

1. Fear of Failure

It is true that there is no such thing as failure for the creative entrepreneur, but there is certainly such a thing as the fear of failure. When we fear failure, we sabotage ourselves, in an attempt to mitigate how bad we might end up feeling should we fail to meet our goals.

Fear of failure comes from the core of our egos, our identities, our self-esteem, and our feelings of emotional wellbeing. Giving into it doesn't have the desired effect of protecting yourself. It actually makes us feel worse about ourselves. And it makes us more fearful again, next time out.

Some signs of fear of failure:

- You worry about what other people think about you if you don't get it right: whether they'll laugh, or be disappointed, or no longer be interested in you.
- The thought of failing makes you over-analyze your skills, your ideas, your right to do what you want to do. How smart or capable are you, really?
- You lower expectations in advance, telling people beforehand why you don't expect to succeed.
- When something goes wrong, you have trouble imagining what you could have done differently or how to correct course.
- You get physical symptoms such as headaches, stomach aches, or other ailments that prevent you from doing your work or preparing properly for an important event.
- You get distracted by tasks that, in hindsight, were not urgent, though they seemed to be at the time.
- You procrastinate until you "run out of time".
- You aim low.

We get frustrated with ourselves when we "fail". But recognizing this fear is important, as is knowing that some degree of fear can ignite our creativity. What happens when you start to turn a doorknob that won't budge? You know if you fail, you are stuck. You might take a moment to absorb the fear or scold yourself for your negligence. Then, you turn to the doorknob again, twisting it harder. Perhaps you pull up on the knob or push it down. When that fails, you might wiggle it. Eventually, you shove the door with your shoulder, or kick it with your foot, or… What you try will be a combination of your experience, your creative inclinations, and the conditions of the moment. But your fear of being stuck had you creatively problem solving. And your creativity is what gave you the idea that blew the door wide open.

In creative mode, failure and rejection can be accepted, even *welcomed*. To want to create something is to acknowledge that we have, so far, failed to have it. Going through "no" is the spark that highlights your path to "yes".

> **DO THIS:** *Make a list of the times you felt the fear of failure and tried to protect yourself, ultimately injuring your chances of achieving what you'd set out to do. F-r-e-e-write what the task was, what you did to protect yourself, why you did it, and why you thought you would fail.*
>
> **TRY THIS: Foster More Fails**: *To accelerate creative flow, deliberately put yourself in difficult (but physically safe!) situations—real and imagined.*

---

2. Fear of Success

If success isn't coming to you, despite your best efforts, there may be a part of you that is, subconsciously but very deliberately, keeping success at bay. Unlike a fear of making mistakes or not meeting expectations, fear of achieving success is rooted in ideas about the changes that come with success.

Each of us has an internal compass that guides our success, a "success-setting" that determines how much income, impact and influence we currently allow ourselves. It's held in place by our beliefs about how much we can achieve, and the risks and downfalls that success might bring. If our creative activity looks likely to break through our current success-setting, we can become uneasy and retreat back to where we feel safer and more comfortable.

This is fine, unless we have a creative intention that requires us to expand our success-setting. In that case, we need to challenge our beliefs about what constitutes success. A common idea is that success will make you arrogant or dislikeable, or separate you from others whom you love; friends, family or community who might be awed or alienated.

Some signs of fear of success:

- You talk about what you are going to do more than what you do or have done.
- You aim too high: every goal's a stretch goal.

- You work hard on several projects at once, not focusing deeply enough on one.
- Your work is never quite good enough for you.
- You say you'll get started on your real work once you've more qualifications/experience/contacts.
- You have competing definitions of success.
- You're vague about goals and outcomes.
- You don't complete your projects.
- Whenever you're on the verge of success, things start to "go wrong".

The very concept of success may trigger feelings of inadequacy, anxiety, and self-doubt which lead to self-sabotage or avoidance of risk. Take some time to reflect on what beliefs you hold about success that may be holding you back.

Write them down and ask yourself if they are really true. How do you know they are true? What would happen if you didn't believe that belief?

Imagine yourself succeeding in whatever you are working towards. Visualization can help you build confidence and reduce fear, as can surrounding yourself with people who believe in you and your definition of success.

3. Fear of Creativity

When I teach a planning workshop, my first challenge is to get each member of the group comfortable enough—with me, with my teaching style, with the space we're in, with the other people in the room—so that creative breakthrough can be facilitated. Sometimes there's someone who just can't go with the flow. They shuffle, squirm, and balk at, or refuse to do the tasks. They may verbally protest with statements like: "This is too stupid", or "I really don't have time for this kind of thing", or "You need to grow up". Often, they let their raised eyebrows or passive-aggressive slouching say what they think. On more than one occasion, I've had personal abuse hurled at me. And too at individuals in the class who'd been visibly enjoying the activities.

Of course, we all have different styles, and creativity is very personal, but the *anger* is the giveaway. Where there's anger, there's fear.

What's feared here is the change that creativity always requires. The person wants to change, otherwise they wouldn't have signed up for the class, but they also fear the change they long for.

Some signs of fear of creativity:

- You find people who self-identify as creative (hipster types) irritating.
- You don't like talking about your creative work, you're not that big-headed, entitled or delusional.
- You keep busy-busy and don't take time to go deep.
- You've been working on books that haven't gone anywhere for years.
- You say things like: "Not everyone can do or be what they want".

Fear of creativity arises from anxiety and self-doubt. It's the fear of being judged or criticized, or of not living up to one's own expectations.

Overcoming our fears—of failure, of success, of creativity itself—requires recognizing and challenging these fears, developing a creative mindset, and taking small steps towards one's creative goals.

Creative Mindset

A creative mindset fosters positive growth. It recognizes the power of creative process. It allows us to work creatively, rather than pushing us to work hard.

Opening to the possibility of growth and development is the most important skill we can develop as creative writers and publishers. Then we need to do the work that takes us there.

You don't get a creative mindset just by saying so. You have to do something. It's natural to fear going public with our ideas. It makes us feel vulnerable, like walking down a city street stripped of our clothes and a layer of skin. But we do it. And once we do it often enough, what would be a momentous experience for somebody else—including younger you—becomes everyday.

What do we do then but push our boundaries further? Head off in a new direction that's just as, or even more, scary. Take off another layer.

We fear exposure, yes, but we also desire it. We want to be naked to ourselves as well as to others. The urge to create is a move towards our own emotional and spiritual expansion. The most courageous and expansive part of ourselves knows this. It integrates the concerns and cares of our more fearful, conservative, emotional selves.

This is not about setting up an internal battle with yourself. Be seen versus hide away; reveal all versus reveal nothing. Neither is it about finding a middle ground. It's about allowing your contractive self to voice its concerns (that's one of the many functions of f-r-e-e-writing). All the parts of you—the conceptual, the caring, the creative—want the same thing, for you to be happy and fulfilled. It's just that they have different ideas about how to get there and what's best for you.

You don't have strong thoughts and feelings for no reason. Your fears want to protect you and keep you safe. But you cannot expand by suppressing a part of yourself or cutting it away. What looks like resistance and self-sabotage is always an internal conversation that needs to happen.

TRY THIS: Fears of Publishing and Creative Business

F-r-e-e-write about your fear of failure, of success, of creativity itself, particularly in relation to publishing and business. What are your fears trying to tell you? How do you integrate them with your drive to expand and grow? What are your next steps?

Resources

If you need more support, I run a private online program, including a monthly workshop, based around the concepts and exercises in this book for a small group of **Planning for Profit patrons**. You can join this program (places permitting) on Patreon: Patreon.com / ornaross

Find out more here: Selfpublishingadvice.org / workshops /

---

1. Samuel Taylor Coleridge. 1815. Biographia Literaria.

27

FINDING CREATIVE FLOW
INTEGRATE AND BALANCE

One of the most important things a creative business planning program can do is help you achieve creative balance. Every creative business needs to find the balance between profit and pleasure, collaboration and solitude, drafting and deepening, and other aspects of the creative process.

If a challenge is too difficult, we get frustrated; if it is too easy, we get bored. Flow rises from that place of optimum balance between ability and challenge.

As an indie author, you are responsible for all the aspects of the publishing process: writing, editing, designing, formatting, distribution, marketing, promotion and selling rights. You must balance your creative vision and artistic integrity with the need to make your book appealing to readers and understand the market for your genre.

Should you do another round of self-editing or move to hiring a professional editor? Answer: balance. Should you do your own book advertising, or should you spend money on a service? Answer: balance. Should you focus on your current readers or chase new ones? Answer: balance. Should you innovate new products or focus on selling the existing ones? Answer: balance. Should you keep your profits or reinvest in promotion? Answer: balance.

What balance looks like, in these and other situations, will be unique to you, and your current writing and publishing situation: the stage of the project and your emotional state. And it's ever-changing. Creative balance is a moment-by-moment endeavor. You may be in a state of flow and producing pages of high-quality work one moment, but the next, feel uninspired and blocked.

It sounds impossible but the key to achieving balance is good planning and good creative practice. This chapter explores these two key aspects for authors: balancing your creative work, rest and play; and planning your work in a way that creates balance between the three hats you must wear.

This is not just about managing day-to-day creative challenges. When you work from balance, harmony, and integration, that energy imprints itself on your work. The resulting simplicity, unity and clarity generates writing that deeply resonates with your readers and stands out in our crowded marketplace.

Creative balance can also help a self-publisher develop a unique brand identity that is deeply reflective of their writing vision and values.

Balancing Creative Work, Rest and Play

Anyone who is consciously creating anything soon realizes that the best ideas surface more often during rest and play time, not when at work. Without sufficient rest and play time, creativity dries up. When we take time and space to explore and experiment, rest and relax in the right ways, creative flow ensues.

Our consciousness expands, our awareness deepens, and we come into the presence of what Albert Einstein described as the most beautiful emotion we can experience, the underlying power that advances art and science. For centuries, it was thought that such qualities were the innate gifts of a special elite. Now neuroscience is showing through brain mapping that such qualities are available to all who engage in the right kind of activities: creative rest and play.

Creative rest is any activity that rests the thinking mind e.g. sleep, retreats, down time vacations, all forms of meditation. It is fostered by solitude, silence, and space. Many studies confirm that *mindfulness* (consciously immersing yourself completely in this moment), and other forms of *meditation* (using any point of mental focus to still the mind), are particularly effective in fostering flow.

Creative play is any activity that is freely chosen and is your idea of fun e.g. swings, comedy, puzzles, flirting, cartwheels, dressing-up, daydreaming, games, coloring. Creative play that optimizes flow state includes *childlike play* like dressing-up or coloring or particular kinds of *aerobic exercise*—jogging, walking, swimming, dancing—that are repetitive and rhythmic.

Neuroscience has revealed why creative rest and play feel so good, showing the rush of feel-good hormones and connective neurotransmitters that are released when a brain moves into the create-state. In that state, a shift happens within. Our self-censor and inner critic are silenced. Creative solutions rise and present themselves to us, unbidden. We learn more easily, perform at a higher level, see patterns, make connections, gain perspective.

The inspiration, intuition, and insight that are surfaced by creative rest and play are the qualities that mark out the good writer and publisher from the average, the great writer and publisher from the good.

Creative rest and play are most beneficial when we're intentional around them, when we relish the contrast with our work and recognize their value, rather than thinking we should be doing something more "productive".

That's why effective creative business planning must include time for rest and play, alongside creative work. Rest and play are not breaks from the creative process. They *are* the process.

CONSIDER THIS: *Are you making time for creative rest and play in your weekly and daily routine?*

BALANCING CREATIVE WORK: THREE HATS

Another principle of effective business planning for authors is recognizing the three roles we must play, best described as **Maker, Manager,** and **Marketeer**.

As an indie author, you must balance the time and effort you spend on writing and editing your book with the time and effort you spend on marketing, promoting, sales and licensing. Writing takes a significant amount of time and energy, and it's vital to spend sufficient time on editing and polishing your work so that it's as good as you can get it, before you publish it. It's easy to become so focused on getting the words down, or so focused on getting the books sold, that you neglect other important aspects of the publishing process.

When we wear the three hats of maker, manager, and marketeer, we perceive more clearly what the job of being an indie author actually asks of us, day by day, week by week, month by month. In order to understand and integrate these three roles, let's first separate them out by imagining ourselves donning and doffing the hat for each role.

- You put on your **Maker Hat** for the work you do *in* your business, making the products you sell and the materials that help you to sell them. Your key Maker task is *production* —writing words and creating books and other products from those words. You may also make audio and video as part of your creative mission and to promote your books.
- You put on your **Marketeer Hat** for the work you do to *grow* your business, as you pitch, publicize, and partner with others to reach more readers and sell more books. Your key Marketeer task is *promotion*—attracting readers with compelling content and communications that bring them to buy.

- You put on your **Manager Hat** for the work you do *on* your business: as you harness time and money, tools and team into making and selling your products. Your key Manager task is *processing*—actioning, organizing, improving, maximizing.

Mapping our creative intentions under the three hats shows us just how disparate the different aspects of our work are and, most importantly, how they all hang together. It all begins to make more sense.

Not understanding how these different roles operate and work together, seeing ourselves primarily as writers, or even as writers who publish, is a common reason why indie authors get stuck.

Let's look more closely at how your Maker, Manager, and Marketeer think—what they believe, how they spend time, what they need to watch out for, and what they most want.

The Indie Author Maker

Your Inner Maker works *in* the business. Wearing this hat, you are a creative artist overseeing *writing and publishing craft*. As Maker, you believe that finding and keeping readers happy is a matter of creating great books.

For Maker, the job is to write the best possible words and produce the best possible books and other products. Maker has three kinds of craft work:

1. Producing the words and the books and other products that you sell.

2. Producing marketing content like blurbs, press releases, explainers, trailers, adverts.

3. Working with editors and designers on publishing craft decisions.

- **Fears**: Maker fears that they are not a good enough writer or publisher to succeed.
- **Focus:** Maker is focused inwards.

- **Money:** Maker prefers not to think about money except for believing that someday they'll "make it".
- **Quote:** Maker's motto is: *"If you build it, they will come."* [1]
- **Success:** Maker defines success in terms of productivity.
- **Time:** Maker's time frame is *now*. "What I produce today could change everything tomorrow." Maker pushes the pace, feeling there's never enough time to make all they want to make.
- **Wants:** Maker craves the solitude and space to create.
- **Blocker**: The "I'm creative, not commercial" duality; blaming others, or conditions, for lack of creativity or production; thinking books sell themselves if they're "good enough"; forgetting about money until the need becomes critical; neglecting or even disdaining the need for management, money, or marketing.

For Maker, the creative question is: *how do I find enough time and creative space to make my stuff?*

The Indie Author Marketeer

The Marketeer works to grow the business. Wearing this hat, you are a creative communicator, overseeing *pitches, publicity,* and *partnerships*. As Marketeer, you believe finding and keeping happy customers is about getting sales and getting read.

For Marketeer, the job is to turn ideas and products into impact and influence.

- **Fears:** Marketeer fears all of Maker's craft and productivity will go unseen and unrewarded.
- **Focus:** Marketeer is focused outwards, on partnerships and publicity that enable the books to be more findable and widely disseminated.
- **Money:** For Marketeer, money is a measure of whether the books are reaching enough readers.
- **Quote:** Marketeer's motto is: *"The reader is King."* CJ Lyons.

- **Time:** Marketeer is future based, starting with a picture of a desirable future, and then working back to the present to make the changes that will measure up to that vision.
- **Success:** For Marketeer, success is fame and fortune.
- **Wants:** Marketeer craves income, influence, and impact.
- **Blocker:** Too much focus on the market and other people's opinions. Shiny object syndrome. Brash claims and crass schemes. Forgetting that business serves life, not vice versa.

For Marketeer, the creative question is: *how do I reach more readers and sell more books?*

The Indie Author Manager

Your Inner Manager works on your publishing business. Wearing this hat, you are a creative director overseeing *time, money,* and *energy.* As Manager, you believe that finding and keeping readers happy is a matter of getting pricing, features, availability, and support right, and having good problem-solving processes for when things go wrong.

For Manager, the job is to integrate money and mission, passion and profits into a sustainable, scalable business. The features of the business itself, not just the products it makes, are what's important.

- **Fears:** Manager fears Maker and Marketer will run the business into trouble if not attentively directed.
- **Focus:** Manager takes a holistic view. They see the business as a system that should deliver commercial profit and creative pleasure to all involved.
- **Money:** Manager thinks of money as foundational, funding and protecting the processes that allow Maker's production to happen, and Marketeer's growth to happen. To Manager, how money is spent, invested, or withheld is the truest statement of the business's values.
- **Quote:** Manager's motto is: *"You don't build a business. You build people and processes, and they build the business."* Zig Ziglar.

315

- **Success:** For Manager, success is running an integrated business that supports a secure and happy lifestyle.
- **Time:** Manager thinks about the past and your demonstrated capacity. What's been achieved so far is the best indicator of what's to come. Manager's pace is measured.
- **Wants:** Manager craves order, safety and security.
- **Beware:** joylessness, anxiety, rigidity. Over reliance on data. Underestimating the power of creative spontaneity. Being risk averse.

For Manager, the creative question is: *how do I set up and maintain processes that allow this business to succeed?*

These are the three hats you must wear as an indie author.

In your making, you communicate from your deepest experience, using your own voice, telling your own truths, being as unique and as creative as you dare to be. In your marketing, you focus on real connections with other human beings—your readers, the authors in your niche whose work you most admire, literary influencers who can take your books to more readers. In your managing, you are kind and fair to your team members, the services you use, and are considerate and true to your readers.

In all three, you draw on your creative passion and mission, your publishing values and framework, your intention to grow creatively and commercially.

Creative work can be an act of self-love, but it can also turn into the opposite: a stick to beat yourself down. The fast-paced nature of social media and publishing schedules puts authors at risk of burnout.

It's not necessary, or productive, for a creative to overwork. Working *well* rather than *hard* is what you want, which means valuing yourself and the values you offer.

At its most fundamental, this means valuing yourself and looking after your mental and physical health.

CONSIDER THIS: Valuing Yourself. *How we manage our money in our creative business is a great indicator of how much we value our work and ourselves. Do you:*

- charge enough for your products to pay your team and yourself properly? i.e. make a profit.

- focus on return-on-investment, not just costs?

- only offer free stuff as part of a marketing strategy?

- pay yourself first?

- ensure you enjoy enough creative rest and play, taking scheduled down days and fun days?

Don't worry if you're not there yet. Achieving and maintaining creative balance is a constant process of adjustment and readjustment, a dynamic act that requires presence and awareness and the ability to find inner equilibrium, no matter what crazy conditions are raging outside. This is what allows your creativity to keep flowing, and what allows you to find peace and satisfaction as you work.

Finding a balance between the different aspects of a creative business allows you to evolve and continuously improve, so you stay relevant and innovative in the constantly changing publishing landscape.

Opt for what you believe will bring the most success but know that there is no single right answer. You don't need to be perfect to do well, to be a good enough writer, to be a good enough publisher. It's okay, more than okay, to make mistakes, that's how we learn and grow. Get things right as much as you can, celebrate successes, learn from failures, and keep moving—while also being patient and enjoying the ride.

It's good to have an end in mind, but what truly matters is how we travel. Each step holds its own reward, and it greatly enriches our work if we can find that payoff, step by step. That's how we enjoy the process: we learn from our fears and failures, and continue to expand our skills and our reach.

You have a unique perspective and voice that can add something new to the literary world. Once you have taught yourself to write and publish well and identified your readers, your books have what they need to find and influence the readers you want.

On the twisty, uphill road towards the next level of writing and publishing success, let balance be your guide. You can't know what's ahead, but you do know what feels right and good, in this moment. You can trust in your intuition, in your work to date, and in the power of taking the next small step.

Let the four measures—productivity, platform, profits, and personal satisfaction—guide your next steps when you have a decision to make.

1. Productivity. How does this option fit with my writing goals and schedules? Will it introduce distractions or streamline my creative process?

2. Platform. Does this option help me to reach my particular readers more effectively, or enhance my relationships and engagements with my readers?

3. Profits. What is the potential return on investment (ROI) for this? Bearing in mind immediate costs and potential future returns, how does it align with my long-term financial goals?

4. Personal Satisfaction. Does this choice resonate with my passion and purpose as an author? Will it make me happy or lead to undue stress? The measure of personal satisfaction often serves as a tiebreaker for other measures.

None of this is easy but with fun work, serious play, and focused rest, it happens.

---

1. From the movie, *Field of Dreams*

PART VII

BRINGING IT ALL TOGETHER

The last six sections helped you lay the foundation for your creative author-business. This next part will help you begin building on this base. The following chapters talk about how authors become good publishers, the different business models and income streams for self-publishing writers, and how a product mix gives you a more sustainable foundation on which you build a publishing business. Finally, it offers some thoughts on our creative future as authors and creators.

28

BECOMING A GOOD PUBLISHER

Becoming a successful publisher is not just about knowing how to publish books in three formats. That is essential knowledge, of course, and that's what this book has concentrated on up to now. Most self-publishing guides stop there, but to succeed in a sustainable way, you need to integrate your tasks, tools, and team into a publishing business that can grow with you, as you become a more skilled writer and publisher.

Authors, like many creatives these days, are becoming business people by default. A few of us set out that way from the start, but for a lot of authors, it's a shock to realize that the day you sell your first book on one of the platforms–Amazon, Kobo, IngramSpark, wherever–you've just gone into business. Yikes!

It's especially shocking if you're the kind of author who doesn't identify as a business person. If in your mind, you are an artist author or a career author, you may have very out of date expectations about how publishing operates.

This part of the book, about running a creative business, and the next, about creative planning, aim to give you the best chance of making a living as an author in the 2020s and beyond. They aim at helping you become a good publisher and run a successful creative enterprise. Later books in this series, particularly Book 7, go into this huge subject in more detail. Here we'll be taking a top-level overview.

Through my work with ALLi, I see many indie authors working hard but not making a lot of progress. For some, their books are not selling. Others are unclear about the skills or resources they need to succeed as writers who also publish. Some are stressed or confused, overwhelmed or even despairing. Few pay themselves a decent salary.

It's a sad truth that most of the indie authors who read this book *won't* succeed. I want to be supportive and encouraging—but also realistic. Most businesses fail within the first three years. Passion-powered businesses are arguably more prone to failure than the average.

Yet many are succeeding. In Chapter 2, we outlined the inspiring successes of some indie authors, and ALLi's research into author income shows the median self-publishing income has increased by 53% over the prior year. How has this become possible? Before you embark on the practical aspects of running your own creative business enterprise, let's look at how authors came to take over publishing in this way.

THE HISTORY OF SELF-PUBLISHING

The self-publishing era began at the end of the 20th century, just when I started writing, though I—and most writers—had no awareness of it until many years later. Back then, writers worked on typewriters. Drafts were composed and edited on paper, then cut and pasted back together with amendments, to be retyped all over again. And again, for as many drafts as necessary.

Yes, young authors, there was a time when cut-and-paste meant cut with actual scissors and glue. Then along came the first word processors, making it possible to manipulate text, fix mistakes, and create page layouts on a computer screen before the pages were printed off. It saved us *hours* of time and tedium.

Alongside this magic called word processing came "desktop publishing" (DTP). Instead of having to do a big print run, you could now publish a few books at a time from your own desktop, using your own computer and printer. Enterprising authors were soon running off copies of books and pamphlets, and selling them via mail order.

The consumer DTP market exploded in 1985 with the Apple LaserWriter printer but still it was difficult for authors to make the finances work. Distribution was a major, time-consuming headache involving returns and complex invoicing, and the mainstream books world refused to engage with self-published books. Most writers preferred to focus on writing, and get a third-party to concentrate on the publishing. While some non-fiction authors set up successful businesses around desktop publishing, most steered clear.

Then in the 1990s, US company Ingram launched Lightning Source as a printer and distributor of what became known as **print-on-demand** (POD) books. While other industries had long established build-to-order businesses, it was never going to be economical to print single copies using traditional technology such as letterpress and offset printing. Now digital technology allowed printing of books in single or small quantities, at the time when the order was made. Lightning Source was set up for independent publishers but it wasn't long before authors and other micro-publishers were queuing up to be served. SelfPub1 was born.

SelfPub1 wasn't just about print, though. Most people don't realize that ebooks have been around as long as paperbacks, first surfacing in the 1930s when, after watching his first "talkie"—movie with sound— writer and impresario Bob Brown had become obsessed with what he called the "readie—"a simple reading machine which I can carry or move around, attach to any old electric light plug, and… allow readers to adjust the type size and avoid paper cuts".

Brown's ideas didn't gain traction at the time but forty years later on the 4th July 1971, author Michael Hart launched Project Gutenberg with an electronic copy of the US Declaration of Independence, typed by him into his computer, and transmitted to his colleagues on the computer network at his workplace, the University of Illinois. Others soon jumped in, producing these electronic books on their own websites for sale to readers.

Again, take-up was low. The average reader of fiction or poetry didn't delight in reading on a computer and was wary of online commerce. But in 1998, around the same time as Ingram was developing POD, the first digital bookstores and publishers on the newly popular World Wide Web emerged. Mass-market "e-paper technology" and the first ebook reader were released by Sony in 2004.

SelfPub2 arrived with a bang in 2007 when Amazon delivered a technological trifecta that changed everything for authors—the Kindle e-reader combined with KDP, a digital publishing platform that gave authors direct access to Amazon's online bookstore, the largest in the world. The Kindle was different to any previous e-reader because it came with this vast online bookstore attached. It was suddenly easy for readers to buy an ebook and download it immediately on purchase.

Amazon already had a publishing wing, and e-readers and online stores had existed before. But Kindle Direct Publishing (KDP) was not a publisher. This meant that the intellectual property rights, the source of all publishing income, were not licensed, assigned, or transferred. They remained with the author.

In addition, the business model was completely different to royalty-based publishing income. No money exchanged hands until a book was bought by the reader, then KDP took a commission on each sale. They soon added a subscription model, Kindle Unlimited, to the mix, which offered readers all-they-could-read packages for a monthly payment, and paid authors according to the number of pages read. They also bought CreateSpace (later KDP Print) for print book production and launched ACX (Audiobook Creation Exchange), as a platform for audiobook production on similar principles to KDP, and added a marketplace to facilitate authors and narrators to collaborate in audiobooks.

Other self-publishing platforms also came into the ebook marketplace around this time: Apple Books and Google Play (2010), Kobo Writing Life (2012), Nook (2013), as well as thousands of smaller publishing platforms and services around the world, and aggregator services like StreetLib (2006), Smashwords (2008), Draft2Digital (2013) and PublishDrive (2015) to service them. And Ingram, long the dominant player in print-on-demand with Lightning Source, started a division called IngramSpark, expressly for small and micro-publishers, including indie authors.

Like Amazon, none of these platforms invested in the publishing process as a trade publisher would—but neither were they licensing any intellectual property. This was the radical change at the heart of **SelfPub2**: the author, not the publishing service, became the publisher. Readers and computer algorithms became the arbitrators of what reached the top of the bestseller list.

The combined effect of digital books, online bookstores, and author empowerment turned publishing on its head. Retaining all publishing rights, authors could now reach their readers through various online retail stores in three formats: audio (audiobooks), electronic text (ebooks) and print (print books) formats. Emerging at the same time were social networking tools like Facebook and Twitter, Goodreads and Wattpad, facilitating social-media marketing. Open-source software made website building cheap and easy. Every aspect of how authors produce, market, and sell their books opened up.

SelfPub2 opened unprecedented opportunities for authors. The involvement of "big tech" companies like Amazon, Apple and Google who were, of course, no more pro-author than Manhattan and London trade-publishers, abounded opportunities. "There has never a better time to be an author" was the truism on everyone's lips even though big tech's insouciance troubled many.

Other challenges for the SelfPub2 era included vanity publishing, digital rights management (DRM), internet piracy, poor print-on-demand quality, self-publishing contract terms. Around 2018, attempts to solve these challenges, combined with more new technology, growing author empowerment and business acumen ignited the **SelfPub3** era.

SelfPub3 (formerly called Self-Publishing 3.0)

At ALLi, SelfPub3 is a concept and a campaign.

- The *concept* is that Web3 tools and technology makes it possible for authors to earn a good living from writing and publishing books.

- The *campaign* encourages each author to examine what they want to achieve with their books and to explore all their options.

Our campaign also advocates for author education about the literary and publishing sectors. Through our blog, podcast and other communications, we encourage our members and community to develop their own "real estate" on the web: websites, apps and other online creative assets that allow for direct sales, complementary income streams and patronage, alongside selling books on retailer platforms.

SelfPub3 shatters the publishing framework that many people outside the author community, and some within, still hold: that for an author, book publication is a dualistic choice between trade (traditional) publishing on the one hand versus self-publishing services on the other.

It is the era of author enterprise: authors setting up as creative business owners, building independent publishing enterprises which focus on attracting and engaging readers through high-level publishing skills in the creator economy.

Since the arrival of the Internet, all the improvements for indie authors have been driven by technology. Web 1 brought us websites, blogs, word-processing and private online boards and lists. Web 2 brought us personal audio and video, blogs and social media, ebooks, POD, and e-commerce, dominated by Big Tech. Web 3 is bringing decentralized platforms, creator ownership and direct trading of digital assets.

SelfPub3 is part of Web3, a more decentralized internet that is not owned and controlled by large Big Tech entities. It will expand using blockchain-based technologies, machine learning and AI (artificial and augmented intelligence) to empower a more adaptive world wide web.

Web2 giants like Amazon, Google and Meta grew quickly by collecting, centralizing customer data, and monetizing it in myriad ways. Web3's global peer-to-peer network gives individuals more control over content, and who can access and profit from personal data.

For indie authors in the SelfPub3 era, working life now has more in common with other creative entrepreneurs who run passion-powered businesses—visual artists, film-makers, healers, performers, activists and musicians—than with authors who choose to exclusively license all their rights to one traditional publisher or to one self-publishing service.

SelfPub3 is explained in more detail in ALLi's campaign book: *SelfPub3: Author Empowerment Through Creative Business*. Find out more here: AllianceIndependentAuthors.org/selfpub3

SelfPub2 and 3 are currently overlapping. Many authors are still bound in exclusive relationships with Amazon and trade publishers while other authors are already selling directly from their websites, publishing wide, distributing through an increasing variety of outlets and in a variety of languages, selectively licensing non-exclusive rights, and trading on blockchains.

These authors use the retailers and self-publishing platforms to distribute their books as widely as possible, with the intention of taking them off these other businesses' websites and back to their own.

Readers are also beginning to appreciate the new publishing landscape, becoming more comfortable with purchasing directly from creators, joining crowdfunders, becoming patrons through Patreon and other outlets, relishing premium products and opportunities for access and closer connection with authors.

At its simplest **SelfPub3** is about author-publishers building sustainable enterprises, with a diversity of earning streams, through our own websites. This means putting our own author websites at the hub of a successful publishing and media enterprise, and not spending more time and money on other people's websites than we do on our own.

Cryptocurrency, AR, VR, Metaverse: all the new words, jargon and technology can be scary, but having a business mindset and strong business fundamentals underpinning our IP, asset-based businesses becomes ever more important as we set up our own transactional websites, get to grips with digital money, mint NFTs on a blockchain, and explore whatever other options are waiting in our publishing futures. Through computers, smartphones, e-readers, and audio devices, millions of readers are now directly available to us, if we can capture and hold their attention.

Mostly, SelfPub3 is about the mindset shift needed to take control of our author enterprises rather than unthinkingly assigning all our intellectual property, our most valuable creative asset, to a business owned by another, whether that is a trade-publisher or a self-publishing service.

SelfPub3 is typified by a free and empowered mindset that is creatively enterprising.

Your Books, Your Way

Does all of this sound overwhelming? Don't worry, there are as many ways to be an indie author as there are authors who want to self-publish.

As publishing economies transform from being scarcity driven (where demand is controlled by supply), to being abundance driven (where demand is cultivated through relationship), each of us can create our own market forces, our own readership, our own books, in our own way. We can go as fast or as slowly as our creative development and personal circumstances allow.

And we don't do it alone. We have the support of other authors, and publishers, and publishing services. From traditional publishers to hybrids to digital-only imprints to an abundance of self-publishing services, there have never been so many ways to create books and reach readers. Whatever stage you're at, as a writer or as a publisher, you can quite easily unfold the next step—once you know the pros and cons of the different options that are open to you.

29

BUSINESS MODELS AND INCOME STREAMS

To run any successful creative enterprise, you need to shape your skills, talents, services, and expertise into something you can sell, otherwise known as a product. The product indie authors sell, obviously, is books—and for some authors that is the beginning and end of their business. Many other authors, out of need or want, though, go beyond the book to sell other products too.

Earning a living from book sales alone has always been rare, particularly for authors working in genres like literary fiction and poetry. Traditionally, given the limitations of shelf space and sale-or-return policies in physical bookstores, only a few authors writing in such genres could sell enough books to make a living. The global audience and infinite shelf-life now available through digital publishing has changed the game. Self-publishing incomes are increasing year on year. Every genre now offers enough global readers to support a skilled author-publisher, one who knows how to write and publish well.

SELFPUB2 BUSINESS MODELS FOR AUTHORS

In the world of Web2 and SelfPub2, indie authors chose two categories of business model: an **exclusive self-publishing model,** publishing books exclusively with one self-publishing platform, usually Amazon, or a **wide self-publishing model**, publishing books non-exclusively with a range of self-publishing platforms and aggregators e.g. Kobo Writing Life, PublishDrive etc.

For diversity and stability, ALLi recommends a wide publishing model as best for most authors, while also recognising that's not always practical, depending on circumstances.

Let's look at the advantages and disadvantages of exclusive and wide publishing a little more closely.

1. Exclusive Self-Publishing Model

You self-publish your books through one distributor only. Authors who employ this model often write in a popular genre and for many exclusive authors, their favored outlet is Amazon—Amazon KDP for ebooks and print, often in Kindle Unlimited for ebooks, and using Amazon ACX for audiobooks. The author focuses on publishing fast and often. They always keep a close eye on Amazon's algorithm and on the marketing methods that send a book up the charts on Amazon, harnessing the power of the algorithms to find new readers.

Some authors employing this model publish only in ebook and do not buy their own ISBNs, relying on Amazon's internal book numbering method (the ASIN: Amazon Standard Identification Number).

This model has delivered excellent sales for authors in genres with whale readers. In fiction, that's romance, crime, and science fiction/fantasy. In non-fiction, it's self-help and business books. And in poetry, it's love poetry, self-help and inspirational. Writers who do well in these genres can find it impossible to keep up with their readers, which is why several are now commissioning other authors to write in their fictional world, or for their publishing companies.

Non-Amazon authors include those who choose to go exclusive

using only one aggregator, like Draft2Digital, PublishDrive, StreetLib, or one publishing service, that handles their distribution. It also includes a growing group of authors who only publish through their own websites. And of course, those who sign exclusive publishing contracts for a title to a third-party publisher for a particular duration.

The advantage of the exclusive model is its simplicity; 44.6% of self-publishers prefer this model according to the Independent Author Income Survey 2023. The disadvantage is that you are likely losing sales on alternative platforms, and you are very vulnerable if your exclusive outlet changes its terms of trading or goes out of business.

2. Wide Self-Publishing Model

This is a books-only business model too but here authors publish through multiple outlets. The indie author community refers to this model as "going wide": using a variety of distributors to be available to as many readers as possible. The wide publisher aims to reach as many readers as possible, by being available not just through as many distributors as possible, but also in as many formats as possible, and across as many territories as possible.

The most common kind of wide publishing is directly uploading to retailers like Apple Books, Google Play, IngramSpark and Kobo in addition to Amazon KDP and ACX, then using aggregator distributors like Draft2Digital, PublishDrive and StreetLib to reach hundreds of other outlets around the world.

Two popular community Facebook groups focus on this business model: Wide for the Win, run by authors Erin Wright, Suzie O'Connell and Skye MacKinnon who use this model. And for audiobooks, Marketing Audiobooks Wide, run by audiobook author Rebecca Hefner.

The advantage of the wide model is its diversity and stability, allowing the author to grow a consistent readership steadily over time. The disadvantage is that it can be time-consuming and complex yet 33.9% of indies use this business model as of 2023.

Those who don't write in genres that attract "whale readers"—readers who consume a lot of books quickly—can complement their royalties earned with other sources of income. These sources can be a part of their 'book business' brand or be separate.

SELFPUB3 BUSINESS MODELS FOR AUTHORS

As we saw in the last chapter, Web3 has decentralized resources, and is now focusing on individuals, which is becoming known as the creator economy. Many authors are now jumping aboard this trend, moving to having their own transactional websites and selling books directly to readers.

This gives us the **creator business model**. As well as publishing books through third-party self-publishing platforms, you also sell books (and perhaps other products and services) directly to readers and other customers through your own website and/or other outlets e.g. Shopify, Kickstarter, WooCommerce, Patreon.

A fourth business model for authors is the **rights licensing model**, used by those who often call themselves "hybrid authors". As well as using self-publishing platforms and/or selling direct, you license rights to third-party publishers, producers and other rights buyers, but on a non-exclusive basis that allows you to also self-publish other formats and titles.

And finally some brave authors are using the skills they have acquired to publish other authors and this gives us the fifth business model for authors, the **publisher model,** in which you publish other authors' books as well as your own for business purposes.

Let us study these three newer models for author sin more detail.

3. Creator Model

The Creator Economy is the term given to that section of the economy where consumers directly fund the work of artists, musicians, filmmakers and, yes, authors. Sam Yam, the co-founder of Patreon, a platform that facilitates such direct payments and a pioneer of this creator economy, describes this economy as: "value directly exchanged for creativity."

The creator economy in publishing sees authors selling directly to readers, and includes various products and services alongside books e.g. premium digital content (including NFTs on a choice of blockchains), subscriptions, memberships, reader clubs, paid video and audio content, as well as crowdfunders and patronage.

A proportion of these authors are also seeing their books as just one part of a bigger business ecosystem and incorporating other activities into their publishing business. By incorporating other products and services, it becomes easier to create an author business that lasts over the long term, and is capable of ongoing growth and expansion (in business lingo, an enterprise that is sustainable and scalable).

Being a creative entrepreneur in this way is different from being a freelancer, working a day job to pay the bills. You integrate activities that support your creative values, your mission as a writer, and your personal passions, into one for-profit business. These models and income streams work on the understanding that our books are just one way to fulfil our mission, passion, influence, and impact working in this world. It understands the power we have as authors, takes hold of it and gets more creative. It's all about the building of creative assets over time.

As of 2023, only 12.6% of indies use this model (according to the ALLi author income survey) but this is the fastest growing sector not just in publishing but across the creative industries. The advantage of this model is dependable income from many readers and fans.

The creator model promises a more human and less automated interaction than social media "influencing" and anonymous online bookselling. Instead of fans or customers, you have supporters or patrons. You can rely on more dependable income. You can choose which kinds of work you take on, and mould your publishing business around your skills as an author, and your other interests and talents, and the needs of your readers.

The downside is that reader expectations need to be managed so that they don't interfere with your creative process and the business can get too complex.

4. Rights Licensing Model

In this model, in addition to publishing your own books, you license your publishing rights to third-party rights buyers. Limiting the format, term and territory, you license a variety of rights, across the world, to maximize income.

The advantages of this model is that your licensing partners bring expertise and new opportunities which expand the reach of your book. The disadvantage is the need to be constantly pitching and vigilant about all contracts and agreements. In ALLi's 2023 income survey, 6.6% of indies said rights licensing made up more than 50% of their business income.

5. Publisher Model

Authors employing this model not only publish their own books but other authors too, becoming a third-party publisher themselves, on a traditional publishing (licensing authors' rights and paying royalties) or hybrid publishing (charging for publishing services) model. Only 2.4% of authors employ this business model in 2023.

The upside of this model is the ability to trade in more work that you can ever produce yourself, making your publishing business more sustainable and stable. The downside is the management and responsibility of other writers' expectation and careers.

INCOME STREAMS TO INCLUDE IN YOUR PRODUCT MIX

Ways in which these authors are earning include (but are not limited to):

Products

- Books - Ebooks, audiobooks, POD books and/or volume/Consignment Print
- Book Box sets - digital and/or print

- Crowdfunded products
- Memberships or subscriptions for readers - on their own website or through platforms like Patreon
- Merchandise linked to publications (self-commissioned)
- Translations (self-commissioned)

Services

- Freelancing - Writing, copywriting etc.
- Journalism - print, podcasting/radio, video/TV
- Publishing Services - Editing, formatting, design etc.
- Referrals/affiliate marketing
- Speaking and appearances
- Sponsorship or other influencer income
- Teaching writing or publishing craft

Licensing

- Book publishing rights at home or overseas
- Broadcasting rights (TV/film)
- Dramatic Rights (Theatre or radio plays)
- Merchandising Rights
- Translation rights

In this rapidly evolving landscape, it's crucial to stay informed and cautious when securing contracts for the future. Be specific about the rights you're licensing, avoid the vague term "digital rights," and be wary of contracts that aim to restrict future formats without fully understanding them.

SO WHICH BUSINESS MODEL?

Some of the models and ideas mentioned in the previous chapter and this one might be anathema to you, some might be more appealing. The important thing is to know which model you are working, or want to work with, and set up your publishing business around that.

You choose how you run your business. If something doesn't work, or stops working, you can experiment and iterate until you get it right.

DO THIS: Which Business Model? *In the future, when you hear about an indie author's success, look closely and observe which model and revenue streams they are using.*

TRY THIS: Which Model is Right for You? *F-r-e-e-write your answer to this question. Take in all your ideas about writing, publishing and creative business. What best suits your writing process, your life routines and lifestyle? What do you ultimately want to create?*

30

YOUR PRODUCT MIX

Now that you understand the different business models an author can employ, you are free to envision a new publishing landscape for yourself, where the way you license and monetize your books transforms into something more dynamic and innovative.

If you've enrolled in Kindle Unlimited, ask yourself what you're truly accomplishing. By doing so, you're granting Amazon a 90-day contract to license your book subscription rights. Is that the best thing for you and your books? Your answer may well be yes and that's great —Amazon KDP provides a unique suite of valuable tools for authors— but don't do it mindlessly, without considering your options.

As a creator in the creator economy, you might want to bring more readers directly to your own mailing list instead. And so you might change your attitude to Amazon and the other platforms and use a free first-in-series book there to build a readership, then guide those readers at the end of the book towards your website for subsequent books.

And also to purchase other products.

Instead of paying for advertising that directs readers to other retail platforms like Amazon, you might think about directing them to your own website where you can sell directly to them, or get them to sign up to your mailing list. This gives you more profit, faster payment into your account, and you and not the platform get the valuable customer data.

In this way of thinking, online platforms shift from primarily being where you sell your books to sites of discoverability. You use the platforms to being more readers to your website.

Other advantages are that the limitations imposed by platforms, such as price restrictions on box sets and reduced prices on Audible, will no longer be a concern. And nobody can shut down your business, overnight. You keep the commercial and creative control.

FOUR KINDS OF PRODUCT

Lots of business research shows that enterprises with a single product type see less profit, grow more slowly, and are less resilient to market changes. Those with a mix of products and projects are more likely to succeed.

To be clear, a *product* is any valuable insight or idea that you package up so that readers and other customers can access it easily, repeatedly and in a desirable way. Say you are a poet, whose niche is love poetry that encourages single young women to be more courageous in finding love. Each poetry book you make, in ebook, print or audio form, is a product.

You've also trained as a life coach and you offer relationships coaching advice. And you do a spoken word, one-person performance which you show at fringe festivals each year. The latter two are more in the nature of services than products, They require you to turn up and spend time, each time. Again, that may be fine by you.

Alternatively, you may want to turn your coaching practice into a digital course e.g. "How to Date with Daring", in which you package up your poems with advice and coaching videos that will now be delivered through digital download.

Now your advice coaching is a product, not a service. You wrote the books and recorded the course once and now they sell again and again.

The most successful businesses offer four distinct kinds of products:

1. Gift product — anything you give freely, no strings attached
2. For prospects product — a free or cheap product in return for a sign-up or small sale.
3. Core product or service
4. Premium product — higher ticket items for sale that are connected to your core product

Translating these four into author-publishing, we get:

1. **Gift giveaways:** anything you give freely, no strings attached, e.g. donations to charity, social media posts, mentoring or coaching aspiring writers
2. **Reader magnet**: anything offered in exchange for a sign-up or sale, e.g. free book or other publication
3. **Core products:** your books (for sale).
4. **Premium products**: higher ticket items for sale that are connected to your books, e.g. courses, memberships, merchandise.

This is a numbered list because it's scaled (from cheapest to most expensive), and it's sequential (designed to progress the reader through your funnel, from receiving a freebie to spending money on your books and then on your more profitable products).

The gift enables them to know, like and trust you and creates interaction and interest, while at the other end of the chain, premium products make your author business more resilient by providing additional income streams.

Your books are at the core of the ecosystem. People, products and services all work in harmony, in an integrated creative business. As a whole, they deliver the positive experience that will keep readers coming back for more.

Your publishing business will take off when you've got a mix of products and services like this that work together to maximize the value exchange with your readers. When those products complement each other and work symbiotically in an integrated way, everything becomes easier.

CONSIDER THIS: Your Product Categories: *Think about the four product categories. Which ones have you got on offer? What is your reader's journey through your product types?*

Here are some final tips to set yourself up for success.

- When choosing your publishing model (volume, craft or engagement), your business model (exclusive, wide, creator, rights or publisher), and your income streams, you must understand your readers and what they value. Take every opportunity as your business grows to understand more about where your readers come from, what they like, and what you should offer them.
- Consistently creating good content is how you increase your following and engagement. Resolve to learn and grow through regular content creation and feedback. Build your author platform on the foundation of reader trust. Do what you say you'll do. If you pivot or swerve (and you probably will) take the time to communicate and explain.
- Build a good publishing team—editors, designers, assistants —and a good arsenal of publishing tools, including AI tools. Web 3 technologies make our jobs easier. Using artificial and augmented intelligence we can produce better books, faster, and market and promote them more easily. Identify what only you can do, and source good tools, tech or team members for the other tasks.
- Remember your personal definition of success. You're not trying to do everything. Author opportunities have so expanded in the creator economy to such a degree that's it's simply not possible to do everything. What you're trying to

do is uncover your own unique niche, your own best business model, you own perfect product mix so you can settle in and draw your readers around you.

- Making a living in the creator economy means valuing yourself enough to ask for the sale. People will pay you in the currency you ask for. If you ask only for clicks and likes, that's what you'll get. If you use your Facebook ads only to send people to Amazon, that's where they'll go.
- Be rigorous. If something isn't working, stop doing it and try something else. Don't do things that have little value for you, commercially or creatively. Delete all "busy work" and resolve to only do value work.
- Don't get enthralled by others' success. You'll never know their full story, their background, advantages, hard work or struggles–and these doesn't matter anyway. There's only one you. Tune into your own creative spirit and follow what others are doing to learn, not to compare or contrast.
- Think about incorporating audio or video, where you cannot help but reveal yourself, into your marketing and promotion. If that isn't right for you, fine, but find a way to be open, revealing and authentically you, in a way that is entertaining, inspirational or at the least informational. Personality, personal values, personal branding: these become ever more key in the age of SelfPub3.

I know it can be challenging to keep on keeping on, constantly improving your writing craft *and* your publishing craft. The final section of this book offers my personal method for bringing it all together and creating an integrated and balanced writing and publishing life.

———

31

THE CREATIVE AGE

Our generation of writers is the latest in a long line of humans through history who have harnessed the power and magic of the written, published word. From Egyptian hieroglyphics through illuminated manuscripts to digital text, the job has always been the same: to express some aspect of body, mind, heart, or soul, in words. And in so doing, to connect with other minds, hearts, and souls. The only thing that has changed, across countless generations, is the tools we use, and the reach they afford us.

By the time they're in process, revolutions are unstoppable. So it is for SelfPub3 now. We can bemoan it, or we can upskill to benefit from it. It's our choice.

As we move more deeply into SelfPub3, advances in technology will bring new opportunities and tools for authors will keep on improving. Shouldn't you set up your business so you can avail of them?

Author Collaboration

If we choose the creative option—to learn, grow and benefit—we have each other for support. The Alliance of Independent Authors is built on author collaboration. Every day, we witness our members paying forward tips about tech, tricks, and tools, knowledge that gives real competitive advantage to others. Our team, our advisory board, and our member structure are set up to do precisely that.

The entire self-publishing space is full of entrepreneurial authors openly sharing sales numbers, tools, and techniques, and promoting each other through blog posts and podcasts, email lists, and social networks. We are also increasingly seeing indie authors enter formal writing and publishing collaborations.

Traditionally published authors have solidarity, of course, but they also must compete with each other for agents, publishing deals, prizes, and bookstore co-op and shelf space. Today's digitally published indie author has nothing to fear from cooperating with others. No single writer can ever satisfy all the readers. And the right kind of collaboration can increase the odds of getting discovered, noticed, and read.

So when indie authors speak about "author comps", we mean comparable, not competing authors. We enjoy "coopetition" (cooperating with perceived competition so that both parties benefit) and know that, in working and educating together, we learn faster, and respond and adapt more nimbly. In short, we do better together than by going it alone.

Author collaborations can be in *writing* (e.g. creating a book together, creating a shared universe or world, creating a single pen name that many authors contribute to, creating anthologies) or in *publishing* (e.g. banding together to make box sets, swap author promotions, put together themed collections, share ad space, host takeovers on each other's platforms, and many other options).

When a collaboration works, writers inspire one another and the creative process becomes less lonely, but when it fails it can be disastrous, commercially and creatively. Having a thorough discussion about hopes and expectations in advance, and writing the salient details into a collaboration agreement, improve the odds of success. (ALLi Members can log in to see ALLi's Contracts section for sample agreements to use.)

We're already seeing powerful examples of what happens when

authors band together around goals like hitting a bestseller list, producing a box set, and cross-promoting each other's work. We can get together through old-style campaigning—petitions, emails, and lobbying—or in whole new ways.

To take one current example, subscription reading. Subscription models are seen by many as a threat to author income. Instead of fretting and berating readers for their choices, a band of authors in a particular niche could come together to offer a direct subscription model to their most loyal fans, sharing workloads and advertising costs, enjoying a shared email list and the opportunity to offer their fans closer connection and premium products.

This is just an idea, to illustrate that we have the means now to be proactive and creative. Resisting what our readers want can never work, but valuing ourselves, and coming up with good ideas, will see readers more than willing to follow.

The Empowered Author

At time of writing, author Brandon Sanderson has just finished a crowdfunder in which he asked fans to help him raise $1 million on Kickstarter to self-publish four novels he wrote during the pandemic. His campaign has just topped $41.7 million from more than 185,000 backers, the most-funded Kickstarter in the crowdfunding site's history.

Sanderson's lengthy fantasy epics and intricately thought-out systems of magic have won him legions of fans. He has made much of magic and lore over the course of writing more than fifty novels in which he follows his own "Laws of Magic" when writing. He has taken what he does and run with it. "Err on the side of awesome," he says. "Readers want to see cool things happen."

He is also a big believer in following your passion where it takes you. "If you give up what you want most for what you think you *should* want more, you'll end up miserable." Sanderson's writing career, and now publishing business, perfectly demonstrate how using the same strategies as everyone else is not the best way to gain attention for your work.

Creative originality gets you noticed for all the right reasons (price is no longer your only selling point) and it's more enjoyable, sending your creative happiness up and up, right off the charts. Your CHQ is your most important measure, remember. Going creative is essential to score high. It's why you got into this business in the first place.

Commercially also, it gives you the advantage you need. Creativity cannot be copied. The one thing that AI, and other authors, can never do is be you. As AI makes text generation ever easier, being uniquely you, uniquely human, becomes your best selling point.

So embrace your own creativity, your own unique circumstances and character, your own niche readers. Specialize in giving your writing and publishing your own particular stamp.

Creative Support

It's quite a journey from aspiring author to creative director of an author enterprise, and it requires quite a mental, emotional, and practical shift, and takes the writer on a steep learning curve. To make the necessary shifts, many authors need support—but as I write (at the beginning of 2023), the literary, publishing, and industry bodies responsible for creative business, entrepreneurship, culture, and intellectual property have not yet tuned into the needs and influence of the self-publishing, independent author. Many such bodies are overseeing conservative publishing policies and practices that fail to recognize how swathes of books are actually produced and sold, bought and read, in today's digital reading environment.

Reframing publishing and literary research and policy so that it properly accounts for how self-publishing authors *actually* work, trade, and negotiate today is a task that's now overdue.

ALLi's SelfPub3 campaign recognizes the challenges today's authors face and works with writers and others to overcome them.

- The campaign encourages authors to make the transition from being a content provider to running a business.
- The campaign also works with other author associations and representatives, and literary, publishing, and creative

industry organizations, to foster author empowerment and entrepreneurial authorship—and to lobby the literary, publishing, and creative industries to support this shift.

SelfPub3 recognizes that writing and publishing books is a long-term endeavor, that each author starts at zero and must produce the first words, then the first book, then continuously develop their books and their business, all the way to profitability. It acknowledges that publishing is always a team effort, as much for the author-publisher as for any publishing house, and that good self-publishing services and assistance are key to sustainable success in publishing today.

More than anyone else in the publishing sector, the indie author is key to unfolding a new, more diverse, more accessible, and more equitable publishing landscape. Many authors are already embracing the principles of SelfPub3—selling directly from their websites, publishing widely in three digital formats, distributing through an increasing variety of outlets and in a variety of languages, selectively licensing non-exclusive rights to publishers and other rights buyers, using AI in their writing, book production and marketing.

As readers become more comfortable with purchasing directly from creators, joining crowdfunders, becoming patrons, paying monthly subscriptions for personal newsletters, purchasing premium products, our opportunities increase. And our mindset and emotional landscape shifts. This author empowerment is the most significant development of the self-publishing revolution, yet it is the least talked about.

It is something that even indie authors ourselves have been slow to grasp.

It's time to discover what's possible when we fully inhabit the creative and commercial opportunities now opening to us. I highly recommend The Creative Penn podcast, TheCreativePenn.-com/podcasts where ALLi Enterprise Adviser, Joanna Penn, keeps the indie author community appraised of new tech, digital money, and what it all means for writers.

Stepping into opportunity means:

- Being aware of our biases and natural fear of change

- Choosing non-exclusivity
- Publishing wide and selling direct
- Investing in our publishing businesses and in ourselves
- Reading all contracts and agreements, and getting advice as necessary (contact the ALLi contracts desk, any time, for general advice)
- Holding out for fair terms and conditions
- Employing selective rights licensing
- Asking for change where there is unfairness
- Refusing short-term wins that lead to long-term losses
- Working together, in a community
- Choosing the creative way

The creator economy can deliver a more human and less automated interaction than the social media influencing and online bookselling of the past decade, and the trade-publishing era before that. But only if we insist upon it—through our work, and through mutual support. Instead of anonymous followers or customers, we have fans, supporters, and patrons—and we have each other.

B efore I leave you, I beg your indulgence for a suggestion I'd like to make. A suggestion born out of *my* personal values, mission, and passion. The global maker movement, of which self-publishing is a part, is seeing independent creators become a force in every industry as never before and is the most important movement of our time. Given its head, it can have the most transformative political, sociological, and economic consequences.

What makes a creative business unique is that it is composed of equal parts passion and profit. What has poisoned so much human interaction, and is poisoning our planet, is the single-minded pursuit of commercial profit, without the balancing force of a deeper creative or spiritual purpose.

Even *The Financial Times*, "the world's leading global business publication," is climbing onboard. Its latest advertising billboard reads:

"Capitalism. Time for a Reset. Read why business must make a profit but should serve a purpose too."

Purpose, as we've seen, is composed of passion, mission, and values. The values of liberty, equality and justice can feel very far away sometimes, and are always in danger of being eroded. Privilege exerts destructive power everywhere. Old elites cling to power, long after time has eroded the value they once brought, and engrained ways of thinking and doing are hard to shift.

Our leaders go to war defending democracy against various threats, real and bogus, but the truth about democracy is that it's not yet a done deal. It's an unfinished creative project.

Digital tools and creative community are leading a great upswelling of personal, creative expression around the world. This movement has its downside, and those dangers have been well aired, but the upside for countless authors is rarely acknowledged in mainstream media—especially books media (for which see old elites, above).

A truly empowered creative class, with a sense of its own significance, making choices from creative as well as commercial imperatives, could shift the world of business and commerce from its current profit-before-people imperative. Publishing, the container of ideas and inspirations, books and stories, is a most important player here.

We can realize the human potential to evolve to a higher level of thought and action than ever before. This is not a utopian view, but a considered analysis of human development to date. We've come so far, so fast. It's not even a century since some Western democracies "gave" women a vote. Free secondary education for all is even more recent. And now here we are today—anyone can now write a book and publish it themselves, reaching real readers with ideas born out of their own real experience. Already, a more positive, connected, and creative world is ours, on an unprecedented scale.

And we now have the necessary creative conditions for a levelling up: an understanding of brains and bodies afforded by a century of research in a multitude of disciplines; a network of communication that is instant and global; a vision of a world where the industrial-military complex and its patriarchal hierarchy is retired in favor of a more diverse, decentralized, and democratic world.

Yes, it's challenging. Conflict, war, and its attendant suffering is everywhere. Victimology wallows in its own hurt while vested interests drive the agenda. The privileged few know how to conserve their privilege and meanwhile, the planet cries out for what's needed.

Creativity is our best tool to liberate us from this social conundrum and it's happening. In every industry, old business certainties are breaking down and the pace of change is picking up. Smaller and less-developed groups, companies, and nations are jumping forward, using digital technology to leapfrog larger entities that are less nimble and weighed down by debt, or complexity, or by once enriching but now encumbering physical assets.

We are close to the centuries-old dream of the democratization of knowledge. AI will play its part in that and, as indie authors, we have our own key role to play. Doing our work well—writing good books, creating successful publishing businesses, building creative communities—gives us influence on our readers, on other writers and publishing partners, and on society at large.

We need creative will and intention to harness that opportunity and open it to more people. Just because anyone can, in principle, learn how to read, write, think, publish, and progress, doesn't mean everyone *actually* can. Different people need different levels of support, and we have a way to go before we see the interests of the disinherited fairly represented.

From this perspective, making good creative choices—an action that seems so personal—has repercussions beyond ourselves and our own individual desires and drives. Everyone needs to become more creative, to get by in this world. Conditioned for collaboration and contribution, a growing creative class is expanding the experience of collective humanity.

Even if you're at the very beginning of your writing path, you have your part to play in this expansive evolution. Indie authors and others who are creating passion-powered businesses are leading the way, not as commentators or analysts, but as doers and makers. Fully exposed, taking risks, putting our living on the line, we offer our personal passion or mission to the world, and do creative business the creative way.

In doing so, we not only change ourselves, and the minds and hearts of our readers, we transform mass consciousness. Who knows where this transformation will take us?

The Creative Moment is Now

Everyone knows a book—and a business—grows one step at a time. It's a truism because it's true. One day the step is sure and strong, the next, uncertain and wobbly. We take the next step, anyway. We won't get anywhere by waiting, by thinking we'll be more ready soon, by saving up to start later. The creative moment, the creative risk is always here, now. Lighten up. Let go. Leap in. Spend your creative energy now.

Yes, you're going to go wrong, make mistakes, fail but the longer you do this job, the more often you see how the wrong step, with hindsight, turns out to be the best step taken. And how every step matters, every step deserves acknowledgement, and what deserves most acknowledgement of all is the decision to keep going, not to be derailed. A team member leaves, the accountant says no, the publishing swerves into unplanned territory, the computer crashes, you didn't get your writing done today... Onwards.

That's what I'm most proud of, myself, more than a decade into my self-publishing life. How my books, and my publishing business, and ALLi have steadily, consistently grown, through so many days when things failed to cohere, and I failed to get it together.

We don't wallow in feelings of failure (or not for too long, anyway). If we lambaste ourselves, get too critical, all we're doing is leaching our own creative energy. Instead, we look at our four measures—productivity, platform, profits, and personal satisfaction—and get back to growing them. We look at our creative publishing plan for this year, this quarter, this month, this week, this day, this moment, and take the next small step. We do what we need to do, to foster the create-state, and find flow again and again and again.

I wish you all good things in your writing, in your publishing, and in your author business. If you need assistance anywhere along the line, do get in touch with us at ALLi via our website: AllianceIndependentAuthors.org. We'd love to be your ally and support your work.

If you're serious about growing your publishing business, and earning a living from your writing, find out about my *Go Creative! Planning for Profit* method, at SelfPublishingAdvice.org/planning. You'll have to try it for a while to see if it's a fit for you.

And wherever you go with your writing and publishing, with your making, managing, and marketeering, don't forget to go creative.

AUTHOR'S NOTE

Hello dear reader,

Thank you for taking the time to read this book. I hope you found it helpful for your author-business, and that you'll now feel more empowered as an author-publisher. I've filled this guidebook with thoughts and opinions, balanced with facts and figures—all as starting points for you to brainstorm and build your own publishing business.

You can find further support at ALLi's Self-Publishing Advice Center, SelfPublishingAdvice.org.

*As part of our community outreach, ALLi emails non-member subscribers with a monthly summary of publishing news highlights, marketing, tech, legal, and more. Sign up and you'll also receive a **free, comprehensive publishing glossary** immediately, explaining all the terms today's indie authors need to know. To join, please visit* <u>SelfPublishingAdvice.org/</u> <u>BookSignUp.</u>

ALLi's guidebooks are for human creators and crafted by human creators and also supported by various tools and technology, including technology artificial and augmented intelligence (AI). For this guidebook, we used Google's search engine, Apple Pages, Vellum, and Zoom for meetings. We picked ChatGPT's brain, and used it to interrogate our own thoughts about various facets of creative self-publishing. We used ProWritingAid, but also human editors. I am grateful to them all.

Thank you most especially to the book production and promotion team: Shanaya Wagh and Sarah Begley.

When talking to authors, we always stress the importance of online book reviews. They are as important to us as they are to you. Every authentic review enables our non-profit to reach more indie authors and advocate for self-publishers' rights and benefits. Together, we're stronger.

If you found this guide useful, please give it a review online on our website at Selfpublishingadvice.org/creative. It doesn't have to be long or complicated, just a star rating and a few words about what helped you.

We really appreciate your feedback and as well as letting other authors know the book is useful, it helps us create better guidebooks for indie authors, going forward.

(Do put a similar request in the back of your own book, if you haven't already!)

From all at ALLi, thank you so much for reading. But mostly, thank you for writing.

Sonas!

Orna

OTHER GUIDES

Browse and buy more publishing guides for indie authors on our
website: SelfPublishingAdvice.org/Bookshop

ALLI SUPPORTS AND RESOURCES

This book is first in series from the Alliance of Independent Authors (ALLi)'s **Publishing Guides for Authors** series. It is the foundational text which outlines the method and mindset that underlie all our services to our members, readers, and subscribers.

Alliance of Independent Authors

ALLi is pronounced "ally" (al-eye not al-ee), and we aim to be an ally to self-publishers everywhere. Our name is spelt with a big ALL and small i because our members are like the three musketeers in Dumas's eponymous novel: ALL working for each individual "i", and each for ALL. Our mission is ethics and excellence in self-publishing.

ALLi is headquartered in London and unites thousands of beginner, emerging and experienced indie authors from all over the world behind this mission. Most of our members are in the US and Canada, followed closely by Europe, Australia and New Zealand, and South Africa. We are a Community Interest Company (CIC) and all profits are invested back in for the benefit of our members and the wider indie author community.

Our work is fourfold:

- ALLi *advises*, providing best-practice information and education through our online Self-Publishing Advice Center, SelfPublishingAdvice.org, offering a daily blog, a weekly live video and podcast, a bookstore of self-publishing guidebooks, and a quarterly member magazine.
- ALLi *monitors* the self-publishing sector through a watchdog desk, alerting authors to bad actors and predatory players and running an approved partner program.
- ALLi *campaigns* for the advancement of indie authors in the publishing and literary sectors globally (bookstores, libraries, literary events, prizes, grants, awards, and other author organizations), encouraging the provision of publishing and business skills for authors, speaking out against iniquities and inequities, and furthering the indie author cause wherever possible.
- ALLi *empowers* independent authors through community and collaboration—author forums, contract advice, sample agreements, contacts and networking, literary agency representation, and a member care desk.

Whether you're self-publishing your first book or your fiftieth, ALLi is with you every step of the way, with a suite of member benefits that includes free guidebooks, discounts and deals, member forums, contract consultancy, advisory board, literary agent for eligible members, a community watchdog desk and more.

As well as offering access to ALLi's supportive, dynamic community and wide range of services, your membership also supports our advocacy work for indie authors globally, from Alaska to New Zealand the long way round, and everywhere in between.

When you join ALLi, you're not just joining an organization, you're becoming part of a transformative, self-organizing, global, author movement. If you haven't yet, I'd like to invite you to join us.

Find out more at: AllianceIndependentAuthors.org

AskALLi: Advice Campaign

In 2013, ALLi launched its #**AskALLi** campaign, in which we pledged to answer, with evidence-based authority, *any* self-publishing question *any* author might have. We continue this work today, through our email support desk, our member forums, and our blog posts and podcasts in the **Self-Publishing Advice Center.** Key in any search term there to get a best-practice answer to your question.

As an ALLi member, you can also jump onto our closed forum and ask other members, ALLi team, and advisors who are on hand, 24/7, for their advice.

Resource Links

Blog: SelfPublishingAdvice.org/blog: How-to blog posts, analysis and opinion on all seven processes of publishing

Podcast: SelfPublishingAdvice.org/podcast: Advice on Fridays and Inspirations on Sundays

Conference: SelfPublishingAdviceConference.com: The largest annual online gathering of independent authors, each October

Planning: Small group creative planning programs run by Orna Ross: Patreon.com/OrnaRoss

---

INDEX

A

D

R